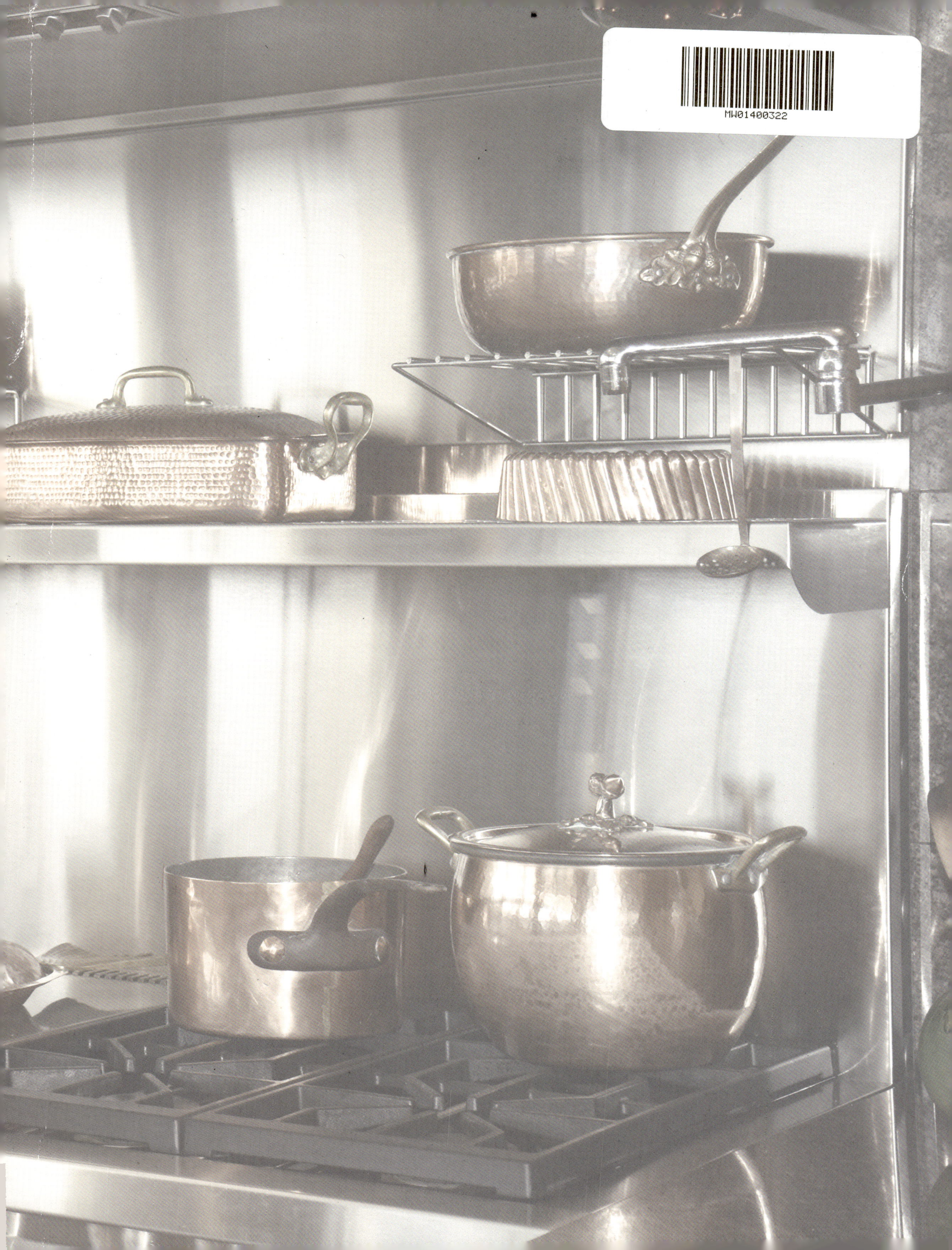

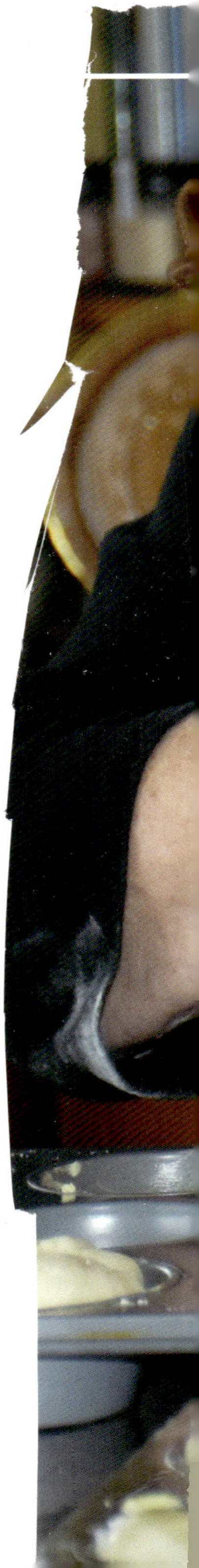

LIFE HAPPENS WHEN
You're Cooking

Empty Pots... Endless Possibilities

Empty pots are waiting pots, longing to be filled.
They hang regally above the kitchen island,
Or take precedence there beside the grill.
Beside each other on pantry shelves they stand.

Nestled in drawers they wait day by day,
As they long to be called to culinary service.
They yearn to do their duty and show the way
To an excellent plated dish with perfect garnish.

The well-seasoned black cast iron skillet,
Gifted to Granny when first she wed,
Says that no cook today dares question it
For making roux or crusty cornbread.

The red Le Creuset perfect gumbo pot
Doubles for stew and soup and chili.
Which surely means it's used a lot
For bold recipes that are never frilly.

Silently clamoring, others plea their case:
The skillet, for frying bacon in the morn,
A saucepan used so many ways,
For peas and beans and boiling corn.

Springforms for cheesecakes and special pies,
Muffin tins – mini, regular, and large – you see,
Cake tins and cookie sheets for cooks so wise,
Casserole and cobbler dishes definitely.

So the empty pots and pans await,
Needing a cookbook with lots of recipes.
Empty pots that implore one to cook and bake,
Wait to be filled with endless possibilities.

Sue Collins Cannon

Acknowledgments

Of all the accomplishments and credits that one accumulates during a lifetime, none can compare to the blessings of family. Therein lies an unbreakable bond that enables each member to grow from a foundation of love and support.

I am blessed with the joys of a family that has grown from three children to their spouses, five grandchildren and five great-grandchildren. Theirs are the recurring names linked to the stories and recipes of my life's journey. Without exception, they have inspired and supported, encouraged and motivated as I have endeavored to put words to the inner music of a passion for cooking.

My granddaughter Kelli Cannon planted the seed that has grown into full fruition. My writing this cookbook was originally her idea. She invested herself in aid and support. Not only did she set up my study as a lovely spot for writing, she taught me how to easily use the computer!

Especially noteworthy is the contribution of my daughter, Connie Cannon Valerius, who has spent innumerable hours of her summer helping me prepare this work for publication. She is responsible for the vivid colorful photographs that bring out the visual beauty of my recipes and reflections.

Dedication

FRED HAROLD CANNON SR.
March 20, 1925 - February 19, 2011

I'll be loving you, always,
With a love that's true, always.
When the things you've planned
Need a helping hand,
I will understand, always, always. . . .

Days may not be fair, always,
That's when I'll be there, always.
Not for just an hour,
Not for just a day,
Not for just a year,
But always.

"Always" - Irving Berlin, 1925
Recorded by Frank Sinatra, 1942

During our "courting" season Fred and I chose "our song." From the young love and promises of that time grew a lifetime of love and commitment. On this love we founded our home where both family and friends could gather at any time, knowing they would always share fellowship, fun, and food.

Although many dear people have touched my life along the way, none ever rivaled my husband for his impact and influence. Through the many seasons of our life together, I was blessed by his support and understanding, his humor and his love. He played a major role in my success as a cook through encouragement and praise.

I would, therefore, like to dedicate this cookbook to the person who supported me in so many endeavors and who "raised me up to more than I could be."

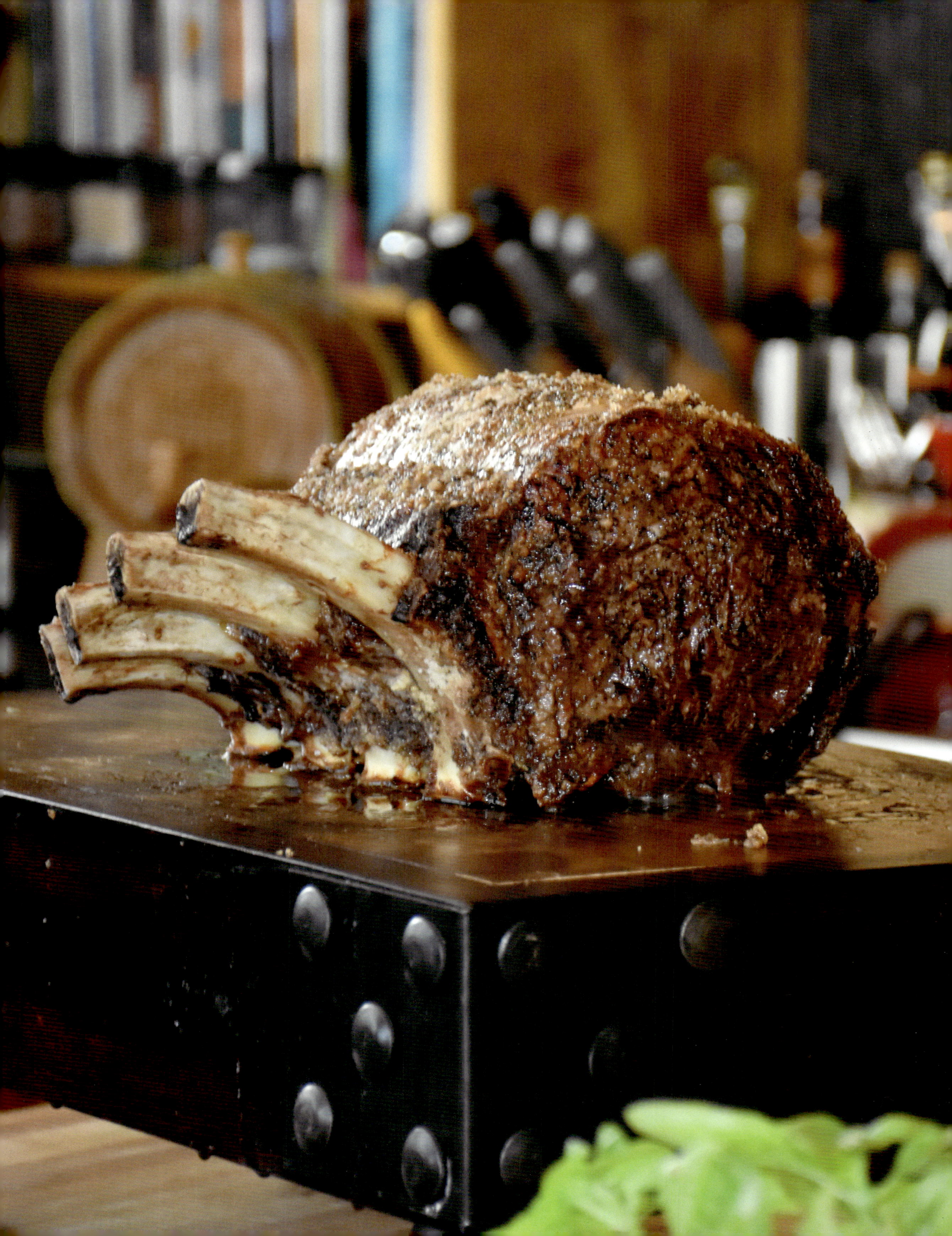

Foreword

Generous love and great food are the epitome of Sue Cannon. And the two cannot be separated with Sue, but are one of the same and an outpouring of each other.

Sue, affectionately known as Nan to those who hold her dear (and all of their closest friends) is a devoted wife, loving mother, adored grandmother and great-grandmother, respected teacher, generous friend. Nan is my grandmother and I am blessed to receive the bountiful gift of love and devotion she is. My life is marked and better for it by the love served out of Nan's kitchen.

My childhood memories with Nan are full of love and encouragement and always involve great food. One of my favorite memories is making cookies with Nan, in my mind, what is hundreds of times. Just picture the Norman Rockwell scene with me... a free-standing mixer sitting on the counter in the heart of the kitchen with the makings of yummy goodness in its bowl flocked with a giggling grandchild on each side and standing at the helm, Nan, a patient, smiling grandmother orchestrating the sweetness of the moment. Note that my memory does not include the worry of messes or life, only a devoted grandmother and yummy treats.

There are countless other memories that flood my mind when I think of Nan. As a teenager, the enchanting aroma of Nan's Banana Nut Muffins would call me out of bed after spending the night at her house. I treasured coming home from college to the comfort of my favorite Peach Cobbler she would make specifically to celebrate my return. On my 21st birthday, Nan made Stuffed Flounder and I felt special! She taught me to make my husband's favorite dessert, Apple Pie, in our early years of marriage. And I vividly remember our phone pep-talk to attempt her Cheesecake Supreme for my first dinner party. Christmas Eve dinner simply would not be complete without Nan's Frozen Pink Salad. She sent ice chests full of savory Seafood Gumbo for James and me to enjoy during the newborn days with our first child (and each child following).

I still treasure each opportunity I have to be in the kitchen with and under this master. The experience is always personal and quite delicious. In fact, it has grown sweeter with time as Nan now shares her love through cooking with my girls and gives them their own keepsake moments. Nan has often told me that people will not remember if my floors are spotless or my décor is perfect, but they will remember how I loved them and the food they enjoyed. The fruit of Nan's life proves this truth.

Every time I make one of Nan's recipes, the compliments come rolling in and not just the courteous ones, but the sincere, "I want that recipe" types. With deep love and respect, I get to tell my guests "it's one of Nan's recipes" likening her with the great cooks of our age. I believe my guests have come to expect the response as her recipes consume my go-to repertoire. Shocking to most people, Nan has always generously shared her recipes believing they are not hers to hold under lock and key, but to be enjoyed and grow with each cook that follows her cues. And now, as you hold this book, you receive the ultimate gift of her labor of love. *Life Happens When You're Cooking: Reflections of a Life Filled with Love, Laughter, and a Passion for Cooking* captures the wisdom and recipes from the life of a dedicated cook, infused with the people, places, and moments that she has made unforgettable.

LINDSEY CANNON DARNELL
Granddaughter of Sue Collins Cannon

TABLE OF

18 Appetizers

36 Breads

54 Soups & Salads

80 Veggies & Sides

Empty Pots, Endless Possibilities 4	Introduction 12
Acknowledgments 6	How This Book Began 13
Dedication 7	A Passion for Cooking 14
Foreword 8	The Making of a Cook 16

CONTENTS

98 Seafood

116 Main Dishes

142 Grilling & Smoking

154 Desserts

The Beat Goes On 52	The Magic Ingredient 208
Sweet Home Alabama 96	Favorite Ingredient 228
The Italian Stripe 145	Index 238
The Chopping Block 152	Reflections and Recipes 244

Introduction

Cookbooks? Another cookbook? Really?

A good question! Who doesn't already have multiple shelves housing an extensive personal cookbook collection? You probably have a goodly number written by the first names of cookbook authors – by chefs familiarly known as Ina, Giada, Paula, Rachael, Julia, Emeril, etc. You have cookbooks published by churches, organizations, nutritionists, and restaurants. Everyone surely has at least a few of the old stand-by books that include etiquette, entertaining, substitutions, cuts of meat, and more than you ever wanted to know from a cookbook. My favorite reference cookbook for many years has been Southern Living's *New Ultimate Cookbook*. I am, however, excited every time I add any cookbook to my collection. I just love to read them, look at the pictures, and mark pages for recipes that I would like to try.

My first cookbook, Better Homes and Gardens' *New Cookbook*, was a 1948 gift from a sister-in-law who was helping me learn how to cook. That red and white checkered binder book still holds a place of honor in my kitchen, and it has the stains and wear to prove its worth! I have to give much credit to this excellent comprehensive cookbook, but I have to acknowledge that the majority of my cooking skills were accumulated through associations with good cooks and through a passion that always pushed me to keep trying until I got it right!

I am always excited when asked by family or friends to do a cooking class. Maybe that is a hangover from my twenty years as a classroom teacher, or maybe it is simply the opportunity to be involved with others in an activity that has brought much enjoyment to my life. Nevertheless, interacting with a group while making gumbo combines teaching and learning with entertainment and great fun. On the other hand, the closeness of a private cooking lesson with a granddaughter is a wonderful treasure.

The ultimate goal of this project is to personalize these recipes by using a dialogue, which is identified by the comments in the margin throughout the work. This method attempts to simulate my presence in your kitchen talking with you about the recipes and commenting on my experiences.

Life Happens When You're Cooking! is not an attempt at a comprehensive cookbook, nor does it specialize in one area, nor do the recipes make claim to gourmet cooking. It is, rather, a personal conversation about cooking in which I share the recipes of my lifetime.

How This Book Began

The impetus for writing this cookbook originated with my granddaughter Kelli Cannon. For part of her Christmas present to me, she wanted to help assemble all of my recipes and have two copies printed in a nice hardback presentation with appropriate illustrations. My first thought was, "Well, that won't take long – maybe about thirty recipes!" As Kelli proceeded to go through my recipe folders, however, she listed about 180 recipes.

During the weeks and months that followed, much planning took place. Many fun, animated conversations centered around creating the concept of the book, even sitting on a bench in Radda while enjoying the Tuscany region of Italy.

Since then I have spent many hours on the computer getting my recipes into cookbook form, sometimes beginning with just a list of ingredients! I have loved going back in time and remembering so many good times revolving around finding, developing, and sharing each recipe. Our home was a truly great testing kitchen for recipes. My husband and children loved to bring their friends home with them, and they knew that I would always cook for them. The opportunities for proofing recipes were many.

Although the original plan was to print only two copies of the book, we soon thought about printing enough copies for the family – perhaps like an heirloom to be passed down. The project has consequently grown, and it has taken on a life of its own. As the matriarch of my family, I am so immensely pleased that the passion for cooking is alive and thriving in the next generations.

As word spread that I was writing a cookbook, we received many requests for copies. I feel very honored over each one. Please know that I am happy to share my dialogue on cooking with each of you and wish you "Bon appétit!"

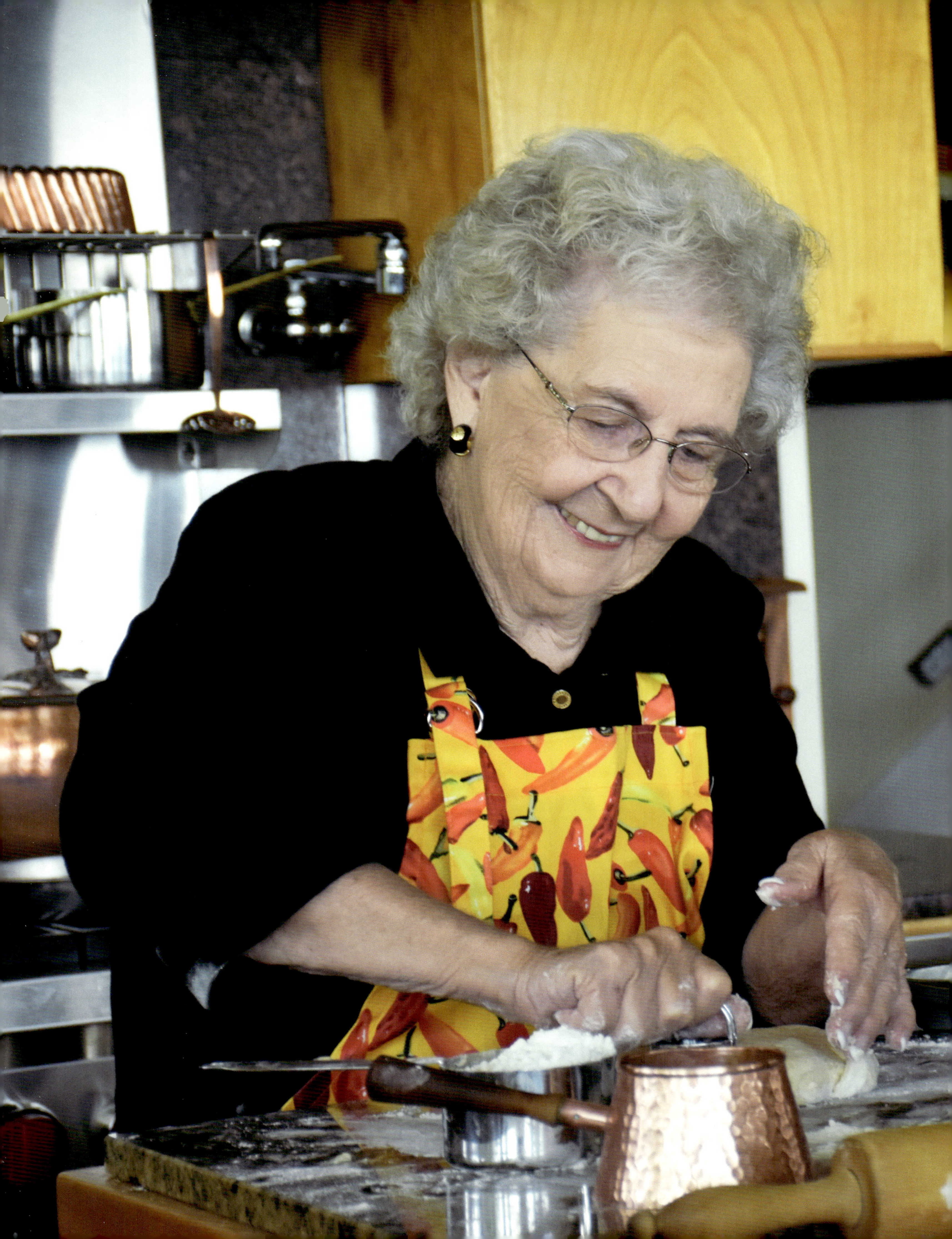

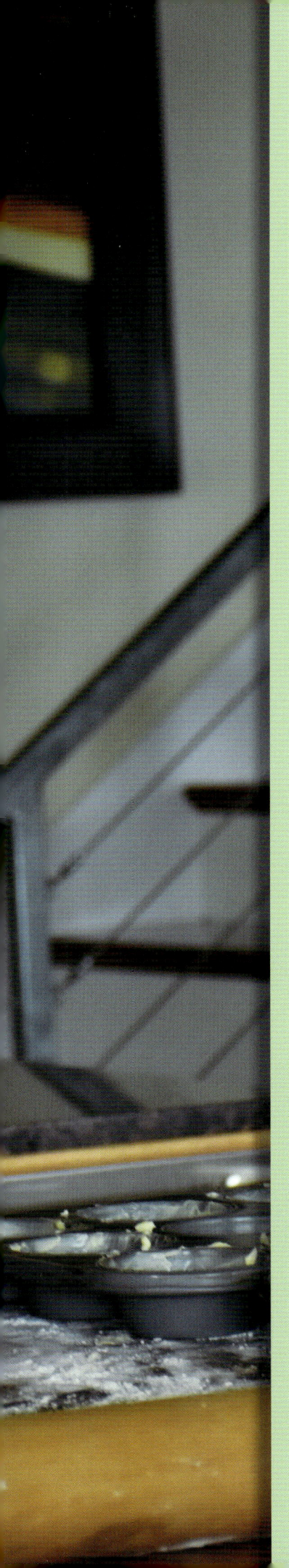

A Passion for Cooking

Day-to-day decisions ultimately create pathways that determine the direction of one's life. From the perspective of my 86 years, I can say with assurance that my life has been greatly enriched by the decision to become more than an ordinary cook preparing ordinary meals.

As the youngest of nine children (six were girls), I should have had many cooking skills. The fact was, however, that while two of my sisters were becoming accomplished cooks, I was always polishing the furniture! Somehow I did learn to make homemade rolls from my dear mother, Elizabeth (Bette) Taylor Collins.

Fred and I married when I was 18, and then began the adventure that was our life together for 63 years. Shamefully, I could not put together a decent meal. I could open a can, fry a pork chop, and make a passable spaghetti with meat sauce. Fred, I discovered, did not like spaghetti. Out of this potentially sad situation, we chose to work as a team. We shopped together and chose simple foods to prepare. Fred always encouraged and supported, and gradually I began to learn.

After a year or so, we began having friends over for dinner. As my culinary reputation was building, I became passionate about wanting to excel at cooking. Fred afforded many opportunities for me to practice. He brought co-workers home for lunch, he invited friends over often, and he loved taking special treats to share at work.

One of the most significant events in our cooking life occurred when Fred started cooking on the grill and the Big Green Egg. We were friends with an older couple whose son-in-law was career military. The son-in-law had shipped them a forerunner to the Big Green Egg, which they kept on their patio but never used. She was such a non-clutter person. One day when we were visiting them, she told Fred she was going to "lend" him that cooker – not "give" as it was a gift to them. Fred enjoyed that cooker from about 1972 until it absolutely fell apart from constant use in the 1990s! Needless to say, a new one immediately took its place.

As our three children – Freddy, Johnny, and Connie – grew into teenagers, they brought their friends after school or after work or hunting trips. Our house became a mecca for our friends and their friends alike. There was always a pot of coffee and homemade treats. Fred and all three children were very social; they were all great at entertaining. And I loved making the cookies, special treats, pies, cakes, etc. Both the impromptu gatherings and our planned parties were opportunities to socialize – to visit, to tell stories (the same ones over and over sometimes), to play cards, occasionally even to dance.

How rich that life was! While the heart of our family was the foremost attraction, the food was an important factor. Food prepared with love creates an atmosphere for happy times and becomes a centerpiece for friendships. Learning to cook well and loving to cook for others lined a treasured pathway in my life journey. It is my joy to see the interest in cooking and the accomplishments of my children, grandchildren, and even my great grandchildren as they travel this same pathway.

The Making of a Cook

A recipe is just a way to start,
Real cooking comes from the heart.

It is more than ingredients, more than measuring,
It is about the ones you're treasuring.

Even more than pots and pans,
More than sous chefs lending hands,

Cooking is backed with real passion
And follows not trend or fashion.

So look who sits down at your table
And seek to show all the love you're able.

For the job description and all required
If your heart is touched, then you are hired!

Sue Collins Cannon

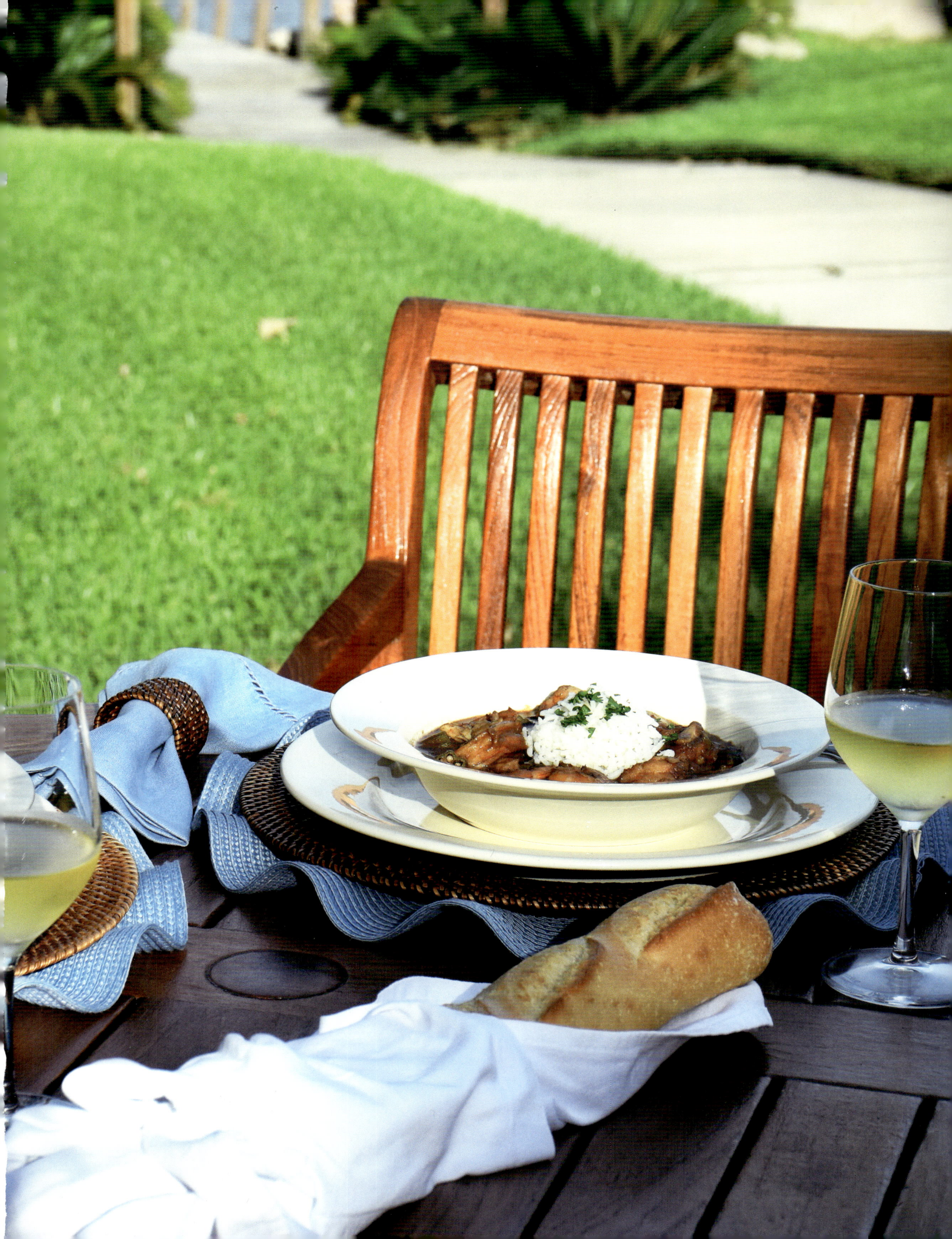

According to Benjamin Franklin, "The best appetizer is a pickle." The man was truly brilliant, but this bit of wisdom continues to baffle me. Does a pickle awaken your taste buds, does it provoke hunger, or does the sour taste send you running for tastier food? Regardless, we love our appetizers not only because they are tasty, but they also provide a great vehicle for socializing before dinner. A glass of wine with a selection of appetizers ensures that good friends gather to share a dining experience.

A few years ago, our family started having heavy hors d'oeuvres gatherings at which each person brings a favorite appetizer. Some exceptional food finds its way to my kitchen island! We especially look forward to the Big Green Egg specialties my nephew Mike Williams brings.

Never discount the versatile cheese tray. Use your imagination in selecting the tray – such as a pretty wooden chopping board, a flat basket, or an unusual piece of pottery. If you have large leaf plants, use some leaves to line the tray. Along with a selection of cheeses and a fruit, place one of the Roquefort Logs beside some flatbread crackers.

From the contents of this section, you may want to choose the Crab, Shrimp & Avocado Cocktail or Smoked Cheddar Cheese Spread as appetizers for a warm summer evening. For a cold winter evening, on the other hand, you might choose Sausage & Cheese Balls or Grilled Shrimp with Bacon. Regardless of climate conditions, freshly Roasted Pecans are always popular in a nut bowl.

APPETIZERS

Hot Crab & Shrimp Dip

Holiday Cheese Wafers

Parmesan & Rosemary Crackers

Swedish Meatballs

Three Cheese Pimento

Firecrackers

Shrimp Dip

Grilled Shrimp with Bacon

Roasted Pecans

Smoked Cheddar
Cheese Spread

Crabmeat Gruyere Tarts

Crab, Shrimp &
Avocado Cocktail

Fajitas Nachos

Roquefort Logs

Sausage & Cheese Balls

Hot Pepper Jelly

Hot Crab & Shrimp Dip

This hot dip combines crab and shrimp with the best seasonings for a delicious appetizer to be served with crostini or your favorite crackers.

1 pound jumbo lump crabmeat

1 small lemon

½ cup sliced almonds, toasted

1 cup Hellman's mayonnaise

1 tablespoon whole grain mustard

1 teaspoon garlic powder

½ teaspoon lemon pepper

Tabasco to taste

3 ounces shredded smoked cheese, such as Gruyère

1¼ cups chopped cooked shrimp

Place the crabmeat in a colander and squeeze the juice of the lemon over the top. Let drain.

In a skillet, toast the almonds and set aside in a small glass bowl.

Combine the mayonnaise, mustard, garlic powder, and lemon pepper in a large bowl. Season to taste with Tabasco. Stir in the cheese and shrimp. Gently mix in the crabmeat with a wooden spoon, taking care to keep the lumps whole.

Carefully spoon the mixture into an 8 x 8 (or equivalent) baking dish. Bake at 375° until bubbly, 20 to 25 minutes. Remove from the oven and sprinkle with toasted almonds. Serve warm.

Yields approximately 6 cups

APPETIZERS

Holiday Cheese Wafers

2 sticks butter, softened

8 ounces sharp cheddar cheese, freshly grated

2½ cups flour

1 teaspoon salt

¾ teaspoon ground red pepper

1 teaspoon Worcestershire sauce

½ cup finely chopped pecans

2 cups Rice Krispies

Using a mixer on medium speed, beat the butter and cheese until well blended. Gradually add the flour, salt and red pepper. Add Worcestershire and pecans. Mix in the Rice Krispies by hand.

Roll into 1-inch balls and place on a parchment-lined cookie sheet. Flatten each ball using a lightly floured fork. Bake at 350° until lightly browned. Check at 12 minutes.

Remove the cheese wafers from the pan and cool. Store in an airtight container.

To freeze for future baking: Instead of rolling into balls, roll the mixture into small logs. Wrap each log in wax paper and place into a Ziploc bag. When ready to bake, thaw the amount needed and proceed to roll into balls.

After trying various recipes for cheese wafers over the years, I combined and tweaked until this recipe emerged.

During the holiday season of 2010, I gave the recipe a formal name.

APPETIZERS

Parmesan & Rosemary Crackers

This recipe is versatile in that other herbs may be substituted for the rosemary.

I particularly like thyme as a variation. One of its attractions for the busy hostess is that the rolls may be frozen, thawed overnight in the refrigerator, sliced and baked when needed.

1 stick unsalted butter, room temperature

4 ounces Parmesan cheese, freshly grated

½ teaspoon natural sea salt

½ teaspoon freshly ground black pepper

1 teaspoon fresh finely chopped rosemary

1¼ cups flour

Using an electric mixer at medium speed, cream the butter until smooth. Turn the mixer to a low speed and add the Parmesan, sea salt, pepper, and rosemary. When the mixture is well blended, add the flour. Mix thoroughly until all flour is incorporated.

Place the dough on a floured surface and form into a ball. Roll into a log about 9 inches in length. Wrap in plastic and place the log in the refrigerator until chilled.

Slice the chilled log into ¼-inch rounds. Place on a parchment paper lined cookie sheet. Sprinkle lightly with sea salt.

Bake at 350° for 10 minutes. Turn the pan and continue to cook until slightly browned, about 8 minutes more.

Yields about 30 crackers

Swedish Meatballs

1½ pounds ground beef

½ pound ground pork

½ cup finely chopped onion

2 eggs

½ teaspoon black pepper

2 teaspoons salt

½ (10.5 ounce) can cream of mushroom soup

1 tablespoon Worcestershire sauce

½ cup bread crumbs

⅛ teaspoon allspice

⅛ teaspoon ground cloves

In a large bowl, mix all the ingredients together. Chill 6 hours. Roll into 1-inch balls and place on a cookie sheet, not touching. Cook at 400° for about 12 to 15 minutes until lightly browned. If desired, make the Savory Sauce and pour over the meatballs. Serve warm.

Savory Sauce:

2 cups catsup

3 tablespoons cider vinegar

⅓ cup Worcestershire sauce

2 tablespoons sugar

1 (10.5 ounce) can cream of mushroom soup

Stir all the ingredients together in a small saucepan. Cook over low heat until well blended. Add water to thin the sauce to desired consistency.

Yields about 100 meatballs

Adding the sauce not only keeps the meatballs moist, it also enhances the flavors.

Three Cheese Pimento

The really great feature of this recipe is the opportunity to experiment with your favorite cheeses.

As a rule of thumb, use one white cheese and one yellow cheese. The combinations are endless. Even consider the likes of smoked Gouda and sharp Cheddar. You can personalize the recipe, thus creating your own.

With the cream cheese, this recipe is more like a spread; leave out the cream cheese, and it is more like a traditional pimento cheese.

The green onion and parsley add a quality of freshness.

Freshly grating the cheese guarantees full flavor.

4 ounces cream cheese, softened

4 tablespoons Hellman's mayonnaise

pinch of salt

black pepper, to taste

garlic salt, to taste

4 ounces Cheddar cheese, freshly grated

4 ounces Monterey Jack cheese, freshly grated

1 (4 ounce jar) sliced pimentos

1 green onion, sliced thin

1 teaspoon chopped parsley

Stir the mayo into the softened cream cheese; add the seasonings. Combine the 2 cheeses with the cream cheese mixture. Drain the pimentos and stir into the mix.

At this point, add extra mayonnaise if needed to achieve the desired consistency. Lastly, stir in the green onion, including some of the green top, and the parsley.

APPETIZERS

Firecrackers

2 sleeves saltine crackers

¾ cup vegetable oil

2 tablespoons red pepper flakes

1 package Hidden Valley dry ranch dressing mix

shake of cayenne pepper

Empty the saltines into a gallon Ziploc bag. Set aside.

Combine the remaining ingredients and whisk until well mixed. Pour the mixture over the crackers and seal the Ziploc bag. Let stand for 30 minutes, turning from time to time to thoroughly marinate the crackers.

Empty the crackers onto a parchment-lined cookie sheet. The crackers do not have to be spread out in a single layer.

Bake for 30 minutes at 200°. Cool thoroughly and seal in an airtight container.

When Marguerite Ference, Steve Valerius' sister, shared this recipe with Connie, she could not have imagined that its popularity would spread so rapidly to Alabama.

Just place a small bowl of Three-Cheese Pimento near a tray of Firecrackers for a tasty appetizer with a kick!

APPETIZERS

Shrimp Dip

An all-time favorite since the early 1970s.

This dip became an instant hit when I brought the recipe back from a visit with friends in Louisville, Kentucky.

It is best served with Fritos.

1 cup finely chopped celery

2 tablespoons finely chopped onion

2 cups finely chopped boiled shrimp or 2 (8 ounce) cans small shrimp

8 ounces cream cheese, softened

½ cup Hellman's mayonnaise

1 tablespoon lemon juice

2 dashes Tabasco, or to taste

Finely chop the celery, onion, and shrimp. Set aside.

Combine the cream cheese and mayonnaise and mix until well blended.

Stir in the lemon juice and Tabasco. Add the chopped ingredients and mix well. Cover and refrigerate until ready to serve.

Grilled Shrimp with Bacon

2 dozen large uncooked shrimp, peeled

2 tablespoons butter, slightly melted

¼ teaspoon kosher salt

¼ teaspoon freshly ground black pepper

¼ teaspoon garlic salt or ½ teaspoon fresh minced garlic

12 slices bacon, regular thickness

1 teaspoon Worcestershire sauce

2 teaspoons soy sauce

Peel and devein the shrimp. In a medium mixing bowl, coat them with butter. Season with the salt, black pepper, and garlic.

Using ⅓ to ½ slice of bacon per shrimp, wrap each shrimp and secure the bacon ends with a toothpick. Place them in a single layer in a shallow container. Sprinkle with the Worcestershire and soy sauces.

Cook on a hot charcoal or gas grill, turning often until the bacon is done.

Served hot from the grill, the combined flavor of shrimp and bacon is an instant favorite.

In our family, this appetizer is the first to disappear!

APPETIZERS

Roasted Pecans

4 - 5 cups pecan halves

1 stick butter, cut into 8 pats

salt to taste

Preheat the oven to 350°.

Spread the pecans in a quarter-sheet jelly roll pan. Place the pan on the middle rack of oven and bake for 10 minutes. Remove from the oven and stir. Place the pats of butter over the pecans and return to the oven. Allow the butter to melt for about 5 minutes.

Remove the pan from oven; stir the pecans and sprinkle generously with salt. Return to the oven and cook for another 5 minutes.

Check for doneness at this time by tasting one of the pecan halves. If not done, return to the oven and check every 3-4 minutes until the desired doneness is achieved.

Spread the cooked pecans onto paper towels to cool. Store in an airtight container. Eat them as a snack, add them to salads, or use them to garnish desserts.

While I have taught a number of people to roast pecans, the most memorable was our friend Fenley Curtis.

When he asked if he could learn to make them himself, I gave him my recipe and five pounds of pecan halves on which to practice. He became quite proud of his pecan roasting skills.

Smoked Cheddar Cheese Spread

5 slices bacon

2 cups grated smoked cheddar cheese

½ cup chopped pecans

3 cloves garlic, minced

4 stems green onion tops, chopped

¾ cup Hellman's mayonnaise, to taste

Cut the bacon slices into ¼-inch pieces and fry until crisp. Drain on paper towels.

Combine all the ingredients in a medium bowl, adding the mayonnaise last.

Yields about 3 cups

Delightful Cherrie Felder from New Orleans shared this recipe with our Girls' Group.

She is well known for her expertise in "frying-up bacon" for many favorite dishes. We love her as chef, sous chef, or just for the great stories she tells over the chopping block.

APPETIZERS

Crabmeat Gruyere Tarts

The basis for this recipe comes from the Houston Coronado Club's *Flavors of Life* cookbook.

Since the tartlet shells are small, I dice the veggies rather small. The mix is very colorful and the taste is outstandingly good!

90 frozen phyllo tartlet shells

4 tablespoons butter

1 cup diced yellow onion

½ cup diced green bell pepper

¾ cup diced red bell pepper

¾ cup diced yellow bell pepper

½ cup diced jalapeno peppers

1 bunch cilantro, chopped

1 cup heavy cream

1½ cups grated Gruyere cheese

1 pound jumbo lump crabmeat

salt & freshly ground pepper

Bake the phyllo shells 3 to 5 minutes to crisp them, as per directions on package. Let the shells cool.

Heat the butter in a pan and sauté the yellow onion until tender. Add the green, red, and yellow peppers and the jalapeño pepper. Continue to sauté for 5 - 7 minutes more. Remove from the heat and place the mixture in a large bowl. Add the cilantro, Gruyere cheese, and heavy cream. Stir together and then add the crabmeat, tossing gently with a wooden spoon. Gently fill the tartlet shells.

Bake the filled tartlets in 375° oven for about 7 minutes or until the cheese is thoroughly melted. Sprinkle with a dash of salt and pepper.

Alternatively, the tarts can be frozen before baking. After filling the shells, place them back in the phyllo packaging and seal before freezing. It's nice to have these frozen tartlets on hand for a quick and delicious appetizer. Before serving, bake in an oven preheated to 375° for 13 to 15 minutes.

APPETIZERS

Crab, Shrimp & Avocado Cocktail

1 pound jumbo lump crabmeat

1 lemon

½ pound large shrimp, peeled

2 tablespoons olive oil

salt & pepper to taste

garlic salt to taste

½ sweet onion, chopped

2 small avocados, chopped

1 cup combined red and yellow cherry tomatoes, halved

2 tablespoons chopped cilantro

White Wine Vinaigrette

Empty the crabmeat into a colander. Squeeze the juice from the lemon over the crab and drain.

Toss the shrimp in a little olive oil, salt, pepper, and garlic salt. Sauté the shrimp until pink, taking care not to overcook. Remove from pan and cool. Cut the shrimp into bite-size pieces.

Layer the ingredients as follows: crabmeat, onion, shrimp, avocado, tomatoes, cilantro, salt and pepper.

Pour the dressing over the top and refrigerate 2 hours in a covered container. Toss before serving.

Connie was in a creative mood, and I was there to observe and take notes.

The cocktail makes a colorful presentation when served individually in crystal stemware.

White Wine Vinaigrette

3 ounces vegetable oil

3 ounces white wine vinegar

4 ounces ice water

Whisk together until blended.

APPETIZERS

Fajitas Nachos

tortilla chips

Famous Fajitas recipe, cooked and cut into small pieces (page 147)

extra sharp Cheddar cheese, grated

white cheese, grated (Monterey Jack, Fontina, etc.)

jalapeño slices

On a cookie sheet lined with either foil or parchment paper, spread a layer of tortilla chips. Sprinkle a fair amount of sharp Cheddar cheese over the chips; then spread the small pieces of beef or chicken fajitas meat on top.

Cook 10 minutes in a 350° oven. Remove the pan from the oven and add jalapeño slices to your taste. Lastly, sprinkle a generous layer of white cheese over the top.

Return the pan to the oven and cook until the white cheese is melted and chips are crisp, about 10 minutes.

Serve while warm with sour cream, guacamole, and salsa.

When making the Famous Fajitas from the Main Dishes section, we always plan enough meat for leftovers to make the nachos recipe.

Actually, this is a "how to" recipe. Simply follow the procedure for any amount, according to your leftovers. John is responsible for this recipe and enjoys the nachos for either an appetizer or lunch.

APPETIZERS

Roquefort Logs

6 ounces cream cheese, softened

2 ounces crumbled Roquefort cheese

2 tablespoons finely chopped onion

few drops Tabasco

dash cayenne pepper

¾ cup finely chopped pecans

In a medium mixing bowl, combine the cream cheese and Roquefort until well blended. Stir in the onion, Tabasco, and pepper. Cover and refrigerate until chilled.

Divide the mixture into 3 parts. Shape each part into a log about 1½ inches in diameter. Gently roll each log in the finely chopped pecans until well coated.

Wrap each log in plastic wrap and refrigerate until firm. Logs may be kept in refrigerator for up to 1 week, but also can be frozen for up to 3 months.

Add one of these savory little cheese logs to your cheese tray — it is always a favorite.

I like to double this recipe in order to freeze some of the logs. After wrapping the individual logs in plastic wrap, simply place a few in a quart Ziploc bag and store in freezer.

APPETIZERS

Sausage & Cheese Balls

Always a favorite appetizer with the flavors of both sausage and cheese.

Remember the tip to shred your own cheese for maximum taste!

2 pounds Jimmy Dean hot sausage

½ cup finely chopped onion

½ cup finely chopped celery

½ teaspoon garlic powder

1 tablespoon Tiger Sauce

⅛ teaspoon Tabasco

24 ounces sharp cheddar cheese, shredded

4 cups Bisquick

Unwrap the sausage and crumble into a large bowl. Set aside while chopping the onion and celery.

Using a wooden paddle, mix the sausage with the onion, celery, garlic powder, Tiger Sauce, and Tabasco. Add the cheese in 3 increments. As the mixture becomes thicker, you will need to mix by hand. When the cheese is thoroughly worked in, add the Bisquick 1 cup at a time.

Form into 1-inch balls. Place on parchment-lined cookie sheets. Bake at 375° for 15 minutes or until lightly browned.

The 1-inch balls can be quick frozen on a cookie sheet; then package in Ziploc bags and place in the freezer for 4 to 6 months. Remove from the freezer and bake as directed.

Hot Pepper Jelly

¾ cup coarsely chopped jalapeño peppers

1½ cup coarsely chopped green bell peppers

1½ cup white vinegar

6½ cup sugar

juice of 1 lemon

1 (6 ounce) package Certo

red or green food coloring, optional

Save a few seeds from the jalapeño peppers. Set aside.

Place the coarsely chopped peppers in a food processor or blender. Using a little of the vinegar, chop and pulse to make a purée.

Using a large Dutch oven or stockpot, combine the pepper purée with the remaining vinegar, sugar, and lemon juice. Cook on low heat for 45 minutes.

Bring to a rolling boil and boil for 1 minute. Remove from the heat and let the mixture rest for 5 minutes. Add the Certo and food coloring, stirring aggressively until well blended. Stir in a scarce sprinkling of the reserved seeds as an aesthetic reminder that you are eating pepper jelly!

Pour into hot ½-pint jars that have been sterilized. Carefully clean the top rims of the jars with a moistened cloth. Cover with lids that have been heated in a pan of water. Screw on the rims to seal the lids, tightening them well. Turn the hot jars of sealed jelly upside down for 5 minutes. Then, set the jars aside and do not disturb them for 24 hours.

Yields 6 to 7 half-pint jars

For an easy appetizer, serve over a log of cream cheese with buttery crackers.

During an October trip to enjoy the beautiful foliage in North Carolina, I became friends with a retired teacher from Florida.

We shared some recipes, and her hot pepper jelly was my prize!

The sealing method is one I learned from my sister Lucile.

APPETIZERS

Having been born in the fateful year of 1929, I have lived through an evolution of breads. "Sliced" loaves of bread at a nickel or dime a loaf were truly a "wonder," as the Wonder Bread Company named their product. My best girlfriend's father drove the bread truck for our area; he became our hero when he took two 7-year-old girls for a ride in his delivery truck.

The best breads, however, were – and still remain – the homemade biscuits, rolls, muffins, and cornbread fresh from the oven. One of my signature recipes is Nan's Famous Yeast Rolls, which is the basis for other yeast breads in this section. Muffins are usually one-bowl recipes and are fairly easy to make. As a bride I learned to make really good crusty cornbread, using freshly ground cornmeal from my father-in-law's gristmill. After he retired, I had to make-do with store bought meal until I discovered Jiffy mix about 10 years ago. (Note the recipe for Speedy Jalapeño Cheese Cornbread!)

I especially love the versatility of a good roll recipe. The dough really fascinated my grandchildren when they were growing up. A cool cooking opportunity for them was making monkey bread. What fun to have their own portion of roll dough to cut into small circles, pile them in a small pan, and brush the tops with melted butter. They took such pride in presenting their own contribution at dinner. Cleaning up the resulting scattering of flour was a small task compared to seeing those proud, happy faces. A new generation, my great-granddaughters, are making monkey bread and cinnamon rolls with me now!

BREADS

Nan's Famous Yeast Rolls

Rosemary Garlic Rolls

Focaccia Bread

Cinnamon Rolls

Speedy Jalapeño Cheese Cornbread

Old-Fashioned Jalapeño Cornbread

Hush Puppies with Crabmeat

Uncle Charlie's Hush Puppies

Pumpkin Bread

Banana Nut Bread or Muffins

Orange Carrot Muffins

Peach or Pear Preserves

Blueberry Surprise with Lemon Blueberry Sauce

Nan's Famous Yeast Rolls

This recipe was passed down from my mother, Elizabeth A. Taylor Collins, who could take four or five simple ingredients and make something delicious!

When I was a teenager, she would invite the entire family for Sunday dinner and make two large pans of these rolls! Later in life I had a tradition of making monkey bread for my grandchildren: we simply cut out very small round rolls and stacked them in a pan. The grandchildren loved to "help" by making their own individual pans to share with their parents.

1 (¼ ounce) packet active dry yeast

¼ cup lukewarm water

1 cup milk

⅓ cup Crisco

¼ cup sugar

1 teaspoon salt

all purpose or bread flour, about 3 cups

½ stick butter, melted

Heat the milk, Crisco, sugar, and salt until the mixture is ready to boil, but do not boil. Remove from the heat and let cool until lukewarm. Meanwhile, dissolve the yeast in the lukewarm water until creamy. Add to the lukewarm milk mixture and stir together.

Add the flour about ½ cup at a time and stir well after each addition. The consistency of the final dough should be stiff, but not dry. Cover and set in a draft-free place for about an hour until the dough doubles in size.

Turn the dough out onto a floured surface and knead until smooth. Cover with a towel for about 10 minutes.

Make into rolls and place on a heavily greased pan or in muffin tins. The versatility of this roll dough allows you to choose your own type of roll. The dough works well to cut with a biscuit cutter, to fold the circle over to form a pocket book, or to form 3 small balls in a muffin tin to make cloverleaf rolls. Brush the tops with melted butter. (If there is a timing issue, the rolls can be refrigerated at this point to slow down the rising process. Remove them about 1½ hours before dinner.) Let rise about an hour until doubled.

Bake at 350° until lightly browned and done, checking at 15 minutes. Remove from oven and brush lightly with melted butter.

BREADS

Rosemary Garlic Rolls

1 cup milk

⅓ cup Crisco

1 teaspoon salt

2 tablespoons sugar

1 (¼ ounce) packet active dry yeast

¼ cup lukewarm water

all purpose or bread flour, about 3 cups

3 tablespoons chopped fresh rosemary

2 tablespoons finely chopped garlic

½ stick butter, melted

coarse sea salt

Heat the first 4 ingredients to boiling, but do not boil. Remove from heat and cool to lukewarm. Meanwhile, mix the dry yeast with the lukewarm water until creamy.

Combine both mixtures. Add the flour ½ cup at a time until the dough is stiff, but not dry. Cover and place in a draft-free place to rise about an hour until doubled.

Punch the dough down and stir in the garlic and chopped rosemary. Turn the dough out onto a floured surface and knead until smooth. Cover with a dishtowel for a few minutes.

On a floured surface, roll the dough out to a thickness of ½ to ¾ inch. Cut into desired shapes: round, square, pocketbook, etc. Place the rolls on a greased pan. Brush the tops with melted butter and sprinkle lightly with coarse sea salt. Let rise about an hour in a warm, draft-free place until doubled.

Bake at 350° for 20 to 25 minutes until done. For softer rolls, cook until lightly browned; for crisper rolls, cook until toasty brown.

Steve and Connie encouraged me to go creative with my regular roll recipe.

Another possibility would be to make petite garlic rolls to serve with soups. Simply follow this same recipe, deleting the chopped rosemary. Roll the dough thinner and cut into smaller rolls – either round or square.

BREADS

Focaccia Bread

Steve and Connie challenged my creativity with this Italian bread!

Using my basic roll dough, I adapted some steps to make my version of the Italian bread that we enjoy so much. It can also be made using olives and prosciutto. I really like making focaccia for special dinners. Bringing the finished fragrant bread to the table usually provokes a few "aahs".

1 cup milk

⅓ cup Crisco

2 tablespoons sugar

1 teaspoon salt

¼ cup lukewarm water

1 (¼ ounce) packet active dry yeast

all purpose or bread flour, about 3 cups

3 tablespoons chopped fresh rosemary

2 tablespoons finely chopped garlic

olive oil

coarse sea salt

Heat the first 4 ingredients until ready to boil, but do not boil. Remove from heat and cool to lukewarm. Meanwhile, mix the dry yeast with the lukewarm water until creamy. Stir into the milk mixture.

Add flour ½ cup at a time, stirring well after each addition. Finished dough should be dense, but still moist. Cover and let rise about an hour until doubled.

Stir in the rosemary and garlic. Turn the dough out onto a floured surface and knead until the dough handles well, using additional flour as needed. Roll out until the dough is approximately the size of the pan.

Grease a quarter-sheet jelly roll pan with olive oil. Place the dough in the pan and use your hands to spread the dough evenly to all sides and corners. Place in draft-free place and let rise until almost double.

Using the handle end of a wooden spoon, dimple the dough. Sprinkle generously with olive oil, then sea salt. Bake in 350° oven until light brown, first checking at 15 minutes. When done, sprinkle with more olive oil and remove from pan.

BREADS

Cinnamon Rolls

1 cup milk

⅓ cup Crisco

¼ cup sugar

1 teaspoon salt

1 (¼ ounce) packet active dry yeast

¼ cup lukewarm water

all purpose or bread flour, about 3 cups

½ stick butter, melted

2 teaspoons cinnamon

3 tablespoons sugar

½ cup chopped pecans

Put the first 4 ingredients into a large saucepan. Heat to almost boiling, remove from the stove, and let cool to lukewarm. Meanwhile, dissolve yeast in lukewarm water until creamy. Stir into the milk mixture.

Stir in the flour, ½ cup at a time, until the dough is dense but still moist. Cover and let rise about an hour until doubled.

Turn out the roll mixture onto a floured surface and lightly knead. Form into a ball shape, cover with a clean dishcloth for about 10 minutes. Roll the dough out into a rectangular shape about ½ inch thick. Spread the rectangle with melted butter, sprinkle with sugar and cinnamon, and lastly sprinkle the surface with chopped pecans.

Starting with the long edge, roll pinwheel-style. Using a chef's knife, cut into equal sections about 1½ inches wide. Carefully lift and place, cut side down, into a well-greased pan. Place the rolls close together. Let rise about an hour until almost doubled.

Bake in a 350° oven until done, usually 20 to 25 minutes. While the rolls are baking, prepare the glaze.

Glaze:

½ stick butter

¼ cup milk

1 teaspoon vanilla

confectioner's sugar, about 2 cups

Microwave the butter and milk until the butter is melted. Add the vanilla. Using a whisk, stir in the sugar ½ cup at a time. When glazing consistency is achieved, spoon over the warm cinnamon rolls. The glaze will harden somewhat as the rolls cool.

These rolls are best when eaten warm.

However, leftovers may be refrigerated and enjoyed either cold or heated. They can also be frozen. Simply cook until rolls are just done, but not browned. Seal with heavy-duty foil and freeze up to 3 months. To bake, partially thaw and cook in a 350° oven until lightly browned, about 15 minutes. Glaze and serve.

This recipe also uses my basic roll recipe which has been adapted into a confectionery treat.

When my granddaughter Ashley married in 2012, she asked for a personal class in making cinnamon rolls. She proved to be an apt student and served them at her Christmas morning family breakfast. I loved her creativity of letting each person glaze his own cinnamon roll!

BREADS

Speedy Jalapeño Cheese Cornbread

My family is always happy to see this bread on the table.

It is a "must" with their favorite country dinner menu of fresh veggies and country fried steak, but also is delicious when served with a bowl of homemade vegetable beef soup.

1½ boxes Jiffy corn muffin mix

⅓ cup milk

1 egg, plus 1 egg yolk

½ medium onion, chopped

⅔ cup creamed corn, slightly drained

4 ounces sharp Cheddar cheese, grated

3 to 4 tablespoons chopped jalapeño peppers (to taste)

¼ cup canola oil

Pour the Jiffy mix into a large bowl, making a well. Add the milk and eggs into the well and stir until just blended. Add remaining ingredients and stir together.

Heat a well-seasoned 10-inch iron skillet over medium heat on top of the stove. Add the oil to the skillet. The skillet is ready when a small amount of batter sizzles in the oil.

Immediately pour the cornbread mixture into the skillet. Let the batter sizzle for a minute or two; then set the skillet into a preheated oven.

Bake 25 to 30 minutes in a 375° oven until crisp and brown. Loosen slightly with spatula around the edges. Turn out onto parchment paper.

BREADS

Old-Fashioned Jalapeño Cornbread

1¼ cups self-rising cornmeal mix

2 tablespoons flour

1 tablespoon sugar

1 egg, slightly beaten

½ cup buttermilk

2 tablespoons oil

4 ounces Cheddar cheese, grated

1 small onion, chopped

2 tablespoons chopped jalapeño peppers

½ cup creamed corn

3 tablespoons canola oil, for skillet

Place the dry ingredients into a large bowl. Make a well in the center. Add the egg, buttermilk, and oil. Stir all together just until blended. Stir in the cheese, onion, peppers, and corn.

Heat a well-seasoned 10-inch cast iron skillet on the cooktop. Add 3 tablespoons of oil. A spoon of the mixture will sizzle in the oil when the skillet is hot enough. Pour the cornbread batter into the skillet.

Bake at 400° for 20 to 25 minutes until crisp and brown. Run a spatula around edges of the pan to loosen. Turn out onto parchment paper immediately.

My first attempt at my family's favorite cornbread was this recipe.

Turning the cornbread out of the hot skillet as soon as it is done will ensure its very crisp crust!

BREADS

Hush Puppies with Crabmeat

During a visit to Dennis and Shane Steger at their Montana home in August of 2014, we were having fun preparing some of our wonderful Gulf seafood.

Along with the usual fried oysters and crab claws, we made Rolanette's Oysters Rockefeller and my Seafood Gumbo. Cherrie suggested that we try a recipe for hush puppies that she had recently found in a magazine. We tweaked the original recipe a bit, and the group absolutely loved the result.

3 cups buttermilk corn meal mix

1 cup self-rising flour

1 teaspoon baking soda

2 teaspoons kosher salt

4 teaspoons freshly ground black pepper

2½ cups buttermilk

1 egg, slightly beaten

1 cup chopped green onions

⅓ cup finely chopped fresh jalapeño peppers

dash of Tabasco

1 pound jumbo lump crabmeat

Combine the dry ingredients in a large mixing bowl. Whisk together and make a well in the center. Add 2 cups of the buttermilk and the egg, whisking until well mixed. Stir in the onions, peppers, and Tabasco. Use enough of the remaining buttermilk to make the batter thick, but not stiff. Carefully add the jumbo lump crabmeat and stir lightly, just enough to distribute the crab evenly.

Heat oil to 355°. Drop heaping teaspoons of the hush puppy mixture into the oil and fry until golden brown.

Yields about 20 servings

BREADS

Uncle Charlie's Hush Puppies

2 cups cornmeal

1 cup flour

1 teaspoon baking soda

1 egg

1 cup buttermilk

1 teaspoon vinegar

¾ cup creamed corn

1 onion, grated

beer, part of 1 can

canola oil

Whisk the dry ingredients together in a large bowl and form a well. In a small bowl whisk the egg, buttermilk, and vinegar until well blended. Pour the liquid mixture into the well of the dry ingredients. Stir until just blended. Add the onion and corn. Thin the mixture to a cornbread batter consistency with a little beer, as needed.

Heat about 2 inches of oil in a deep skillet until hot, or heat a deep fryer to 355°.

Drop the hush puppy batter by teaspoons into the hot cooking oil and fry until crusty brown. Drain well on a wire rack over paper towels.

Uncle Charlie, my brother who was nearest my age and who was also a classmate and friend of Fred's, was always a special family guest in our home.

He enjoyed our children, and they always looked forward to his visits. He also loved to cook – not just on the Big Green Egg, but also in the kitchen. This recipe was especially good with the fresh fish that Freddy was so adept at catching in the rivers and bay waters of southern Alabama.

BREADS

Pumpkin Bread

Vassie Hatchett
of Union Church, at the age of 80, gave me this cherished recipe.

She was a wonderful person and a very accomplished seamstress who specialized in Azalea Trail Maid gowns. I met her in 1984 when she helped me design and sew Connie's antebellum wedding gown, hat, and parasol. In one of our delightful sessions, she served this delicious pumpkin bread and shared her recipe!

3½ cups flour

3½ cups sugar

1 teaspoon nutmeg

1 teaspoon cinnamon

1 teaspoon baking soda

2 teaspoons baking powder

¾ teaspoon salt

4 eggs

1 cup canola oil

2 teaspoons vanilla

2 cups cooked pumpkin, mashed

1 ½ cups chopped pecans

Combine all the dry ingredients in a mixer bowl. Whisk together and make a well. Add the eggs and oil. Beat at medium speed until well blended. Mix in the pumpkin and vanilla. Stir in the pecans by hand.

Pour the batter into heavily greased and floured loaf pans. Bake in a 350° oven until done. Check at 45 minutes; continue to cook until center is firm.

Set the loaves on a cake rack and cool in the pans for 10 to 15 minutes. Run a table knife around the edges before turning out the loaves. Continue cooling with the top side up.

Pumpkin Muffins: Use the same ingredients, but whisk together entirely by hand. Adjust baking time to the size of your muffin tins. Check at 20 minutes.

Yields 2 loaves

BREADS

Banana Nut Bread or Muffins

1 cup flour

½ teaspoon baking soda

½ teaspoon salt

1 teaspoon cinnamon

¾ cup sugar

⅓ cup oil

1 egg

¼ cup buttermilk

1 teaspoon vanilla

1 large banana, mashed

¾ cup chopped pecans

Yields 12 medium muffins

Mix the dry ingredients by whisking in a large bowl and form a well. In a small bowl whisk the oil, egg, buttermilk, and vanilla. Pour into the well of the dry ingredients. Stir just until mixed. Add the bananas and pecans.

Heavily grease muffin tins with Crisco and sprinkle with flour. Fill ⅔ full of batter. Bake in a 350° oven until done – about 25 minutes. Centers of the muffins will be firm when done. Lift the muffins out gently with a fork and place on a wire rack.

In 1955 I worked for a time with a lady named "Jim", who taught me to make banana cake.

Over the years I tweaked her recipe and it became a family favorite, as well as the basis for this recipe.

This recipe is quite versatile as it is easily doubled or tripled.

It adapts to different sizes of muffin tins. The muffins are also delicious when iced with Cream Cheese Frosting (page 187). To make a loaf of Banana Nut Bread, adjust the cooking time to about 45 minutes.

BREADS

Orange Carrot Muffins

In the early 1990's, Lisa and Freddy took me to lunch at the Bay Oaks Country Club in Clear Lake, TX.

They strongly recommended the muffins and especially wanted to see if I could duplicate the recipe. The muffins were the best I had ever eaten, so it was a joy when my version really pleased them.

1½ cups flour

1½ cups sugar

1½ teaspoons cinnamon

¾ teaspoon nutmeg

1½ teaspoons baking soda

½ teaspoon salt

⅔ cup oil

2 eggs

2 cups grated carrots (about 1 pound)

zest of a large orange

¼ cup orange juice

1 cup grated coconut

1¼ cups chopped pecans

Whisk the dry ingredients together in a large bowl, making a well in the center. Combine the oil and eggs and pour into the well; stir until all ingredients are wet. Add the remaining ingredients, stirring until just mixed.

Prepare the muffin tins by heavily coating with Crisco and sprinkling with flour. You may use paper liners instead, but you will not get that nice crust on the muffins.

Bake at 350° until done, about 25 minutes. Test by checking the center tops for firmness with your fingertip (very carefully, of course). Cool on a cake rack for 5 minutes. Loosen the edges with a table knife; carefully lift from the muffin tins with a fork.

Yields 12 to 15 regular size muffins

BREADS

Peach or Pear Preserves

10 cups prepared fruit, either peaches or pears

8 cups sugar

½ lemon, cut into small pieces (rind included)

red food coloring, optional

Prepare the peaches or pears by peeling the fruit and cutting into small pieces.

In a stockpot or a very large Dutch oven, combine all the ingredients. Bring to a boil, stirring occasionally; then lower the heat to keep the mixture at a low boil.

Cook until the fruit is done and the syrup is somewhat thickened. This usually takes about 1 hour. If the preserves need a bit more color, cautiously add a little red food coloring!

Ladle the preserves into hot ½-pint jars that have been sterilized. Wipe the tops of jars with a moistened cloth. Apply lids that have been heated in water on the stove. Screw the bands hand-tight. Invert jars for 5 minutes. Turn the jars upright and leave them undisturbed overnight.

My sister Lucile taught our brother Charlie and me to make jellies and preserves in the early 1980s.

What good times those were: we peeled, chopped, and canned while Fred shopped for supplies and Betty cleaned up after us. What special joy came to me years later — I knew how to make pear preserves when Dennis Steger wanted so much to find some for his father!

BREADS

Blueberry Surprise with Lemon Blueberry Sauce

About 20 years ago, a contest was held in Baldwin County, Alabama, in search of recipes using blueberries.

The idea of adding cooked sausage pieces to a coffee cake came from the winning recipe, which was published in the Mobile Press Register. Adding my citrusy blueberry sauce and serving with crisp bacon has made for a great addition to our breakfast menus.

1 pound Jimmy Dean sausage

1½ sticks butter

¾ cup sugar

¼ cup light brown sugar, packed

2 eggs

1 cup sour cream

2 cups flour

1 teaspoons baking powder

½ teaspoon salt

1 cup blueberries

1 cup chopped pecans

Lemon Blueberry Sauce

Night before: Prepare as follows.

Cut the sausage into slices and fry in a large skillet until brown. Drain and cool. Break into small pieces.

Using a mixer at medium speed, cream the butter and sugars until light and fluffy. Add the eggs and sour cream; blend well. Gradually add the dry ingredients to the creamed mixture, beating at a low speed until blended.

Remove from the mixer and add the cooled sausage; then, gently fold in the blueberries by hand.

Grease and flour a 9 x 13 pan. Sprinkle the chopped pecans over the bottom of the pan. Spread the batter evenly over the nuts. Cover with plastic wrap and refrigerate overnight.

Next morning: Remove the plastic wrap. Bake in a preheated oven at 350° for 50 to 60 minutes until done and lightly browned. Serve warm with Lemon Blueberry Sauce and crisp slices of bacon!

Lemon Blueberry Sauce:

½ cup sugar

2 cups blueberries

1½ cups water, divided

2 tablespoons cornstarch

1 tablespoon fresh lemon juice

1 teaspoon fresh lemon zest

Combine the sugar, blueberries, and 1 cup water in a small saucepan. Bring to a boil. Meanwhile, combine the remaining ½ cup water with the cornstarch and stir until smooth. Lower the heat under the blueberries and add the cornstarch mixture. Stir while simmering until slightly thickened. Remove from the heat and stir in the lemon juice and zest. Serve warm.

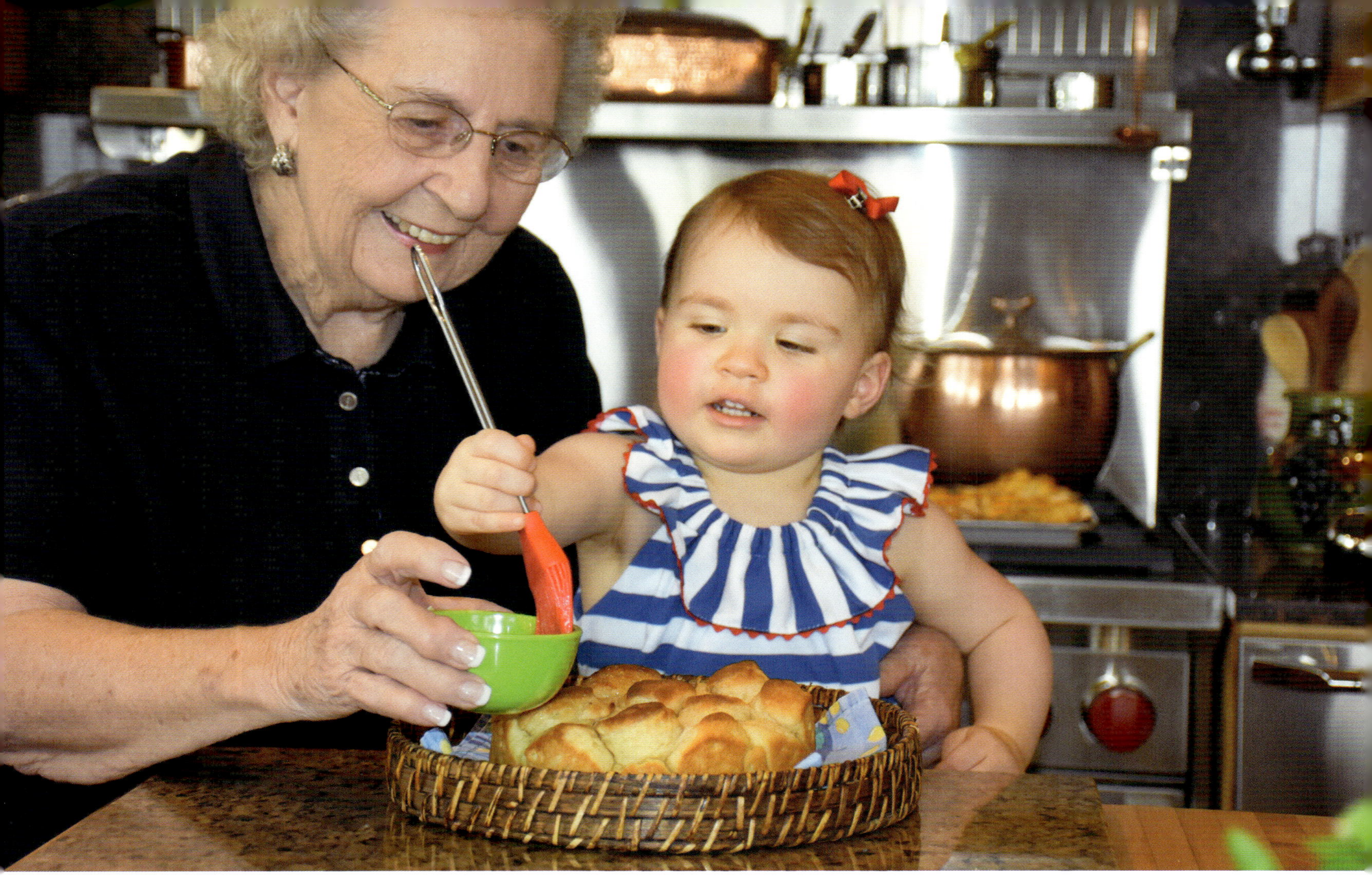

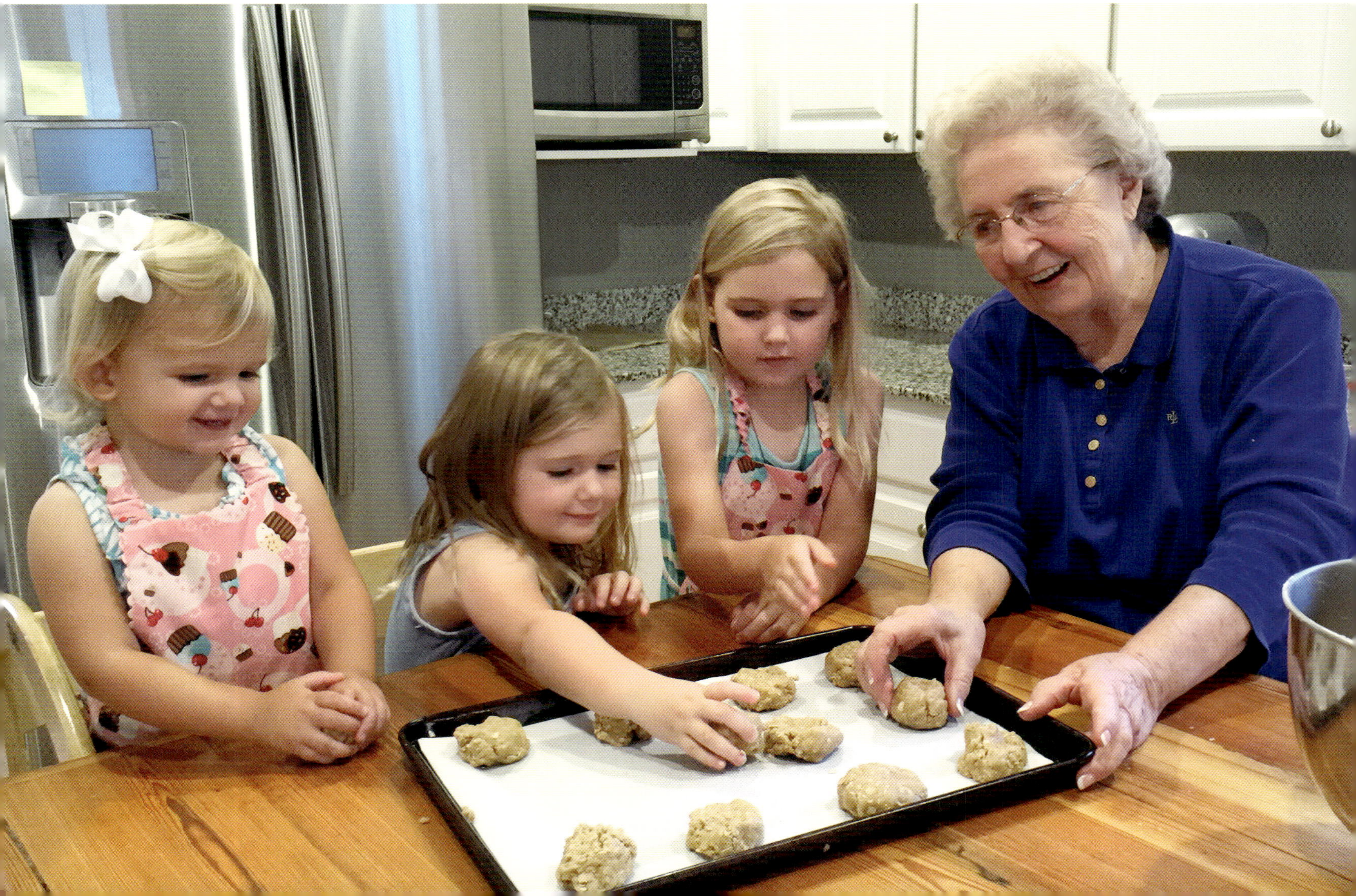

The Beat Goes On...

Maybe unconsciously, and maybe not, I wanted my grandchildren to share my love of cooking. Through them the beaters – the whisks, the spatulas, and spoons – will continue beating and stirring into the next generation and then the next.

When grandchildren spent time at my house, they became the focus of the day. We played. We sang while "just a-swangin" on the front porch swing. We took turns on the riding lawn mower to tour the pecan orchard, stopping to pick wildflowers and weeds alike. We played board games, Battle, Go Fishing, Uno, checkers, and dominoes. But always, always, we spent some time in the kitchen.

With five grandchildren anxious to "help" with a family dinner, they needed to have interesting, fun tasks. We worked together setting the table. They created place cards to mark the seating arrangement. One took drink orders on a cute little pad. Another took orders for dessert, and all were involved in plating and serving dessert.

My grandchildren are all grown now. Through texts and emails, they often consult with me and send me texts with pictures of their renditions using recipes that are in this cookbook. At times I receive SOS texts with questions, or maybe just a need for a supportive word.

I am pleased beyond measure over the next generation of cooks. Moreover, I now have great-grandchildren with whom to cook. I just want to keep passing it on. So let the beat go on!

The soups that I have included in this section are especially good during cooler weather. They are hearty presentations, rich with meat and include tasty vegetables and seasonings. With crackers, garlic bread, or cornbread, the soups are excellent one-dish meals. As an added bonus, the recipes usually provide left overs that seem to taste even better after a day or two in the refrigerator.

Some of the salads, as well, are nice for light lunches. The recipe for Chicken Salad is one of my stand-by dishes for sharing with neighbors, friends, and family. I always make the full recipe and, therefore, have more than enough. The West Indies Salad is also a great starter presentation.

The once-popular congealed salads, I just know, are going to make a comeback. You may want to include one in your next holiday menu!

SOUPS & SALADS

Vegetable Beef Soup

Uncle Charlie's Chili

Poblano Crab Soup

Clam Chowder with Dill

Chicken & Andouille Gumbo

Roux

Chicken Tortilla Soup

West Indies Salad

Absolutely Delicious
Salad Dressing

Comeback Salad Dressing

Bleu Cheese &
Spicy Pecan Salad

Spicy Pecans

Chicken Salad

Shrimp Salad

Crab Tower Salad

Crispy Pickle Slices

Cole Slaw

Southern Broccoli Salad

Coca Cola Party Salad

Pineapple Salad

Blueberry Salad

Ambrosia

Charleston Delight

Frozen Pink Salad

Vegetable Beef Soup

In New Orleans, Mondays were traditionally days for red beans and rice.

At my mother's house in the Mississippi Delta, Mondays were always vegetable soup days. She never used a recipe, and often used ham bones instead of beef stew meat. The memory of one of her bowls of soup far surpasses the reality of any I have ever made!

2 tablespoons canola oil

2 pounds beef stew meat

1 large onion, chopped

3 ribs celery, chopped

½ teaspoon coarse black pepper

2 teaspoons salt

2 tablespoons Worcestershire sauce

3 cups water

28 ounces beef broth

1 (10 ounce) can tomato sauce

1 (20 ounce) can diced tomatoes

3 cups baby carrots, sliced

3 medium potatoes, diced

16 ounces frozen cut okra

3 cups baby green lima beans, cooked

3 cups whole kernel or cream-style corn, cooked

Heat the oil in a large heavy pot. Sear the meat until browned. Add the onion, celery, pepper, and salt. When the veggies are wilted, stir in the Worcestershire, water, and beef broth. Bring to a boil, cover and simmer 2 hours until the meat is tender.

Add the tomato sauce, tomatoes, carrots, and potatoes; bring to a boil. Lower the heat, cover with the lid, and simmer for 30 minutes. Add the okra, beans, and corn. Bring to a boil. Turn the heat to simmer, cover, and cook 20 minutes.

Yields about 5 quarts (plenty for freezing and/or sharing)

SOUPS & SALADS

Uncle Charlie's Chili

2 to 3 pounds ground beef

1 large onion, chopped

1 package 2-Alarm chili seasoning

1 (10 ounce) can Rotel tomatoes with chilies

1 cup water

2 cans chili (I like Wolf brand chili, 1 with & 1 without beans)

tamales, optional

sour cream, grated cheese, chopped onions as optional garnishes

In a large heavy pan, brown the ground beef with the chopped onion. Remove the pan from the heat and drain the excess liquid.

Return the pan to the heat. Using the packets of seasonings from the 2-Alarm chili kit, add all except the red pepper and the mesa. Stir in the Rotel tomatoes and water. Lastly, add the 2 cans of chili.

At this point taste the mixture to determine if you need to add some of the red pepper packet to achieve your preferred taste.

Simmer the chili covered for 25 minutes, stirring occasionally to prevent sticking or scorching.

Serve while hot. Place a tamale in each bowl, if desired. Offer grated cheese, chopped onions, and sour cream as optional garnishes.

Yields 8 to 10 servings

My brother Charlie taught me to make chili by his own special recipe at their mountain cabin in Franklin, North Carolina, during one fall foliage season.

After a hot bowl of this chili, we sat around the fireplace, shelling pecans and sharing memories from our youth. My brother was "Uncle Charlie" not just to my children, but to all their friends. His fun-loving, caring personality drew people to him.

Poblano Crab Soup

This soup ranks among the best in both elegance and flavor.

It is therefore our family's special occasion choice.

For a nice accompaniment, make some petite yeast rolls with finely chopped jalapeño or minced garlic. See the recipe for Rosemary Garlic Rolls (page 39).

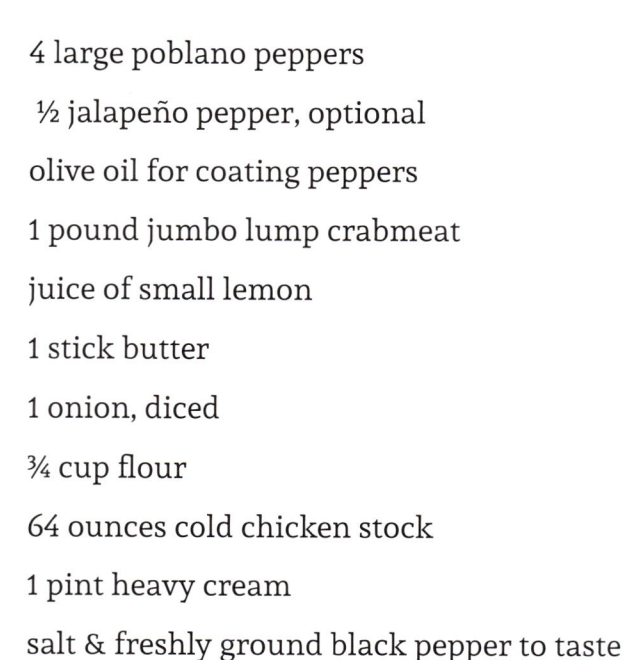

4 large poblano peppers

½ jalapeño pepper, optional

olive oil for coating peppers

1 pound jumbo lump crabmeat

juice of small lemon

1 stick butter

1 onion, diced

¾ cup flour

64 ounces cold chicken stock

1 pint heavy cream

salt & freshly ground black pepper to taste

Coat the peppers with olive oil. Roast them on a hot grill, turning often until they are blistered and blackened on all sides. Place them in a bowl and seal with plastic wrap, allowing them to steam until cool enough to handle. Remove the skins and seeds; cut into large pieces. Set aside.

Carefully empty the jumbo lump crabmeat into a colander. Sprinkle the juice of a small lemon over the crab. Set aside to drain.

Sauté the onions in the butter. Stir in the flour. Gradually whisk in the chicken stock, keeping the mixture smooth. Add the peppers and simmer for 25 minutes, stirring occasionally. Remove from the heat.

Processing in portions, purée the hot soup in either a blender or food processor. Return the soup to the pan and place over low heat. Stir in the heavy cream, salt, and pepper. When the mixture is hot, carefully add the crabmeat. To avoid breaking those succulent jumbo sections of crabmeat, be sure to use a wooden paddle to gently mix in the crabmeat. Continue cooking until the crabmeat is thoroughly heated. If desired, reserve some crabmeat to garnish each serving.

Yields 8 servings

SOUPS & SALADS

Clam Chowder with Dill

Base Recipe:

2 tablespoons extra virgin olive oil

1 cup finely chopped onion

2 tablespoons finely chopped celery

1 teaspoon salt

¼ teaspoon thyme

¼ teaspoon garlic powder

¼ teaspoon freshly ground black pepper

¼ cup flour

1 tablespoon cornstarch

2 (6.5 ounce) cans minced ocean clams

1 cup diced potatoes

2 cups clam juice

In a large pot, sauté the onions and celery until translucent. Season with the salt, thyme, garlic powder, and pepper. Stir in the flour and cornstarch. Add the clams, including the liquid, and the potatoes. Lastly, stir in the clam juice. Bring to a simmer and cook 20 minutes or until the potatoes are done. Cool the mixture in the refrigerator for at least 30 minutes, or until ready to finish for serving.

Finishing:

1 (10 ounce) can baby sea clams

1 cup whipping cream

2 tablespoons butter

4 tablespoons chopped fresh dill

vermouth for splashing

When ready to serve the chowder, remove the base from the refrigerator and place over medium heat. Stir in the clams, cream, and butter. When the chowder is thoroughly heated, add the dill and stir well. Ladle into soup bowls and to each add a splash of vermouth before serving.

After enjoying clam chowder at a restaurant, Fred wanted me to try making it.

I managed to put together some ingredients in a way that he really liked. Over the years I have continued to tweak my recipe. The most recent version, the addition of fresh dill and the splash of vermouth, occurred when my daughter returned from Newport where she had enjoyed the award-winning clam chowder at the famous Black Pearl restaurant.

SOUPS & SALADS

Chicken & Andouille Gumbo

Roux, see recipe on following page

Crockpot Chicken or rotisserie chicken; skinned, deboned, and cut into small pieces

broth reserved from Crockpot Chicken

2/3 stick butter

1 large onion, chopped

3 ribs celery, chopped

½ bell pepper, chopped

2 cloves garlic, chopped

3 quarts chicken broth (use the reserved plus other)

1 teaspoon cayenne pepper

1 teaspoon black pepper

2 teaspoons salt

4 bay leaves

1 (14 ounce) can diced tomatoes

16 ounces frozen cut okra

1 pound Andouille sausage, sliced in ¼-inch pieces

5 tablespoons gumbo filé

cooked rice, optional

parsley for garnishing

Melt the butter in a large heavy pot. Sauté the chopped onion, celery, and bell pepper until wilted. Add the chopped garlic. Stir in the roux. Add the chicken broth (a total of 3 quarts) in 3 parts, stirring well after each addition.

Add the remaining ingredients, except for the gumbo filé. Bring the gumbo to a boil. Turn to the lowest heat setting; cover and let simmer for 1 hour. Using a metal spoon, skim the extra oil from the top of the gumbo pot. Stir in the gumbo filé and cook 5 minutes more. Serve with a scoop of rice and garnish with parsley.

Yields about 5 quarts

On a trip to Connie's in February of 2012, we decided to work on developing a good chicken and sausage gumbo recipe.

Our research included searching several cookbooks plus analyzing my original chicken gumbo recipe. Using these sources, plus a bit of ingenuity, we experimented and were pleased with this resulting recipe.

Roux

1 cup canola oil

1½ cups flour

Have ready a quart-size glass bowl before beginning the roux. Place a large metal spoon so that it rests against the bottom and side of the bowl. Pouring the extremely hot roux onto the spoon prevents the danger of breaking the bowl.

In a heavy saucepan, heat the oil over medium heat until a pinch of flour sizzles when it is sprinkled into the skillet. Add all the flour, stirring constantly with a wooden spatula to incorporate it.

Continue to stir throughout, diligently turning the mixture to prevent the flour from burning on the bottom of the pan. When the roux reaches a rich brown color, much like a dark peanut butter, immediately remove the pan from the heat and pour the roux over the metal spoon in the glass bowl.

After a couple of minutes, remove the spoon and stir the mixture well using a metal whisk. Set the bowl of roux aside until needed. The roux will darken and the excess oil will rise to the top and can be spooned off before adding the roux to the gumbo recipe.

"Roux", a French term meaning reddish brown, is a thickener for soups and sauces. It not only acts as a thickener, but also adds its flavoring to the gumbo.

While cooks vary in their preferred color of the roux when it is done, they all agree on certain tips: use a dry, heavy saucepan such as a cast iron skillet; give the roux your undivided attention; and start over if you accidentally burn the roux.

SOUPS & SALADS

Chicken Tortilla Soup

Connie created this recipe by selecting and combining ingredients from several existing recipes.

2 tablespoons olive oil

1 large onion, chopped

2 garlic cloves, chopped

2 (15 ounce) cans Rotel tomatoes

2 (15 ounce) cans black beans, drained and rinsed

3 cups cooked creamed corn

2 quarts chicken broth

1 tablespoon Minor's chicken base

2 tubs Knorr's concentrated chicken broth

2 packets Sazo'n Goya con Azafran seasoning

1 rotisserie chicken, pulled into small pieces

garnishes: cheddar cheese, tortilla chips, jalapeños, avocados, lime juice

In a large pot over medium heat, sauté the onion and garlic. Add the Rotel tomatoes and continue cooking until heated. Add the chicken broth, chicken base, and concentrated chicken broth. Stir in the black beans and corn. Bring the soup to a boil and add the pulled chicken.

Bring to a simmer and cover the pot. Cook until the soup is thoroughly heated. For the best flavor, continue to simmer for 1 hour.

Ladle the soup into individual bowls. Sprinkle with lime juice. Garnish with grated cheddar cheese and broken tortilla chips or strips. Add chopped jalapeños, avocados, and cilantro.

To make your own tortilla strips, cut soft corn tortillas into strips. Deep fry in hot oil until browned and crisp. Drain the chips and sprinkle with salt.

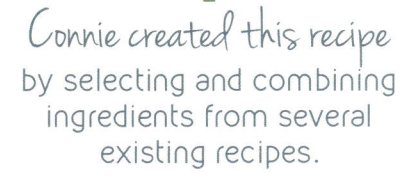

SOUPS & SALADS

West Indies Salad

1 pound fresh jumbo lump crabmeat

juice of 1 small lemon

1 medium onion, finely chopped

4 ounces Wesson Oil

3 ounces cider vinegar

4 ounces ice water

salt and pepper to taste

Carefully place the crabmeat in a colander and squeeze the lemon juice over the crabmeat. Set aside to drain.

Spread half the onion over the bottom of a shallow bowl or plastic container. Next, make a layer of the crabmeat and spread the remaining onion over the top.

Salt and pepper to taste. Whisk the oil, vinegar, and ice water until mixed. Pour this mixture over the layers. Cover and marinate for 2 to 12 hours. Toss lightly before serving.

Yields 6 to 8 servings

This very special recipe dates back to mid-1900s and originated with Bailey's Restaurant on Dauphin Island Parkway in Mobile County.

We have found that, on occasion, adding a few boiled, chilled shrimp and a little basil gives this crab salad extra enhancement. The ultimate key to its flavor, however, lies in the freshness and quality of the jumbo lump meat.

SOUPS & SALADS

Absolutely Delicious Salad Dressing

The catchy title is so appropriate for this light salad dressing that will make the salad greens sparkle and your palate tingle.

My friend Cherrie Felder was happy to pass on the recipe that was given to her by a friend.

½ cup extra virgin olive oil

2 tablespoons lemon juice

2 cloves garlic, minced

1 teaspoon salt

½ teaspoon freshly ground black pepper

4 tablespoons grated Parmesan cheese

2 pinches dry mustard

Combine the ingredients in a small mixing bowl. Whisk until well blended.

Toss with salad greens. Any salad dressing not used may be refrigerated for a few days.

SOUPS & SALADS

Comeback Salad Dressing

2 garlic cloves, minced

1 cup Hellman's mayonnaise

¼ cup catsup

¼ cup chili sauce

1 teaspoon mustard

½ cup vegetable oil

1 teaspoon Worcestershire sauce

1 teaspoon black pepper

1 teaspoon paprika

1 small grated onion

1 teaspoon water

Tabasco – few drops or to taste

salt to taste

lemon juice to taste

Combine all ingredients and chill before serving.

Yields about 2 cups

While I was attending Belhaven College in Jackson, my sister Ruth and brother-in-law Hoy took me on Friday nights to the Rotisserie, a really nice restaurant that was well known for its steaks.

The chopped salad included capers and was topped with this unforgettable salad dressing, for which my sister was able to obtain the recipe.

This dressing is also delicious as a sauce for fried food.

Bleu Cheese & Spicy Pecan Salad

Spicy Pecans are excellent added to salads.

I borrowed this recipe from my daughter, Connie. Her salads are both delicious and eye pleasing. With some fresh spring greens, her choice of cheese, an apple or pear, these pecans, and maybe some crisp pancetta – she only needs to mix together a nice dressing to create an outstanding salad.

5 to 6 cups mixed lettuces

3 green onions, including tops

1 Bosc or red pear or Granny Smith apple

4 ounces bleu cheese, crumbled

⅔ cup coarsely chopped Spicy Pecans

Wash, spin, and chill a mix of your favorite salad greens. Chop the green onions. Select 1 of the fruit options to core and chop.

In a large salad bowl, place the chilled lettuce and remaining ingredients. Add the Vinaigrette and toss to coat.

Yields 8 servings

Vinaigrette:

3 tablespoons apple cider vinegar

⅔ cup white vinegar

⅔ cup sugar

1 teaspoon salt

1 teaspoon dry mustard

2 tablespoons Worcestershire sauce

1½ tablespoons onion juice

1 cup vegetable oil

In a small bowl whisk the sugar, salt, and mustard with the vinegars, Worcestershire, and onion juice. Slowly pour in the oil, and whisk continuously until well blended.

Spicy Pecans

2 large egg whites

1½ teaspoons salt

¾ cup sugar

2 teaspoons Worcestershire sauce

2 tablespoons Hungarian paprika

1½ teaspoons cayenne pepper

4½ cups pecan halves

¾ stick butter, melted and cooled

Beat the egg whites until foamy. Add and blend in the salt, sugar, Worcestershire sauce, paprika, and cayenne pepper. Stir in the melted butter until well mixed. Fold in the pecan halves. Spread the pecans evenly onto a parchment-lined cookie sheet.

Bake at 325° for 30 to 40 minutes, stirring every 10 minutes. When the pecans are toasted, remove the pan from the oven. Slide the parchment paper with the pecans onto a flat surface and cool. Store the cooled pecans in an airtight container.

Hungarian paprika is known for its rich sweet pepper taste.

Chicken Salad

1 whole chicken or 4 chicken breasts *

5 boiled eggs, chopped into small pieces

1 tablespoon finely chopped onion

1 cup chopped celery

¾ cup chopped sweet pickles, optional

½ teaspoon celery seed or celery salt

dash of garlic salt or garlic powder

salt and pepper to taste

¼ cup orange juice

½ to 1 cup Hellman's mayonnaise, to desired consistency

Cook the chicken in a crockpot or on the stovetop. Cool and remove the skin and bones. Dice the chicken and place in a large mixing bowl. * For busy days, a rotisserie chicken is a great option.

Measure all ingredients and combine with the chicken. Chill for maximum flavor.

Yields 10 to 12 servings

This chicken salad recipe is quite flexible.

You may add or delete ingredients to your preference. For example, I sometimes add more celery or I may add a cup of chopped pecans. Since the recipe makes a large bowl, it can be divided and shared with friends or family.

SOUPS & SALADS

Shrimp Salad

1 teaspoon Old Bay seasoning

1 teaspoon salt

1½ pounds medium shrimp

3 hard boiled eggs, chopped in pieces

1 rib celery, finely chopped

1 teaspoon finely chopped onion

⅓ cup chopped sweet pickles, optional

salt, pepper, and garlic salt to taste

½ to 1 cup Hellman's mayonnaise

In a large saucepan, bring about 1½ quarts of water to a boil. Stir in the Old Bay seasoning and salt; then add the shrimp. Bring to a boil and cook about 3 minutes, or until the shrimp turn pink.

Immediately pour the shrimp into a colander to drain. Cover the shrimp loosely with ice. Peel the shrimp and remove the veins. Cover with plastic wrap and set them in the refrigerator while you prepare the other ingredients.

In a large bowl combine the remaining ingredients with the shrimp. Add mayonnaise according to your desired consistency and taste.

The salad is best served cold on a bed of lettuce.

Yields 6 to 8 servings

Shrimp is the basis for many wonderful recipes and is delightful however you choose to prepare this flexible seafood.

It is important to avoid overcooking, as the shrimp will become tough and lose some of its delicious flavor. Covering the shrimp immediately with ice not only stops the cooking process, but also quickly cools them for peeling. Fred especially enjoyed this salad; I made it on his request many times!

SOUPS & SALADS

Crab Tower Salad

An extraordinary salad in both taste and presentation which was created by Connie and enjoyed by all!

Jumbo lump crabmeat is essential for building the towers. Handle carefully to keep lumps whole.

6 ounces cherry tomatoes

2 tablespoons finely diced red onion

salt & freshly cracked black pepper, to taste

extra virgin olive oil

1 pound fresh jumbo lump crabmeat

juice of ½ lemon

Chunky Guacamole

tortilla chips

Prepare each layer separately and set aside.

1st layer: Wash the cherry tomatoes and dry completely. With a small sharp knife, cut each tomato into 4 sections, being careful not to mash. Place the tomatoes into a medium bowl, keeping them free of any liquid. Add the red onion. Sprinkle with salt and pepper to taste. Add just enough olive oil to lightly coat the tomatoes. Gently toss the mixture.

2nd layer: Place the crabmeat in a colander and sprinkle with the lemon juice. Set aside to drain.

3rd layer: Chunky Guacamole

    4 avocados, cut into chunks

    juice of 1 fresh large lemon

    ⅓ cup finely diced red onion

    1 teaspoon minced fresh garlic

    1 tablespoon chopped fresh jalapeño pepper

    1 tablespoon chopped cilantro

    ½ teaspoon kosher salt

    ½ teaspoon freshly ground black pepper

    several dashes Tabasco, to taste

In a large bowl, squeeze the lemon juice over the avocado chunks. Add the onion, garlic, jalapeño, cilantro, salt, and pepper. Toss lightly and add Tabasco to taste. Lastly, carefully mix in the tomatoes and taste for additional salt and pepper.

To assemble: Use 5 or 6 ramekins about 3 inches in diameter. For the 1st layer, divide the tomato mixture among the dishes. Avoid any extra liquid. For the 2nd layer, divide the crabmeat and carefully place on top of each of the tomato layers. For the 3rd layer, divide the guacamole and spread over the crab layers.

Cover each of the dishes with plastic wrap, gently pressing into the guacamole. Set them into the refrigerator until thoroughly chilled. Remove the plastic wrap. Very carefully turn each ramekin upside down to release the tower onto a salad plate. Garnish with tortilla chips.

Yields 5 to 6 servings

Crispy Pickle Slices

Several recipes for these pickles have surfaced over the years, and I have tried most of them.

My very favorite is this one that my friend Cynthia Woodham makes. She gifted "Pop" and me with a jar of these at Christmas 1995! Since that time, my house has seldom been without these sweet and crispy pickles. I cannot even remember how many others with whom I have shared her wonderful recipe.

1 gallon sliced hamburger dill pickles

5 pounds sugar

⅓ cup pickling spices

1 cup Tarragon vinegar

Drain all liquid from the pickle slices. Pour the drained pickles into a large container.

Double a piece of cheesecloth to form a 5-inch square. Pour the pickling spices into the center. Gather the edges to make a bag for the spices and secure with a string.

Insert the bag of pickling spices in the middle of the pickles. Pour the bag of sugar over the top. Lastly, add the cup of vinegar. Cover the container and set aside for 3 days.

Place the pickles in small jars or containers and keep refrigerated.

Yields 1 gallon

Cole Slaw

6 cups shredded green cabbage

¾ cup shredded carrots

4 green onions, chopped

½ cup chopped sweet pickles, optional

2 teaspoons sugar

½ to ¾ cup Hellman's mayonnaise

salt & pepper to taste

In a large bowl, combine the shredded cabbage with the carrots, onions, pickle, and sugar. Toss to mix and stir in the mayonnaise. Add salt and pepper. Cover and chill until ready to serve.

Go light on the mayonnaise, as the slaw will wilt down a bit as it chills.

Yields 8 servings

The old-fashioned way of preparing cabbage is to choose a firm head of fresh green cabbage, perhaps even using a small amount of red cabbage.

SOUPS & SALADS

Southern Broccoli Salad

1 bunch broccoli

¼ pound Swiss cheese, grated

2 green onions including tops, thinly sliced

½ cup Hellman's mayonnaise

¼ cup sugar

1 tablespoon apple cider vinegar

½ pound bacon

Wash the broccoli and cut the tops into bite-sized florets. Combine the florets with the cheese and onions.

In a small bowl make a dressing by whisking together the mayo, sugar, and vinegar. Pour the dressing over the broccoli mixture and toss to coat. Let the salad marinate in the refrigerator overnight or up to several days.

Cut the bacon into ¼-inch pieces. Fry over medium heat until crisp. Drain on paper towels.

When ready to serve the salad, remove from the refrigerator and stir in most of the bacon. Sprinkle the rest on top for garnish.

Yields 8 servings

Even though the elder George Bush did not like broccoli, the veggie has a long history.

Records show that George Washington planted broccoli in his garden at Mount Vernon. Broccoli is so versatile that it can be used as an ingredient in stir-fries or casseroles, or it can be served raw in salads such as this one. I often just zap it in the microwave with a little butter, salt, and pepper.

Coca Cola Party Salad

1 small package cherry JELL-O gelatin

1 small package raspberry JELL-O gelatin

1 can seedless white cherries

1 (20 ounce) can crushed pineapple

1 cup chopped pecans

12 ounces bottled Coca Cola, partially frozen

1 (3 ounce) package cream cheese, frozen

Drain the juice from the cherries and pineapple; heat the juice in a medium saucepan until it begins to boil. Remove the pan from the heat and stir in the 2 boxes of gelatin until dissolved. After the mixture has cooled, pour it into a large measuring bowl. Add Coca Cola to reach the 4-cup level. If needed, add water, juice, or more coke to make the 4 cups.

Cut the cherries in half. Add to the gelatin mixture, along with the pineapple and pecans. Stir until mixed and pour into a mold or rectangular dish. If using a mold, spray it first with Pam. Chill at least 5 hours in the refrigerator.

When ready to transfer the salad from the mold, run hot water into the sink and immerse the mold about halfway into the water for a scant 10 seconds. Immediately turn the salad onto a serving dish. Before serving, grate the cream cheese over the top of the salad.

Yields 10 to 12 servings

Congealed salads were very popular menu items during the late 1940s and on through much of the 1980s.

A nice dinner was seldom without a family favorite. The popular brand for gelatin was the Jell-O brand – so popular in fact that jello has become synonymous with gelatin. Although congealed salads are no longer common menu items, I have included samples for you to try.

Connie worked as a tour guide at Bellingrath Gardens while she was in college.

The older ladies who worked there became good friends to her and shared some wonderful recipes. This one became my favorite congealed salad in the late 1970s. The red salad with its snow-like topping is especially festive for the holiday season.

SOUPS & SALADS

Pineapple Salad

My sister-in-law Louise, who was known for finding great recipes, introduced this delightful one to our family around 1950.

1 (20 ounce) can crushed pineapple

½ cup sugar

juice of ½ lemon

2 tablespoons plain gelatin

6 ounces cream cheese, softened

¾ cup red maraschino cherries, cut in half

liquid from red maraschino cherries

1 (8 ounce) carton Cool Whip

Heat almost to a boil the pineapple, sugar, and lemon juice in a medium saucepan.

Dissolve the gelatin in ¼ cup water and add to the pineapple mixture. Stir in the softened cream cheese.

Refrigerate the mixture in the medium saucepan until it begins to congeal. Add the cherries. Stir in the Cool Whip and enough of the cherry juice to reach a pretty pink color. Pour into a mold or dish and return to the refrigerator to finish congealing the salad.

Yields 10 to 12 servings

Blueberry Salad

2 small packages grape JELL-O gelatin

2 cups boiling water

1 can blueberry pie filling

1 (8 ounce) can crushed pineapple

1 cup sour cream

4 ounces cream cheese, softened

¼ cup sugar

1 teaspoon vanilla

Dissolve the gelatin in the boiling water. Let the mixture cool; add the pie filling and pineapple. Pour into a mold or dish. Refrigerate until congealed.

In a small bowl blend the sour cream, cream cheese, sugar, and vanilla until smooth. Spread this topping over the congealed salad. Return the salad to the refrigerator until ready to serve.

Yields 10 to 12 servings

My niece Betty Murray is my source for this delicious congealed salad recipe.

She has continued to serve it, and her family is glad! Blueberry lovers will delight in this salad.

Ambrosia

1½ to 2 dozen oranges*

1 (20 ounce) can crushed pineapple, including juice

1 (6 ounce) package frozen grated coconut or 1½ cups flaked coconut

small bottle maraschino cherries, cut into halves

sugar to taste, ½ to 1 cup

Prepare the oranges as follows: Remove all peeling, including the white inner peeling. Section the fruit, removing membranes and seeds. *Use enough oranges to yield 6 to 7 cups of prepared fruit.

In a large mixing bowl combine the oranges, crushed pineapple, coconut, and maraschino cherries. Since oranges vary in sweetness, you will need to add sugar accordingly. Begin by stirring in ½ cup sugar; taste, then add more sugar as needed.

Chill in a covered container. The flavors in ambrosia improve when refrigerated a couple of days.

Although ambrosia is no longer a popular holiday fruit dessert, the fresh orange goodness is certainly worth the extra effort to prepare.

Some families enjoy the recipe as a fruit salad. It is also a refreshing snack food, with that "I could have had a V-8" effect!

SOUPS & SALADS

Charleston Delight

1 cup sugar

1 (8 ounce) package cream cheese

1 (8 ounce) carton Cool Whip

1 (10 ounce) package frozen strawberries

1 (20 ounce) can crushed pineapple

3 bananas, mashed

1 cup chopped pecans (may be toasted)

Using a mixer, beat the sugar and cream cheese until smooth. Stir in the Cool Whip by hand.

In a large bowl combine the strawberries, pineapple, bananas, and pecans.

Fold the cream cheese mixture into the fruit and nuts. Pour into a large rectangular dish and freeze. Serve either cut in squares or dipped with an ice cream scoop.

Yields 12 to 15 servings

Before Lisa and Freddy's wedding, she was given a recipe shower.

Her mother, Betty Simmons, gifted her with her own mother's strawberry salad recipe, which was a perennial Christmas favorite in their family. After moving to Houston, Lisa discovered a similar salad on the menu at the Charleston Tea Room. She renamed her recipe Charleston Delight and shared it with family and friends. It became a personal favorite and is frequently on my Christmas menu.

Frozen Pink Salad

1 can Eagle Brand sweetened condensed milk

1 can cherry pie filling

1 (15¼ ounce) can crushed pineapple, partially drained

1 cup chopped pecans

1 (12 ounce) carton Cool Whip

In a large mixing bowl, combine the first 4 ingredients, stirring to mix well. Fold in the Cool Whip. Pour the mixture into a large rectangular dish and seal with foil. Freeze the salad until ready to serve. Cut into squares and serve frozen.

SOUPS & SALADS

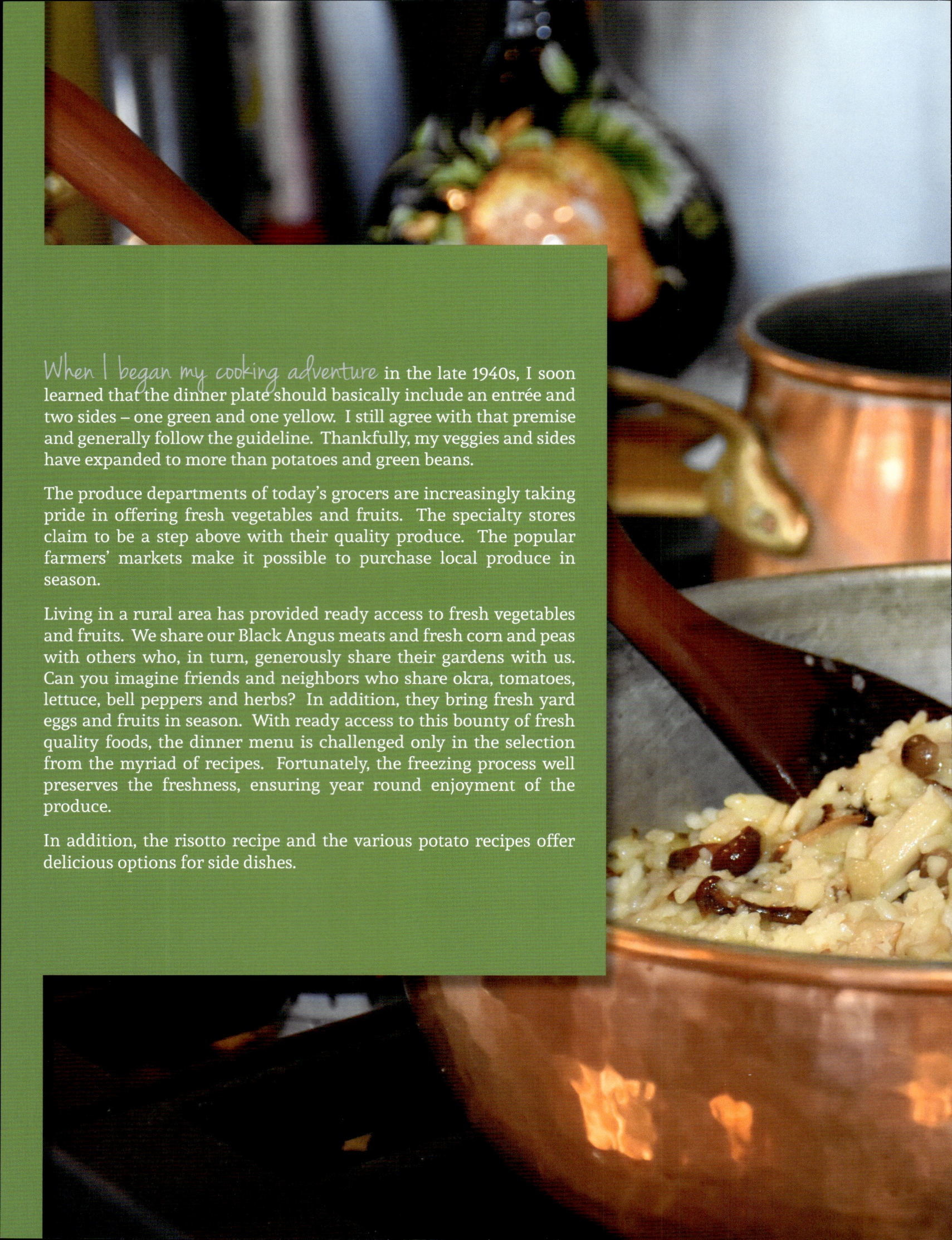

When I began my cooking adventure in the late 1940s, I soon learned that the dinner plate should basically include an entrée and two sides – one green and one yellow. I still agree with that premise and generally follow the guideline. Thankfully, my veggies and sides have expanded to more than potatoes and green beans.

The produce departments of today's grocers are increasingly taking pride in offering fresh vegetables and fruits. The specialty stores claim to be a step above with their quality produce. The popular farmers' markets make it possible to purchase local produce in season.

Living in a rural area has provided ready access to fresh vegetables and fruits. We share our Black Angus meats and fresh corn and peas with others who, in turn, generously share their gardens with us. Can you imagine friends and neighbors who share okra, tomatoes, lettuce, bell peppers and herbs? In addition, they bring fresh yard eggs and fruits in season. With ready access to this bounty of fresh quality foods, the dinner menu is challenged only in the selection from the myriad of recipes. Fortunately, the freezing process well preserves the freshness, ensuring year round enjoyment of the produce.

In addition, the risotto recipe and the various potato recipes offer delicious options for side dishes.

VEGGIES & SIDES

Southern Creamed Corn

Fried Okra

Southern Peas or Butter Beans

Turnip or Collard Greens

Sautéed Squash with Onions

Potatoes au Gratin
with Fresh Herbs

New Potatoes in Cream Sauce

Candied Sweet Potato Rounds

Sweet Potato Casserole
with Pecan Topping

Baked Beans

Risotto with Wild Mushrooms

Spiced Peaches

Fried Apples

Southern Creamed Corn

4 cups sweet corn, cut from fresh ears

1 stick butter

salt and pepper to taste

1 tablespoon sugar

¾ cup milk

Remove the shucks and silks from fresh ears of sweet corn. Prepare the corn by first cutting off the tips of the kernels, then scraping the cobs to remove remaining corn. Depending on the size of the ears of corn, you will need 12 to 18 ears.

Melt the butter in a 10-inch skillet over medium heat. Stir in the corn; add the salt and pepper to taste and the sugar. Gradually add the milk. Cook, stirring frequently, until the mixture is heated through.

Pour into a casserole dish that has been sprayed with Pam. Cook at 350° for about 30 minutes until lightly browned on top.

Family favorite veggie!
We grow our own sweet corn on Cannon Farms.

At harvest time we do our own processing and freezing. Since discovering the E-Z Corn Creamer, we have been able to keep family and friends in frozen corn. Beginning in 2012, John has planted a variety known simply as BC 801. It immediately became our favorite sweet corn.

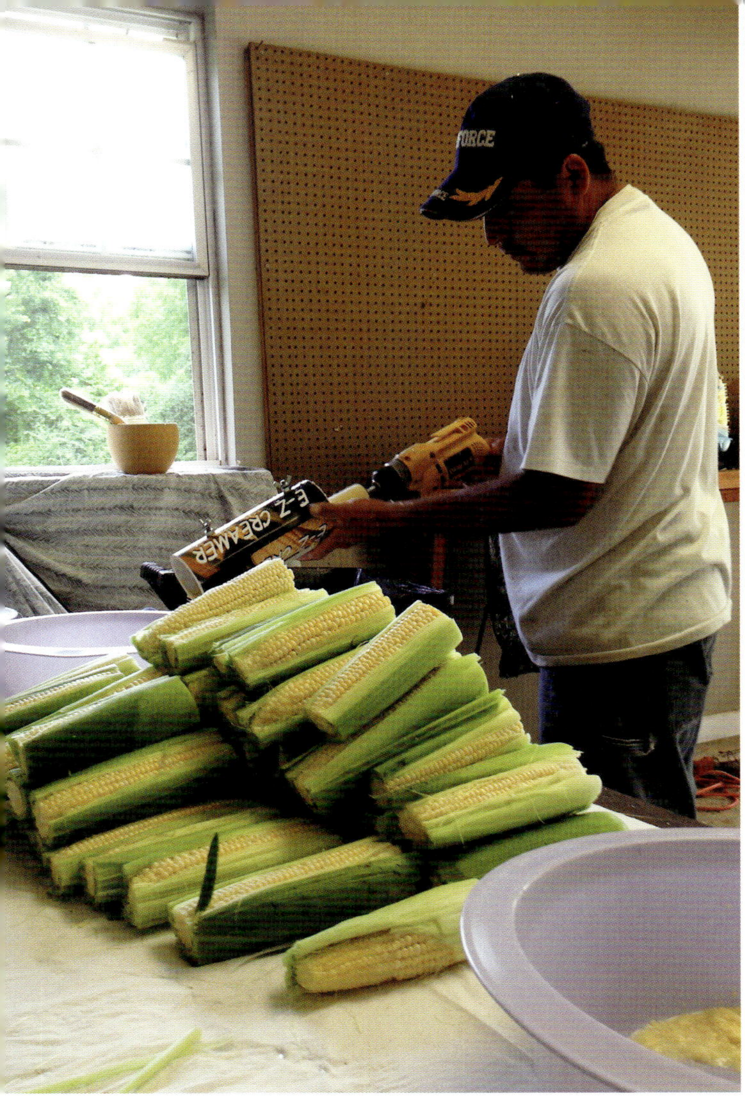
FORCE
E-Z CREAMER
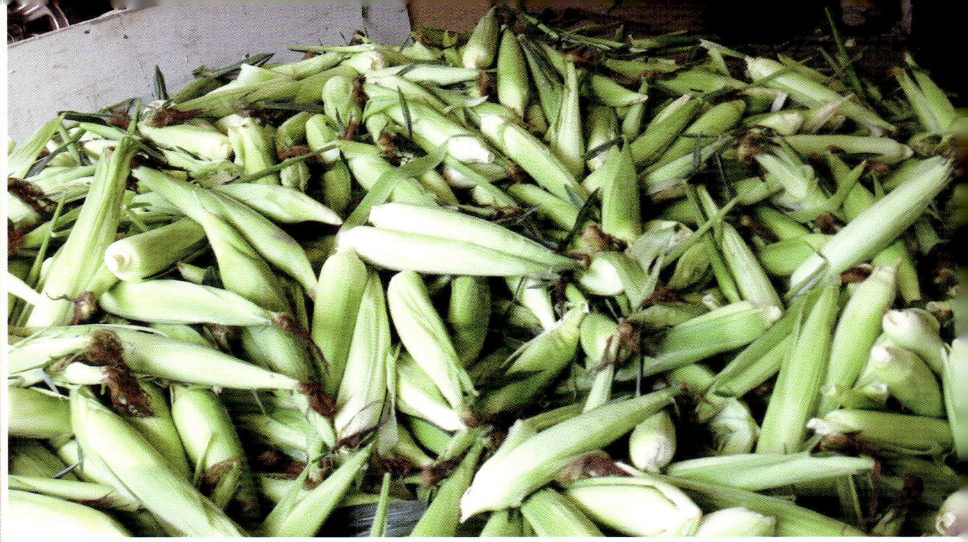
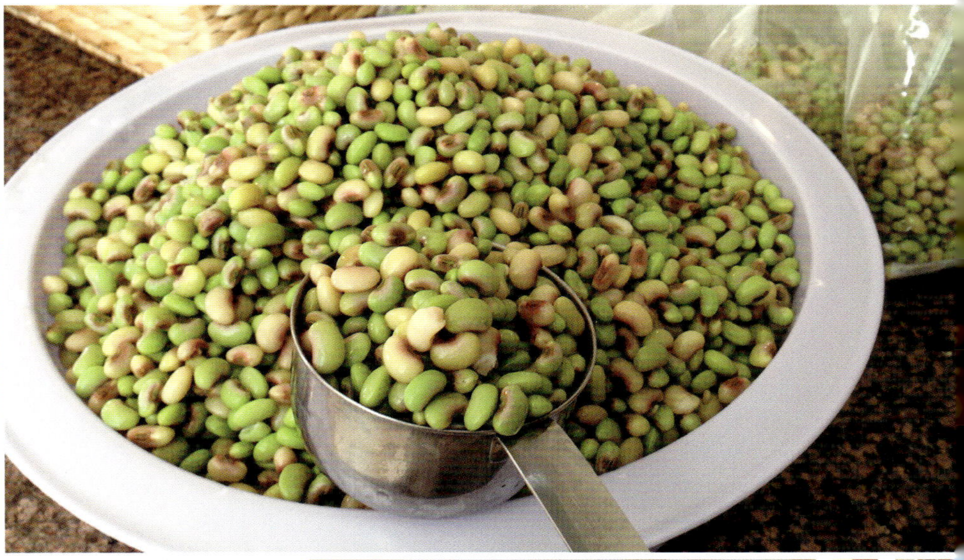
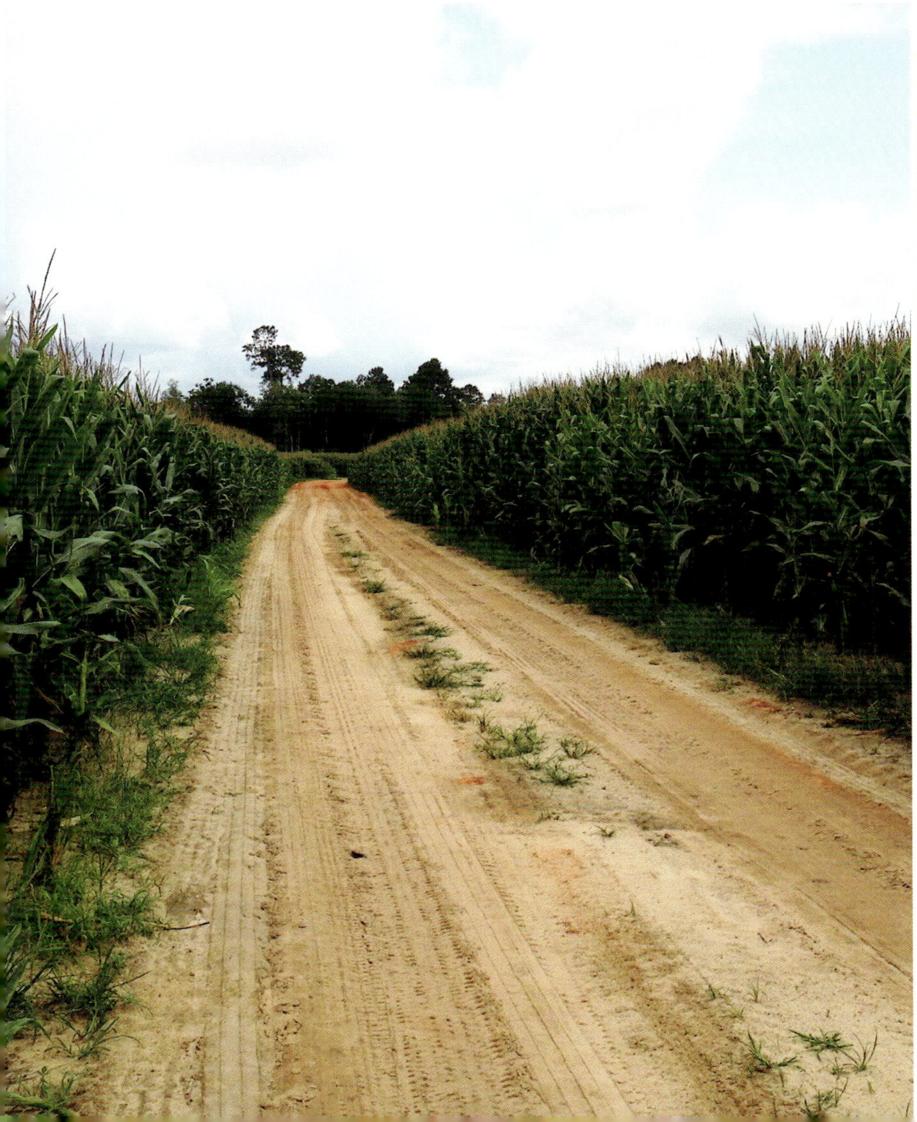
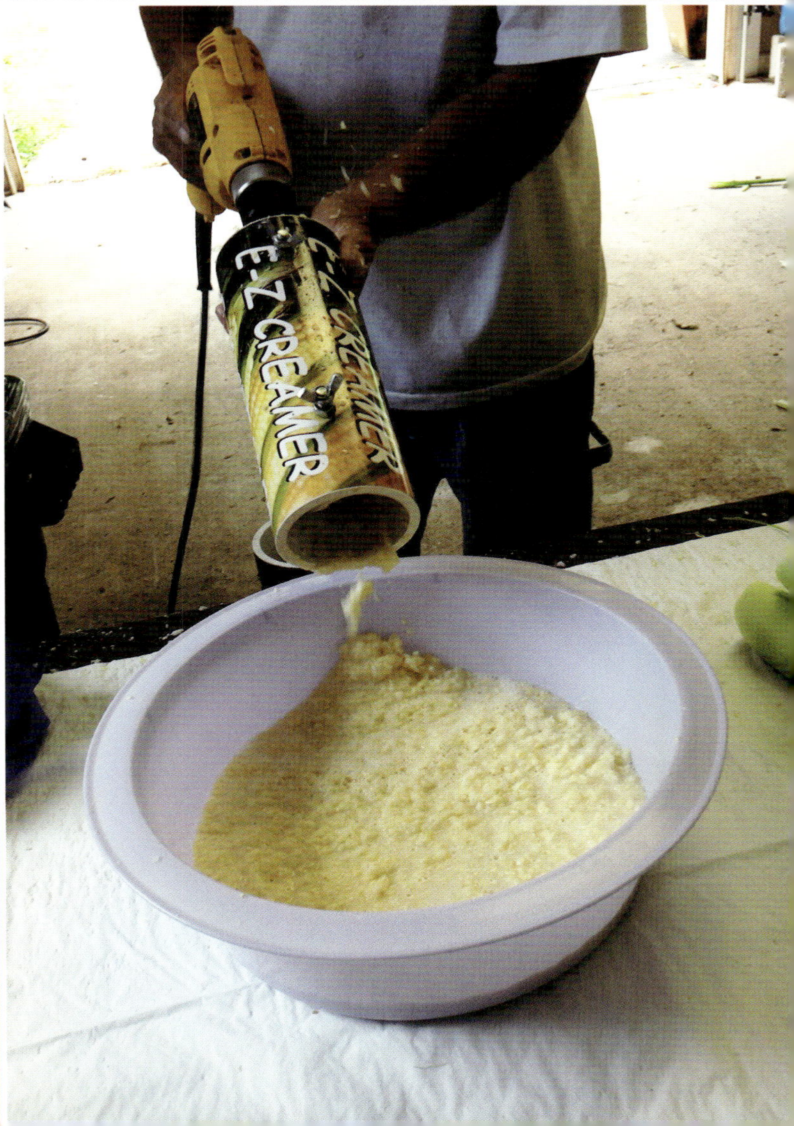
E-Z CREAMER

Fried Okra

1 pound fresh okra

1 egg

1½ cups milk

2½ cups self-rising cornmeal mix

½ teaspoon salt

½ teaspoon pepper

1 teaspoon Tony Chachere's seasoning

canola oil for frying

Wash the okra and dry on paper towels. Remove the stems; cut the remaining pods into ½ to ¾-inch sections. Set aside.

Beat the egg slightly with a whisk. Add the milk and continue whisking. Add the cut sections of okra to the mixture. Refrigerate until ready to fry, overnight if necessary.

Combine the dry ingredients in a medium container. Using a slotted spoon, lift a portion of the okra from the liquid mixture. Dredge in the cornmeal mixture and place on a sheet of foil. Repeat until all the okra is breaded.

Heat the oil to 355°. When using a frying basket, first immerse it in the hot oil. When heated, remove the basket and add 1 layer of breaded okra. Lower into the hot oil and give the basket a little shake a couple of times during the frying process. When the okra is nicely browned and crisp, drain on a rack that has been placed over a cookie sheet. Repeat the process until all okra is fried.

If using a fry pot on the stove, heat the oil over medium-high heat. To test for the correct frying temperature, drop one section of okra into the hot oil. If it sizzles immediately, the oil is ready.

Avoid overcooking as the flavor of the okra will be affected. Practice will teach you the perfect doneness.

Yields 6 servings

Nothing sets off a country vegetable dinner like the crispness of this delicacy.

VEGGIES & SIDES

Southern Peas or Butter Beans

3 cups peas or baby green lima beans, fresh or frozen

3 tablespoons bacon drippings or butter

½ cup diced ham or fried bacon pieces, optional

salt & pepper to taste

1 teaspoon sugar

1½ tablespoons chopped onion

8 to 10 pods fresh or frozen okra, optional

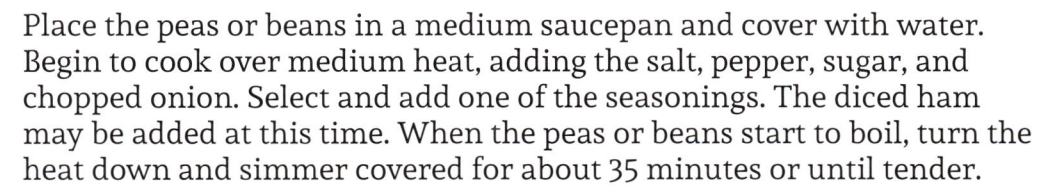

Place the peas or beans in a medium saucepan and cover with water. Begin to cook over medium heat, adding the salt, pepper, sugar, and chopped onion. Select and add one of the seasonings. The diced ham may be added at this time. When the peas or beans start to boil, turn the heat down and simmer covered for about 35 minutes or until tender.

If you choose to add okra, place the pods on top of the peas or beans for the last 10 minutes of cooking. The fried bacon pieces make a nice garnish to sprinkle on top for presentation.

So many kinds of peas and beans! My favorite peas are the pink-eyed purple hull and the Mississippi zipper peas.

Of the two, the zipper peas are creamier; however, both are excellent legumes. My favorite beans are definitely baby green lima beans. Butter peas, a cross between peas and beans, are also family favorites.

VEGGIES & SIDES

Turnip or Collard Greens

3 to 4 slices of thick sliced bacon

1 bunch of turnip greens or collard greens

1 tablespoon sugar

⅛ teaspoon pepper

½ teaspoon salt

3 medium turnip roots, optional for turnip greens

Cut the bacon into ¼-inch pieces and cook over medium heat until the bacon is crisp. Drain on paper towels and set aside. Reserve the bacon drippings.

If you are using a fresh bunch of turnip greens, remove the larger stems. Wash through 3 or 4 sinks of water. If you are cooking collard greens, cut the leaves crossways into 1-inch wide strips and wash thoroughly.

Pour 2 inches of water into a Dutch oven and heat until boiling. Add the sugar, pepper, and salt. (More salt may be needed later.) Pour in the bacon drippings and begin to add the greens. Allow part of the greens to cook a bit before adding more, until all the greens are in the pot. Bring to a boil again; then, turn heat to simmer and cover with lid. Cook 1 to 1½ hours or until the greens are tender.

If you choose to add the roots to the turnip greens, prepare them by peeling and cutting them into ½-inch rounds. Add the roots after the greens have cooked for 1 hour. Taste test for adding additional salt.

Lift the cooked greens out of the liquid into a serving bowl. Using a sharp knife and a fork, cut through the greens a few times. Sprinkle the crisp bacon pieces over the top.

Today's world offers options for convenience.

If you have limited time, or if farm fresh greens are unavailable, take advantage of the packaged greens in the produce department of most grocery stores. Turnip roots may be purchased separately. A pan of jalapeño cornbread goes really great with these greens.

Sautéed Squash with Onions

10 to 12 small yellow squash, sliced into ½-inch rounds

2 tablespoons olive oil

1 medium onion, coarsely chopped

salt & coarsely ground pepper to taste

1 tablespoon sugar

2 tablespoons butter

Pour the oil into a large skillet and place over medium heat. Add the chopped onion and sauté slightly. Add the squash slices and continue to cook over medium heat, stirring occasionally. Sprinkle with the salt, pepper, and sugar. Cook until the squash is crisp tender.

Add the butter and heat until melted. Remove squash from pan to prevent overcooking.

Yellow squash is best when picked young & tender.

Zucchini squash may be cooked the same or mixed with yellow squash for a nice combination.

VEGGIES & SIDES

Potatoes au Gratin with Fresh Herbs

This original recipe, created by Connie, takes the old recipe for Texas Potatoes to a higher level.

2½ pounds red or russet potatoes, peeled and cut into ½-inch cubes

1 stick butter, divided

¾ large white onion, chopped medium

½ large red bell pepper, chopped medium

¼ large green bell pepper, chopped medium

2 cloves garlic, minced

2½ tablespoons chopped fresh oregano

3 tablespoons chopped fresh parsley, divided

1 tablespoon thyme, optional

16 ounces shredded extra sharp cheddar cheese, divided

1 (10.5 ounce) can cream of chicken soup

1 cup sour cream

2 dashes Tabasco

salt, garlic salt, & pepper to taste

In a 10-inch skillet, sauté the onions with the red and green bell peppers in ½ stick butter until translucent. Stir in the minced garlic and set aside.

In another large skillet, sauté the cubed potatoes in ½ stick butter until about half done. Remove from heat, and stir in the sautéed vegetables.

Reserve 1 tablespoon of the chopped parsley and 4 ounces of the shredded cheese; set aside for the topping. Add the remaining ingredients to the potato mixture and stir gently until mixed well.

Pour the mixture into a medium casserole dish. Bake at 375° for 30 minutes. Sprinkle the reserved cheese over the top in an irregular fashion (do not make a solid layer). Lastly, sprinkle the parsley over the top. Bake for 15 minutes longer until the cheese has melted.

Yields 8 to 10 servings

VEGGIES & SIDES

New Potatoes in Cream Sauce

12 to 15 small red new potatoes

1 tablespoon chopped onion

salt and pepper to taste

½ stick butter

3 tablespoons cornstarch

⅔ cup milk

Peel the potatoes; wash and place them in a medium saucepan. Barely cover with water. Add the onion, salt, and pepper. Cook over medium heat until the potatoes are done.

While the potatoes are cooking, combine the cornstarch and milk, stirring until smooth. When the potatoes are done, turn the heat down to low. Stir in half the milk mixture and the butter. When the sauce begins to thicken, add more of the milk mixture until desired consistency.

Yields 4 servings

These new potatoes were always a favorite for Fred, especially in his later years.

I think his mother had made them for him in his youth!

VEGGIES & SIDES

Candied Sweet Potato Rounds

This recipe provides a little different, lighter presentation for candied yams.

8 small sweet potatoes

¾ stick butter

salt to taste

cinnamon to sprinkle

½ cup light brown sugar

Peel the sweet potatoes and cut crossways into ¾-inch rounds.

Using an electric skillet on 300° or a large skillet over medium-low heat, melt half of the butter. Place the sweet potato rounds in a single layer in the skillet. Sprinkle them sparingly with salt and cinnamon. Cook the potato rounds until the bottoms are crusting.

Turn the rounds over, keeping them in a single layer. Again, sprinkle sparingly with salt and cinnamon. Cook for about 5 minutes.

Gently push the rounds to one side of the skillet. Add the remaining butter, allowing it to melt. Add the brown sugar and stir until a syrup forms. Redistribute the rounds in the syrup and cook until tender. Transfer the rounds to a warm bowl and pour the syrup over them. Serve while warm.

Yields 8 servings

Sweet Potato Casserole with Pecan Topping

6 medium sweet potatoes

⅓ cup milk

¾ cup sugar

1 stick butter, melted

2 eggs

1 teaspoon vanilla

Topping:

1 cup light brown sugar (packed)

⅓ cup flour

¾ stick butter, room temperature

1¼ cups chopped pecans

Place the sweet potatoes in a large pan and cover with water. Bring to a boil and cook 30 to 45 minutes until tender. Pour off the hot water and run cool tap water over the potatoes. When the potatoes have cooled enough to handle, peel and cut them into pieces. Place them in a large mixer bowl.

Add the milk, sugar, melted butter, eggs, and vanilla. Use the electric mixer at medium speed and beat until smooth. Pour into a casserole dish that has been sprayed with Pam. Set aside and prepare topping.

Topping: Whisk together the brown sugar and flour. Blend in the butter with a pastry blender or 2 knives until mixture is crumbly. Add chopped pecans and toss until blended. Sprinkle this topping over the casserole.

Bake at 350° for about 35 minutes or until lightly browned and bubbly around edges.

Yields 8 to 10 servings

My sister Lucile sent this recipe to me in the mid-1970s.

Although it was new to me at the time, it is now a traditional recipe with versions in multiple cookbooks. Lucile was the very best cook I have ever known, so her version was always loved by my family!

Baked Beans

6 slices bacon

½ stick butter

1 small onion, chopped

2 tablespoons chopped bell pepper

1 rib celery, chopped

2 (15 ounce) cans pork and beans

½ cup Worcestershire sauce

⅓ cup brown sugar

Cut the bacon into ½-inch pieces and fry in a large skillet over medium heat until crisp. Drain the bacon on paper towels. Dispose of the bacon grease.

Place the butter in the skillet and sauté the onion, celery, and bell pepper until wilted. Add the pork and beans, Worcestershire sauce, and brown sugar. When the mixture is thoroughly heated, stir in the crisp bacon pieces.

Pour into a baking dish and cook in a 350° oven until hot and bubbly, about 45 minutes.

Yields 6 to 8 servings

This is my favorite baked bean recipe. It was shared with me in the 1950s.

I only added the bell pepper to the original recipe. I have, in turn, shared the recipe numerous times over the years. The prominence of the Worcestershire, along with the crisp bacon pieces, makes the beans especially tasty.

Risotto with Wild Mushrooms

6 cups chicken broth (best if made using Minor's chicken base)

6 ounces extra virgin olive oil, divided

1 pound fresh assorted mushrooms, rough-chopped

1 large onion, diced

2 cloves garlic, minced

2 cups Carnaroli or Arborio rice, uncooked

½ cup dry white wine

⅔ cup fresh Parmigiano-Reggiano cheese, grated and divided

sea salt and freshly ground black pepper, to taste

fresh basil, for garnish

Heat the chicken broth in a saucepan. Turn to lowest simmer to keep the broth hot until needed. Sauté the mushrooms in 2 tablespoons of olive oil and set aside.

In a large skillet, sauté the onion and garlic in 4 tablespoons of olive oil. Add the rice and stir until hot and evenly coated.

Keep the rice at a brisk simmer and add the hot chicken broth, ½ cup at a time. Stirring the rice constantly, continue to add more broth each time as the liquid is absorbed. Stir in the white wine and simmer until all liquid is absorbed; then, transfer the sautéed mushrooms to the rice mixture. Cook until the rice is al dente. The rice will be slightly firm and creamy, not mushy.

Stir in ⅓ cup of the cheese. Remove from heat and season with salt and pepper to taste. Let the risotto rest for 3 minutes.

Spoon into individual molds. To serve, remove the risotto from the molds and garnish with the remaining cheese and fresh basil.

Steve Valerius created this fabulous recipe.
Connie has kept his art going, and now her risotto gets rave reviews.

She also adapts the recipe to make a wonderful shrimp version by using fresh shrimp in place of mushrooms.

VEGGIES & SIDES

Spiced Peaches

Many years ago when spiced peaches were a common menu item, this recipe appeared in a local magazine.

I jotted down the ingredients and kept my notes. These peaches are as tasty as the ones my mother and sister made from scratch during my youth, but so very much easier. As a bonus, they also rank high in aroma and eye appeal.

2 large cans of peach halves

1⅓ cups sugar

1 cup cider vinegar

4 cinnamon sticks

2 tablespoons whole cloves

Drain the peaches, reserving the syrup in a medium saucepan. Place the drained peaches in a large mixing bowl.

To the peach syrup, add the remaining ingredients. Bring to a boil; lower the heat and simmer 10 minutes. Pour the hot syrup over the peach halves and set aside to cool.

Chill thoroughly before serving. Store in refrigerator.

VEGGIES & SIDES

Fried Apples

4 Granny Smith apples

2 Roma apples

¾ cup light brown sugar

½ cup sugar

¼ teaspoon salt

1½ teaspoons cinnamon

½ stick butter

Wash, peel, and slice the apples, leaving the peeling on one Roma apple. Place the apples and the butter in a medium size heavy saucepan. Heat until the butter is melted. Combine the sugars, salt, and cinnamon; pour over the apples. Cook over medium heat, stirring frequently, until the apples are tender. Serve warm as a side dish.

Yields 8 servings

Fred and I loved visiting my brother Charlie and his wife Betty in the 1980s at their mountain cabin in Franklin, North Carolina.

In October we would take day trips in all directions to enjoy the colorful foliage. We often had breakfast at the Dillard House. I was immediately charmed by the restaurant and by the fried apples that were a staple on the breakfast menu. On our way back to the cabin, we stopped by an orchard and bought fresh apples. The next morning I created this version for our country breakfast.

VEGGIES & SIDES

Sweet Home Alabama

The State of Alabama has been my home since 1947 when we moved to Mobile as young newlyweds. My children were born and grew up in Mobile County. My children and I earned degrees from the University of South Alabama. I taught in the Mobile School System for almost 20 years. After our marriage of 63 years, my husband was laid to rest in Mobile Memorial Gardens. This brief bio does not begin to reflect the happiness I have enjoyed over my lifespan. The joys of marriage and motherhood have been mine, as well as the delights of friendship and the gratification of teaching 11th grade students.

Alabama is also where I learned to cook. South Mobile County is not only the best seafood locale, it is also a great farmland. I have enjoyed ready access to a plethora of fresh foods from which to prepare delicious meals.

The seafood industry supports the nearby connecting towns of Coden and Bayou la Batre, made famous by Winston Groom in Forrest Gump. The view from the bridge is a bayou teeming with shrimp boats. On the way out to the shrimping waters, the boats make the requisite stop by the icehouse to take on fuel and ice. Oyster shops, both large and small, dot the landscape of the area. Expert shuckers fill buckets with tasty oysters, while motorized conveyor belts dump the calcium-rich shells in growing piles. According to Willie Sprinkle of Johnson Seafood Products in Coden, the "sweetest" crabmeat comes from coastal Alabama. JSP is a fifth-generation family seafood business, dating back to the very early 1900s. The family takes great pride in producing premium crab, oyster, and seafood products. I can personally endorse their success as I frequently enjoy their salty oysters, large crab claws, and superior jumbo lump crabmeat!

On the years that my pecan trees fail to make a good crop, I can always find my favorite ingredient from the many orchards in the county. My friends at Sessions Pecans can always be counted on for abundant supplies of all varieties. Dees Pecans of Union Church is well known for shipping pecans and also has a gift shop. Ken Buck of Bayou la Batre usually has shelled Elliott pecans, my favorite.

One of the cattle farmers in the county, my son John, keeps our family in Black Angus beef. Along with his farm crops, some years he plants sweet corn and peas for the family freezers. He plans for more than we need because we love to share with family and friends. There is fun in the kitchen when we have our "pea day" gathering to blanch and freeze copious amounts of the vegetable. The Corn Creamer tools are a must for preparing the corn for the freezer, and even then several people are required. Our neighboring Baldwin County, across Mobile Bay, is also known for its Silver Queen corn, potatoes, and pecans.

My favorite barbeque sauce is made by Dreamland Bar-B-Que, a restaurant chain which originated in Tuscaloosa, Alabama. For many years barbeque lovers enjoyed their sole menu item of ribs with sauce and two slices of white bread. In recent years the menu includes all the sides you would expect. Dreamland sells its sauce, in quarts or gallons, at each of the 8 restaurants; or they will ship if you are not nearby. If you like a thinner barbeque sauce that is tangy and spicy, try Dreamland.

Conecuh County, located about halfway between Mobile and Birmingham, is best known for the Conecuh Sausage produced there. The hickory smoked sausage is phenomenal, second to no other. Although the sausage is now available in 21 states, every link is still made at the plant located in Greenville on I-65. An impressive daily output ranges from 30,000 to 40,000 pounds. I serve the savory sausage as appetizers, as a breakfast meat, and sometimes with veggies for dinner. I also use the Conecuh Cajun sausage as an important ingredient in my signature recipe for seafood gumbo! This company also ships. They have some great packages, which also include their bacon and ham. You may also stop by their gift shop which is located onsite.

Chilton County peaches, believe me, rank with the best peaches grown anywhere. Traveling south from Birmingham on I-65, the site is marked by a water tower proudly displaying a beautifully ripened peach. At one of the exits, you will see huge markets where you can find all things peach – fresh fruit, ice cream, yogurt, shortcake, etc. I can hardly wait for peach season; I especially enjoy the freestone variety, which are harvested in July. Each year I grab a few baskets and buy the Fruit Fresh that prevents their turning brown. Then, the peaches we do not eat fresh can be peeled, sliced, and frozen in vacuum-sealed bags. These become the basis for the peach cobblers that I love to share with family and friends.

Blueberries also produce well in lower Alabama. While I do not personally have any blueberry bushes, my freezer is usually well stocked due to the generosity of my friend, Larry Shields. We are of the old-fashioned mindset of friends and neighbors who find real pleasure in sharing the bounty. Just so, neighbor Linda Hedrick keeps me supplied with fresh yard eggs from her special chickens. During the summer months, other friends with gardens share fresh okra and delicious tomatoes. On the 4th of July, beautiful striped watermelons appear at my back door, courtesy of neighbor and former student, Clint Clark. After all, Grand Bay watermelons are the best! We know, because our two sons raised and sold them during their high school and college years.

Thusly, "Sweet Home Alabama" is home to many and varied crops and products to the delight of cooks all over the state. I seldom make a trip without taking two or three ice chests loaded with some of these wonderful Alabama products to share with family and friends.

Having grown up in Cleveland, a Mississippi Delta town 17 miles from the river, my perception of seafood was the platter of fried catfish that occasionally graced the dinner table. One of my brothers would first need to make the trip to Rosedale, which was the nearest river town, to get a fresh river "cat." To this day, fried catfish is truly special – not only for nostalgic reasons, but also for its unique texture and taste.

Cleveland residents were somewhat exposed to other seafood. After all, the oyster truck arrived from the coast once a year. News spread by word of mouth that the "oyster man" was in town. Again, the deep fryers were enlisted for duty. Other than these exposures and an occasional shrimp cocktail at a restaurant, my experience with seafood was quite limited.

When Fred and I began our married life in Alabama, the Gulf Coast opened up a bountiful world of absolutely wonderful seafood: trout, red snapper, flounder, shrimp, oysters, and crab. What had previously been a limited exposure to seafood now became unlimited culinary possibilities. For the most coveted freshness, we could meet a shrimp boat coming in with its catch. Or we could visit one of the oyster or crab shops for freshly picked crab or freshly shucked oysters.

Needless to say, my menus were frequently interspersed with seafood. Thus began my adventure into finding, tweaking, and developing seafood recipes that my family and friends enjoyed. I became enlightened to the profusion of ways to prepare succulent offerings of seafood that did not utilize a deep fryer. Even though I will always tend to fry catfish, I have learned some other excellent methods for preparing seafood.

This pathway to learning was a fun trip of its own. The recipes in this section are the favorites that resulted. I am most proud of my Signature Recipe for gumbo, which has evolved over 60 years of culinary pursuit.

SEAFOOD

Fried Fish Fillets or Oysters

Favorite Seafood Cocktail Sauce

Fried Shrimp or Crab Claws

Sue's Seafood Gumbo

Jumbo Lump Crab Cakes
with Lemon Remoulade

Crab Royale

Crab Stuffing

Stuffed Flounder

Barbequed Shrimp

Baked Stuffed Shrimp

Shrimp Fettuccine

Crawfish Etouffée

Oysters Rockefeller

Fried Fish Fillets or Oysters

The most efficient way to fry seafood is to prepare a breading and frying station.

Not only does the area provide convenience, but it also makes for an easy cleanup. Line a large area with wide, heavy-duty foil. On one side, set up the breading station; on the other side, set up the deep fryer and a rack which has been placed over a cookie sheet (for draining the fried seafood).

1 gallon canola oil

fish fillets or fresh oysters

3 cups self rising cornmeal mix

2 teaspoons salt

1 teaspoon coarse ground pepper

1 tablespoon Tony Chachere's creole seasoning

Heat the oil in a deep fryer to 355°. Let the basket heat in the oil.

In a large bowl or pan, combine the cornmeal mix with the salt, pepper, and Tony's. Dredge the fillets or oysters through the meal mixture until you have a nice coating. To avoid moisture seeping through the breading, bread the fish or oysters only in small batches.

Remove the basket from the deep fryer; hold it over your breading area as you place a single layer of breaded fish or oysters in the basket. This step will avoid excessive breading accumulating in the bottom of the deep fryer. Lower the basket into the hot oil and cook until the fish or oysters are brown and crisp. Drain on a wire rack.

Favorite Seafood Cocktail Sauce

¾ cup catsup

¾ cup chili sauce

2 tablespoons Worcestershire sauce

juice of a large lemon

3 tablespoons horseradish, or to taste

Combine all ingredients, taste test, and chill.

SEAFOOD

Fried Shrimp or Crab Claws

1 gallon canola oil

large peeled shrimp or crab claws

3 cups all purpose flour

2 teaspoons salt

1 teaspoon black pepper

1 tablespoon Tony Chachere's creole seasoning

1 egg

1½ cups whole milk

Heat the oil in the deep fryer to 355°. Let the basket heat in the oil.

In a large bowl combine the flour, salt, pepper, and Tony's. In a medium sized bowl, beat the egg and stir in the milk until well blended. In another bowl place the peeled raw shrimp or crab claws.

Follow this procedure for shrimp: Dip the shrimp in the egg and milk mixture. Dredge them in the flour mixture. Prepare in small batches as you fry them.

Follow this procedure for crab claws: Dredge the crab claws in the flour mixture; dip in the egg and milk mixture; lastly, dredge through the flour mixture again. Prepare in small batches as you fry them.

Holding the hot basket over the breading area, place the shrimp or crab claws in a single layer in the basket and fry just until done. Shrimp is much tastier not over-cooked. Crab claws need to be cooked until crisp, but not overdone. Drain on a wire rack. Continue to fry in batches until all are cooked.

My Signature Recipe

My first attempt at seafood gumbo was initiated by a very simple, easy-to-do recipe featured in The Mobile Press Register about 1955.

I followed the recipe strictly, but the result was more like a shrimp soup that was pretty good. Subsequently, each time I used the recipe, I would do a little something different. My daughter-in-law, Lisa, first wrote the recipe down as she watched in 1985. From that time I have continued to experiment, tweak, and develop a gumbo recipe that is a bold blending of rich flavors that enhance our wonderful Gulf seafood. I am most proud of this result.

Thusly, Sue's Seafood Gumbo has become my Signature Recipe. I have shared it with many friends and family members. I have enjoyed teaching hands-on classes at Laborcitas Creek Ranch in South Texas, at Connie's bay house on Galveston Bay, at Lisa's home in Clear Lake, TX, at the Steger's Montana home, and in my own kitchen in the southern part of Mobile County.

I have always loved making gumbo. Making the roux, chopping the veggies, assembling the ingredients, and choosing the perfect seafood turns my kitchen into that special place where creativity reigns and aromas delight! For my 83rd birthday, Connie and Steve gifted me with a dream gumbo pot – a 9 quart red Le Creuset. (Connie also purchased the same pot for me to use at her house and took one as a hostess gift to Montana. Rolanette Lawrence bought the 13-quart one for the classes at her ranch.) The perfect gumbo pot not only makes the gumbo better, it also enhances the pleasure of cooking. Plus, the red Le Creuset looks so pretty on the stovetop!

Making gumbo in this quantity also extends an opportunity to share with others. I can fill a wide-mouth quart canning jar, get on my golf cart, and cruise over to a neighbor to share some gumbo. At any given time, cartons of my frozen gumbo can be found in freezers from Florida to Alabama to Texas to Montana.

Although my family has the recipe, they still prefer their gumbo to be delivered – already made and frozen! It is my joy to receive a text from friends and family telling me that they enjoyed my gumbo for lunch that day, or that the gumbo they had for dinner was the best ever, or that the gumbo was a hit when served at a party. During a year's time, I make more than 20 pots of gumbo. Each one is prepared with love – a love for turning an empty pot into the best gumbo I can make for the people who are most dear in my life.

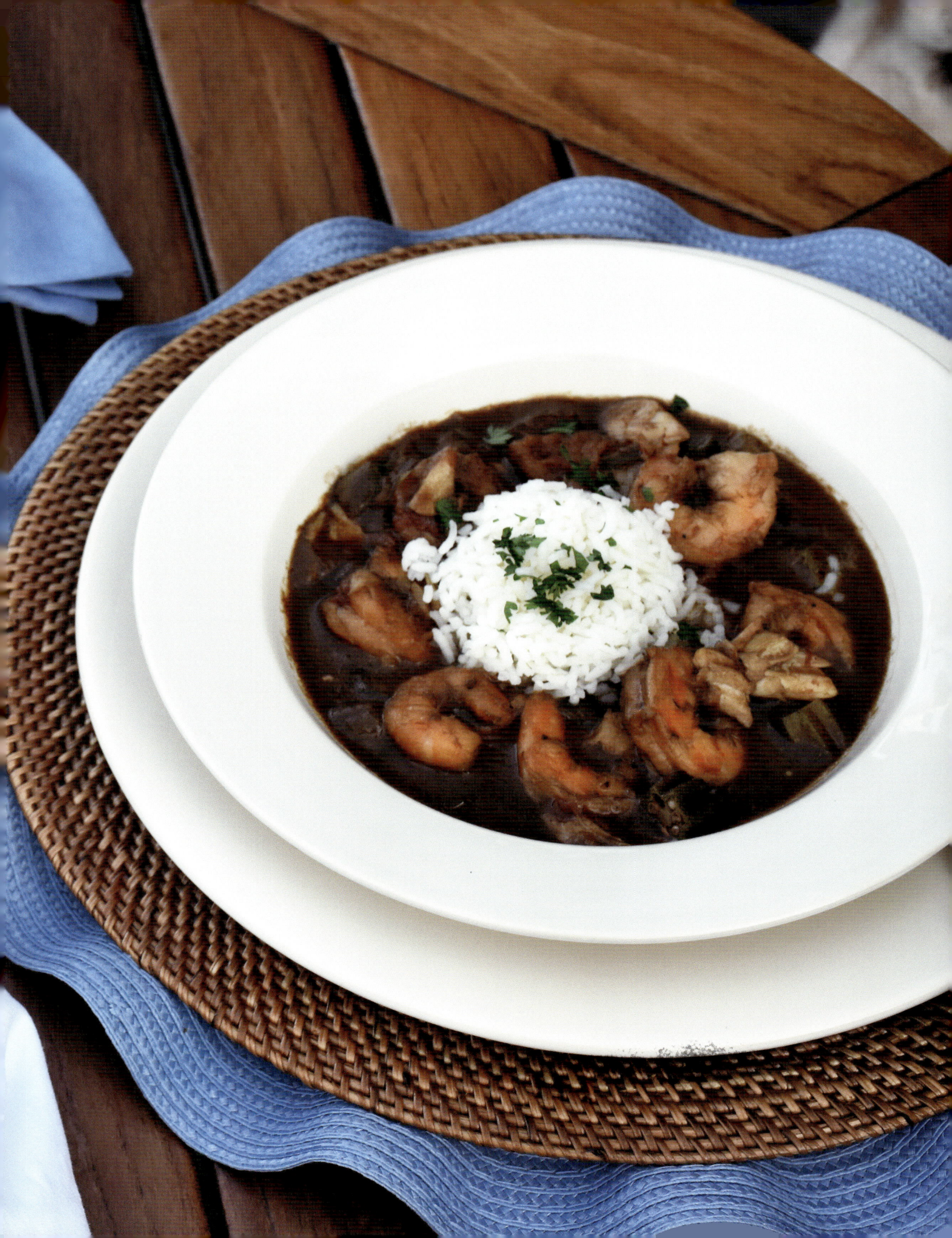

Sue's Seafood Gumbo

1 cup canola oil

1½ cups flour

2 medium onions, chopped

5 ribs celery, chopped

1 bell pepper, chopped

1 stick butter

2 quarts chicken broth

28 ounces canned diced tomatoes

24 ounces frozen cut okra

1 pound Conecuh Cajun sausage

3 tablespoons Worcestershire sauce

3 tablespoons Tiger Sauce

1½ tablespoons salt

1½ teaspoons coarsely ground black pepper

2½ tablespoons Tony Chachere's Creole seasoning

5 pounds peeled and deveined shrimp

2 pounds jumbo lump crabmeat (some may be saved for garnish)

4 to 5 tablespoons gumbo filé

SEAFOOD

Roux: Roux is best when prepared in a cast iron skillet. Over a medium flame, heat the oil until a pinch of flour sizzles when sprinkled into the skillet. Add the flour and stir constantly with a wooden spatula until the roux is a rich brown color, much like a dark peanut butter. Remove immediately from heat and pour into a glass bowl that has a metal spoon resting against the bottom and side. The spoon prevents the hot roux from breaking the bowl. After a couple of minutes, remove the spoon and stir well with a whisk. Set the bowl of roux aside until needed. The roux will darken to a rich, brown color. The excess oil will rise to the top and can be spooned off before using.

Gumbo: In a large 9 quart gumbo pot, sauté the veggies in the butter. Begin with the onions, add the celery, and stir occasionally until translucent. Lastly, add the bell pepper and sauté about 3 minutes. Stir in the roux until blended with the veggies. Slowly add about 2 cups of the chicken broth, stirring until smooth. Gradually add the remaining chicken broth.

Stir in the diced tomatoes and cut okra. Cut the sausage into sections about 5 inches long. Split each section lengthwise; then, cut into ½-inch pieces and add to the gumbo mixture. Lastly, add the Worcestershire, Tiger Sauce, salt, pepper, and Tony's.

Let the pot of gumbo come to a light boil. Turn down the heat and simmer with the lid on for 1 hour. With a large metal spoon, skim the excess grease from the top of the gumbo base.

Add the peeled shrimp and cook uncovered until the shrimp are almost done, usually 10 to 15 minutes. Add the gumbo filé, stirring until well blended. Lastly, use a wooden spoon or spoodle to gently add the crabmeat, taking care to keep the lumps intact. Cook only until the crabmeat is heated.

Serve with rice and garnish with the reserved crabmeat. The flavor of gumbo improves each day, becoming significantly better after 2 or 3 days. The gumbo also freezes well.

Yields about 7 quarts

SEAFOOD

Jumbo Lump Crab Cakes with Lemon Remoulade

1 pound jumbo lump crabmeat

1 small lemon

2 sleeves of saltine crackers

2 large eggs

¼ cup Hellman's mayonnaise

½ teaspoon Worcestershire sauce

½ teaspoon dry mustard

⅛ teaspoon Old Bay seasoning

¼ teaspoon cayenne pepper

¼ cup minced onion

2 tablespoons chopped fresh cilantro

2 tablespoons butter

4 tablespoons vegetable oil

Carefully place the crabmeat into a colander. Squeeze the lemon juice over the crabmeat and set aside to drain.

Place the saltine crackers in a Ziploc bag and seal. Using a rolling pin, crush the crackers. Avoid pulverizing, taking care to leave the crackers in very small pieces. Reserve ½ cup of the cracker crumbs to be added to the crab mixture, and place the remainder of the crumbs in a bowl for coating the crab cakes. Set aside.

In a large bowl, lightly beat the eggs. Whisk in the mayonnaise and Worcestershire sauce. Add the seasonings and stir in the onion, cilantro, and ½ cup cracker crumbs. Using a wooden spoon or paddle, gently fold in the crabmeat so as to keep the large lumps together.

This recipe is the result of an extensive search by Connie and Steve to develop the perfect crab cake.

They tried many recipes – including the most delicious one from their friend, Linda Egan of Edwards, Colorado. To Linda's delightful recipe, they added herbs and tweaked the process slightly. Thusly, we have the "perfect crab cake." We paired the crab cakes with an older family recipe for lemon remoulade.

Shape the mixture into cakes about the size of a mini-muffin, but a little thicker. Coat the crab cakes with the remaining cracker crumbs and transfer to a baking sheet that has been lined with wax paper. Refrigerate until ready to cook. These crab cakes may be assembled and refrigerated overnight.

In a large skillet, melt 1 tablespoon butter in 2 tablespoons oil over medium heat. Cook half of the crab cakes about 3 minutes per side, or until golden and crisp. Repeat the process with the remaining butter, oil, and crab cakes.

Yields 15 to 20 small crab cakes

Lemon Remoulade:

2 cups Hellman's mayonnaise

¼ cup Creole mustard

1 tablespoon fresh lemon juice

2 teaspoons paprika

¾ teaspoon cayenne pepper

2 garlic cloves, minced

¼ cup capers

2 tablespoons chopped fresh parsley

In a medium bowl whisk together the mayonnaise, mustard, lemon juice, paprika, and cayenne pepper. When the mixture is well blended, stir in the garlic, capers, and parsley. Cover and chill 30 minutes.

A versatile sauce for seafood that will keep up to 3 days when stored in a covered container in the refrigerator.

SEAFOOD

Crab Royale

Fit for a queen or princess, Crab Royale is remarkably suited for her luncheon.

Plate this crab delicacy with fresh, crisp garden lettuce that has been tossed with Absolutely Delicious Salad Dressing (page 64). Your guests will be delighted to share this light lunch with you!

1 pound jumbo lump crabmeat

juice of 1 lemon

1 stick butter

½ cup grated onion

½ cup finely chopped green bell pepper

¼ cup finely chopped red bell pepper

2 eggs

½ cup Hellman's mayonnaise

1 tablespoon Creole mustard

sea salt & freshly cracked pepper to taste

1 package frozen phyllo sheets

1 egg, beaten with 1 tablespoon water

Gently place the crabmeat in a colander and sprinkle with the juice of a lemon. Drain and set aside.

In a skillet, sauté the onion and peppers in the butter until just wilted.

Meanwhile, lightly beat the eggs in a mixing bowl. Add the mayo and mustard; whisk until well blended. Stir in the sautéed peppers. Add salt and pepper to taste.

Using a wooden spoon or soft plastic spatula, gently fold in the crabmeat. Keep the jumbo lumps intact.

Make 6 pastry shells. For each one, use 3 or 4 layers of phyllo sheets and cut a 6-inch square. Place the square on a parchment-lined cookie sheet. Carefully scoop the crab mixture into the center. Fold the edges of the pastry under to form a round shell. Use a pastry brush to lightly coat the edges of the shells with the egg wash.

Bake at 350° for 15 minutes.

Yields 6 servings

Crab Stuffing

1 pound jumbo lump crab meat

1 fresh lemon

1 stick butter

1 tablespoon red bell pepper, chopped

1 tablespoon green bell pepper, chopped

⅓ cup flour

1 teaspoon salt

½ teaspoon black pepper

1 tablespoon Worcestershire sauce

2 teaspoons yellow mustard

1½ tablespoons prepared horseradish

1½ cups milk

1 tablespoon fresh lemon juice

chopped fresh parsley to taste

1 cup Pepperidge Farm herb seasoned stuffing

paprika, optional

Carefully place the crabmeat in a colander, taking care to keep the jumbo lumps intact. Squeeze the fresh lemon over the crabmeat. Set aside.

In a large skillet, sauté the red and green bell pepper in the butter. Stir in the flour, salt, and black pepper until smooth. Add the Worcestershire sauce, mustard, and horseradish. Gradually add the milk, stirring to keep the sauce smooth.

Remove from heat and stir in the lemon juice, stuffing, and parsley to taste. Gently fold in the crabmeat, using a wooden paddle to avoid breaking the jumbo lumps.

The stuffing is excellent for flounder, shrimp, mushrooms, or for individual servings. For 4 to 6 individual servings, spray the ovenproof dishes with Pam. After dividing the mixture, sprinkle paprika over the tops. Bake at 375° for 25 - 30 minutes.

The basis for this recipe came from a mother whose children I taught in the 11th grade.

She was a great PTA president. At an appreciation luncheon for teachers, she served a crabmeat casserole that was delicious. With a few tweaks to convert it to a versatile stuffing, this recipe has been a family favorite since 1972.

SEAFOOD

Stuffed Flounder

When my sons were teenagers, they loved gigging flounder.

Grand Bay, in southern Mobile County, Alabama, was a favorite place to take all their gear for this night sport. They went equipped with lights and gigs, and they always returned with flounder. Their success meant that stuffed flounder was a frequent menu item.

4 individual size flounder, about 1 pound each

8 large lemons

salt and coarse ground pepper to taste

Slap Ya Mama Cajun seasoning, to taste

1 stick butter, divided

4 to 6 ounces white wine

1 recipe Crab Stuffing (page 109)

12 large shrimp, optional

Prepare the lemons. Using 3 lemons, cut into thin slices to make lemon rounds. Using 2 lemons, cut into wedges. Juice the remaining 3 lemons. Set aside.

Wash the fresh flounder and prepare them for stuffing. Using a sharp knife, cut the dark side of the fish from the tail to the front. Make the cut all the way to the bone. Next, use the knife to slit a pocket to either side of the bone.

Prepare a large jellyroll pan by heavily greasing with butter. Pour the white wine into the pan. Arrange the flounder in the pan so that they do not touch.

Working with each fish, spoon lemon juice over the entire area. Fold back the pocket. Salt and pepper to taste; sprinkle lightly with the Slap Ya Mama seasoning.

Work with the crab stuffing, using your hands to form ¼ of the stuffing into a football-shape while taking care not to press the crabmeat. Place into the pocket and shape the fish around the stuffing.

Melt the remaining butter and generously brush over the top of each fish. Arrange the lemon rounds along both sides of the fish. Sprinkle with paprika.

Bake at 375° for 35 minutes. Serve on warmed plates. Garnish with lemon wedges and parsley.

Optional shrimp: Coat the peeled shrimp with a little melted butter and salt to taste.

Set the timer to add the shrimp after the flounder has cooked 25 minutes. Gently push 3 shrimp lightly into the stuffing of each flounder. Return to the oven and cook 10 minutes.

Barbequed Shrimp

2 sticks butter, melted

¼ cup minced garlic

Tabasco to taste (lots of it!)

2 teaspoons paprika

2 tablespoons salt

3 tablespoons black pepper

½ cup barbeque sauce

1 lemon, sliced

dash of dried oregano

1 tablespoon chili sauce

5 pounds large unpeeled shrimp with heads on

3 sticks butter, melted

1 tablespoon black pepper

In a large mixing bowl, combine the first 10 ingredients. Whisk together until well blended. Place the shrimp in a large flat container and pour the mixture over them. Marinate for about 1½ hours.

Remove the shrimp from the marinade, and place them in a large casserole dish. Stir 1 tablespoon black pepper into the melted 3 sticks of butter and pour over the shrimp.

Bake at 300° for about 40 minutes, basting often. Avoid overcooking.

Yields 8 to 10 servings

This is an authentic New Orleans recipe and was given to Fred and me by a friend who lived there.

After a Saints game in the 1970s, he served barbequed shrimp at a party we attended. The shrimp are a bit messy to eat, but are quite succulent.

SEAFOOD

Baked Stuffed Shrimp

2 pounds large shrimp (15-count per pound)

5 tablespoons butter, divided

2 tablespoons minced shallots or green onions

¼ cup minced onions

1 green bell pepper, chopped fine

1 cup soft breadcrumbs

1 teaspoon salt

⅛ teaspoon black pepper

1 egg, beaten

parsley for garnishing

Shell and devein 6 of the shrimp. Sauté them in 3 tablespoons of the butter for 2 minutes or until pink. Remove the shrimp from the pan and chop finely. Set aside.

Into the same pan, add the shallots, onion, and green pepper. Cook until translucent, about 4 minutes. Remove from heat. Stir in the breadcrumbs, chopped shrimp, salt, and pepper. Blend in the egg and set the mixture aside.

Shell the remaining shrimp, leaving the tails on. Make a split along the inner sides, but do not cut completely through. Mound the stuffing into the split of each shrimp. Curl the tail back over the stuffing, forming the shrimp into a "C" shape. Place all the shrimp into a buttered baking dish with the tails pointed up. Drizzle with the melted 2 tablespoons of butter. At this point, the stuffed shrimp may be baked or may be covered and refrigerated for baking later.

Bake at 400° for 15 to 20 minutes, just until the shrimp is done.

Yields 6 servings

My daughter-in-law Faye is family-famous for this delicious shrimp presentation.

We have been enjoying her special dish for over 25 years. She sometimes prefers using slightly smaller shrimp, as they are moister and sweeter. Currently, she is working on tweaking the stuffing as a recipe for shrimp cakes.

SEAFOOD

Shrimp Fettuccine

3 pounds shrimp, boiled and peeled (do not overcook)

2 sticks butter

3 onions, chopped

2 bell peppers, chopped

3 ribs celery, chopped

3 garlic cloves, minced

4 teaspoons chopped parsley

¼ cup flour

½ teaspoon each salt & pepper

3 cups half & half

½ cup plus 1 tablespoon evaporated milk

12 ounces jalapeño cheese, grated and divided

12 ounces fettuccine, cooked al dente and drained

In a large pan, sauté the veggies in butter until translucent. Add the parsley and garlic; cook slightly.

Stir in the flour; gradually add the half & half and evaporated milk. When the mixture is smooth, stir in 8 ounces of the cheese. Simmer about 5 minutes to make the sauce.

Add the shrimp to the sauce. Lastly, stir in the fettuccine. Pour the mixture into a buttered casserole dish. Bake at 350° for 15 minutes; sprinkle the remaining cheese over the top and cook another 15 minutes.

Yields 10 servings

Clemmie, my brother Roy's wife, brought the original recipe into the Collins family around 1983.

The fettuccine quickly became a truly delicious addition to our family favorites.

SEAFOOD

Crawfish Etouffée

After enjoying crawfish etouffée served over stuffed flounder at Willy G's in Houston, I couldn't wait to create my own recipe.

The result is a dish that is easy and quick. Just pick up a pound bag of fresh or frozen crawfish tail meat from the seafood section of the grocery store.

1 stick butter

1 large onion, finely chopped

½ cup chopped celery

¼ cup chopped bell pepper

2 tablespoons flour

¾ cup hot water

¾ teaspoon salt

¼ teaspoon each of black pepper and cayenne pepper

½ teaspoon garlic powder

½ teaspoon Tabasco

1 pound peeled crawfish tails

½ cup chopped green onion tops

½ cup chopped fresh parsley

Sauté the onion, celery, and bell pepper in butter for about 5 minutes. Stir in the flour until slightly browned. Gradually add the hot water while continuing to stir. Add the seasonings and the crawfish. Cover and cook over low heat about 20 minutes until heated. Lastly, stir in the green onions and parsley; continue to cook another 5 minutes. Serve over hot cooked rice. Garnish with extra green onion and/or parsley, if desired.

SEAFOOD

Oysters Rockefeller

1½ quarts raw oysters

2 sticks butter

2 ribs celery, chopped fine

1 medium white onion, chopped fine

3 cloves garlic, chopped fine

¾ cup parsley, chopped fine

¼ teaspoon anise seed

2 teaspoons crushed red pepper or to taste

¼ cup Worcestershire sauce

juice of ½ lemon

1 pound frozen spinach, thawed

salt, black pepper, cayenne pepper to taste

splash of white wine

1½ cups grated Parmesan cheese

¼ cup breadcrumbs

French baguette

Drain the oysters in a colander while you prepare the sauce.

In a large skillet, melt the butter and sauté the celery until soft. Add the onions, garlic, parsley, anise seed, crushed red pepper, Worcestershire sauce, and lemon juice; continue sautéing until the onion is soft. Stir in the spinach; add the salt, black pepper, and cayenne pepper to taste. Splash the mixture with a bit of white wine. Set the sauce aside. This mixture may be made ahead of time and refrigerated.

Pat the oysters dry. In a shallow baking dish, arrange them in a single layer. Cover the oysters with the Rockefeller sauce as thick as desired.

Bake at 350° for 30 minutes. Remove from the oven; cover with the cheese and a thin layer of the breadcrumbs. Return to oven for 10 minutes or until the top is lightly brown.

Serve with warm French bread sliced into ½-inch pieces.

This recipe is one of my most favorite ways to serve oysters.

Perhaps that is partially due to the fond memories of visits with the Stegers at their Montana home. On our seafood (brought from Johnson Seafood in Coden, Alabama) day, Rolanette Lawrence taught us to make her fabulous recipe, with her sous chef Connie adding a special twist. From the spacious deck at happy hour, we feasted visually on the magnificent views of Glacier National Park while we feasted gastronomically on this amazing delicacy.

SEAFOOD

The hard times experienced in America during the Great Depression years were marked by frugality in most families. The "when I was young" stories, told by the older family members, abound with redundant examples of hardships during that era. Along with the tales of how far they walked to school and how hard they had to work for long hours, were the stories about the scarcity of meat in the weekly menus. With good cause, the politicians from that time always promised "a chicken in every pot." Chicken, whether fried or baked, was the real treat for Sunday dinner.

After World War II, the country began to experience a return to prosperity. By the time I was learning to cook in 1947, I could plan each meal around the main dish. How fortunate I was to live on the Gulf Coast with its abundance of fresh seafood, as well as the availability of beef and pork. Chicken, in all its versatility, was still a perennial favorite.

Since my son John began to raise cattle on his farm, he has kept our freezers supplied with Black Angus meat. From the lean ground beef to beef tenderloin, we enjoy the various cuts of meat from cows who graze in fields of abundant green grass. All of my family still favors what we always called our "country dinner," consisting of country fried cube steak, creamed corn, peas with okra, and jalapeño cheese cornbread. Either peach or berry cobbler is our idea of the perfect dessert with this favorite meal.

MAIN DISHES

Standing Rib Roast

Boston Butt, Oven Roasted

Party Chicken

Classic Chicken Pot Pie

Osso Bucco

Country Fried Steak

Savory Bolognese

Lasagna

Herb Buttered Quail

Tangy Meat Loaf

Bacon Quiche

Baked Ham

Holiday Dinner
Roasted Turkey
Cranberry Sauce
Giblet Gravy
Classic Cornbread Dressing

Pizza

Standing Rib Roast

7 to 9 pound prime rib roast, with 6 or 7 ribs

2 garlic cloves

3 to 4 tablespoons kosher salt

1 tablespooon coarsely ground black pepper

1 teaspoon Tex Joy steak seasoning

Line a shallow roasting pan with heavy-duty foil. Cut 2 deep slits in the meat and insert the garlic cloves. Place the roast in the pan with the rib side down. Generously coat the meat with the kosher salt and pepper. Sprinkle with the steak seasoning.

Place the roast in a preheated 450° oven and cook 20 minutes. Reduce the heat to 300° and continue cooking.

Total time of cooking, including the first 20 minutes, is 20 minutes for each pound. For example, an 8 pound roast has a total cooking time of 160 minutes, or 2 hours and 40 minutes. Meat thermometer should read 145° for medium-rare.

Remove the roast from the oven, cover with foil, and let rest for 20 minutes.

Allow 8 ounces per serving

My nephew, Bobby Collins, taught me to cook this grand roast in 2002, and was I impressed by his expertise!

The high heat for the first 20 minutes sears the outside, while the lower heat slowly roasts the meat to a moist and flavorful medium-rare doneness.

MAIN DISHES

Boston Butt, Oven Roasted

6 to 8 pound Boston butt roast

⅓ cup olive oil

kosher salt

coarsely ground black pepper

1 (5 ounce) bottle Tiger Sauce

Prepare a roasting pan by lining it with heavy-duty foil and placing a rack inside the pan. Prepare a work surface by placing a large piece of heavy foil on the counter space; then, place the Boston butt on the foil. Begin by coating the entire surface of the meat with the olive oil. Generously (really generously) coat the entire surface with kosher salt. Next, do the same with the pepper.

Place the Boston butt, fat side up, on the rack in the roasting pan. In a zigzag motion, pour the Tiger Sauce over the top and sides of the meat.

Start cooking the roast in the oven at 400° for 30 minutes. Turn the oven to 300° and continue cooking for about 4 hours or until done. Pork is well done when a meat thermometer inserted into the center reaches 165° to 170°. Check to see if the meat shrinks back from the bone for an additional test.

If the meat begins to get too brown, make a tent of foil to loosely place over the pan. When the meat is done, remove from oven. Cover the Boston butt with foil and a large dishtowel until you are ready to serve.

Yields 12 to 15 servings

Fred used to say that if there was anything better than pork, it was more pork!

This Boston Butt recipe certainly verifies that "more pork" theory with its slow cooking and flavor-enhancing, simple ingredients. Whether served sliced or the more popular pulled pork style, this meat consistently gets rave reviews. See the Grilling and Smoking section for an alternative smoked version of Boston butt.

My favorite barbeque sauce is made by Dreamland Bar-B-Que, a restaurant which originated in Tuscaloosa, Alabama.

Dreamland sells its sauce, in quarts or gallons, at each of its 8 restaurants; or they will ship if you are not nearby. If you like a thinner barbeque sauce that is tangy and spicy with lots of black pepper, try Dreamland.

Party Chicken

This chicken recipe has been a family "go to" entrée since my sister-in-law, Louise Collins, served it in the 1960s.

The slow-cooked combination of beef, bacon, and chicken results in an extraordinary blending of the 3 meats into a unique taste sensation. The fresh mushrooms and parsley are an update to this favorite.

2 cups sliced fresh mushrooms

1 tablespoon extra virgin olive oil

salt & pepper to taste

1 (2.25 ounce) jar dried beef, cut in ½-inch pieces

8 chicken breasts, skinned and deboned

8 slices bacon

1 can cream of mushroom soup

1 (8 ounce) carton sour cream

2 tablespoons chopped fresh parsley

Sauté the mushrooms in the olive oil. Sprinkle with salt and freshly cracked black pepper to taste. Set aside.

Cover the bottom of a greased casserole dish with the dried beef.

Wrap each chicken breast with a strip of bacon and place in the casserole dish over the dried beef. Sprinkle half of the sautéed mushrooms over the top. Reserve the remaining half for garnishing.

Blend the soup, sour cream, and 1 tablespoon parsley; pour over the chicken. Cover with foil or plastic wrap. Refrigerate overnight.

Cook at 300° for 2½ to 3 hours. Use the remaining mushrooms and parsley for garnishing the cooked chicken breasts.

Serve plated with Pecan Wild Rice.

MAIN DISHES

Classic Chicken Pot Pie

2 refrigerated pie crusts

2½ cups cooked chicken, cut into bite-size pieces

1 (10.5 ounce) can cream of chicken soup

1¼ cups milk

1 cup combined English peas and diced carrots, cooked

salt to taste

coarse ground black pepper to taste

Line the bottom of an 8 x 8 square or a regular round pie dish with 1 pie crust. Set aside.

In a large bowl, combine all the other ingredients. Pour the mixture into the pie crust.

Place the remaining pie crust over the chicken mixture, crimping the edges around the baking dish. Make several slits in the top for steam to release during cooking.

Bake at 375° until the mixture is bubbly and the crust is crispy, about 45 minutes.

For a super easy one-dish comfort food, try this tasty version of a traditional classic.

I have made it for so many years that I have forgotten how the idea originated. My mother asked for my recipe! It was also one of Fred's favorites in his retirement years.

Osso Bucco

⅓ cup butter

1½ cups finely chopped onions

½ cup finely chopped celery

½ cup finely chopped carrots

2 cloves garlic, minced

½ cup olive oil

6 to 8 (2½-inch thick) veal shanks, each tied with kitchen string

salt and freshly ground black pepper, to taste

1 cup flour

1 cup red wine

¾ to 1½ cups beef stock

3 cups canned tomatoes, drained and chopped coarse

2 tablespoons fresh basil, chopped

2 tablespoons fresh thyme, chopped

4 tablespoons fresh parsley, chopped

2 bay leaves

Gremolata

Select a Dutch oven that has a tight cover and is just large enough to hold the veal shanks standing up in 1 layer. Sauté the veggies in the butter until translucent, stirring frequently with a wooden spoon. Remove from the heat and set aside.

Sprinkle the shanks with salt and pepper and dredge with flour. In a heavy skillet over medium high heat, brown half of the shanks in 6 tablespoons of the olive oil. Add the remaining oil and brown the remaining shanks. Place the browned meat, standing up side by side, on top of the vegetables in the Dutch oven.

My first exposure to osso bucco was a delectable dinner at Brennan's of Houston, which featured the perfectly prepared veal shank served over risotto.

To my great joy, however, Mary Ruth Valerius graciously shared her recipe that is equally as delicious. While the shanks are in the oven cooking, prepare the Wild Mushroom Risotto for a scrumptious presentation for your dinner table.

MAIN DISHES

Pour off the oil remaining in the skillet, leaving only a film to coat the pan. Add the wine and boil over high heat, scraping the bottom for the browned bits left from frying the meat. When the wine is reduced to about ½ cup, stir in ¾ cup of the stock, the tomatoes, and the herbs. Bring to a boil and pour this over the veal shanks. Add enough of the reserved stock so that the shanks are half covered.

Cook over medium heat until the liquid comes to a boil. Cover the pot with a tight fitting lid. Bake on a lower shelf in a 350° oven for approximately 1 hour and 15 minutes, basting occasionally. When done, the meat will have no resistance when pierced with a fork. Remove from the oven and increase the oven temperature to 450°.

Carefully transfer the veal shanks to a large ovenproof serving dish, keeping the marrow intact. Cut and remove the string. Bake the shanks at 450° for 5 to 10 minutes, until browned and glazed.

In the meantime, strain the contents left in the Dutch oven to extract all liquid. Boil over high heat, stirring frequently, until the liquid is reduced by half. Pour this sauce over the veal shanks. Sprinkle the top with gremolata.

Yields 6 to 8 servings

Gremolata:

1 tablespoon grated lemon peel

1 teaspoon minced garlic

3 tablespoons fresh parsley, finely chopped

Combine the ingredients until evenly mixed.

Country Fried Steak

Cubed steak anchored our family's "country dinner" menu.

As far back as I can remember, I prepared this meal once a week. To this day my grown children and their friends still request that I cook their favorite meal of cubed steak, peas with okra, corn, and jalapeño cornbread. In season, of course, I also fry some fresh okra and slice vine ripened tomatoes!

1½ pounds cubed steak

salt and pepper to sprinkle

1 cup flour

¼ teaspoon salt

¼ teaspoon pepper

¼ cup canola oil

¾ cup water, optional

Trim the cubed steaks of any fat or gristle. Lightly sprinkle with salt and pepper.

Pour the canola oil into a large non-stick skillet and place over medium heat.

In a shallow pan combine the flour, salt, and pepper. Dredge each cubed steak through the flour mixture and place into the hot skillet. When the meat is browned on one side, sprinkle a little of the flour mix on top and turn the steaks to brown on the other side. Serve warm.

Optional: After the steaks are brown on both sides, turn the heat to low and add ¾ cup of water. Cover and simmer for 30 minutes. This steaming will enhance tenderness as well as add a bit of gravy.

Yields 4 to 5 servings

Savory Bolognese

2 pounds mild Italian sausage

2 pounds lean ground beef

2 medium onions, chopped

2½ tablespoons chili powder

1 teaspoon garlic salt

salt & freshly cracked black pepper to taste

2 large cans Centro stewed tomatoes or 2 quarts freshly stewed tomatoes

3 tablespoons Worcestershire sauce

1½ jars Emeril's home style marinara sauce

2 tablespoons finely chopped fresh garlic

½ cup pesto (page 127)

½ cup fresh chopped oregano

½ cup fresh chopped basil

½ cup fresh chopped parsley

If the Italian sausage is packaged in links, first remove the casings. Pull into bite-size pieces.

In a large heavy pot on medium heat, begin to brown the sausage and ground beef. Avoid overworking the meat, leaving the sausage in bite size pieces. As the meat cooks, add the onion and cook until translucent. Stir in the chili powder and garlic salt. Add salt and black pepper to taste.

When the meat is mostly cooked, add the stewed tomatoes. Stir in the Worcestershire, marinara sauce, and garlic. Continue to cook for about 10 minutes.

Turn heat to simmer for 20 to 30 minutes. Add the pesto and herbs. Continue to simmer for 1 hour and 15 minutes. Taste and add additional salt and pepper if needed.

Yields 4 to 5 quarts

As a result of several years working toward making an ultimate meat sauce, my daughter, Connie, has produced a recipe that is both excellent in taste and versatile for serving.

She uses the meat sauce with great success in pasta dishes. It is outstanding as the meat sauce for lasagna. This recipe makes enough to freeze some containers for future use.

Connie and Steve shared a passion for cooking and entertaining. They participated in many cooking classes in France and Italy, as well as in the California wine region. They took advantage of numerous classes in Houston and New Orleans. As a result their dinner parties were legendary, and the food was beyond special. I have learned a great deal about food from them. In my opinion, Connie should write her own cookbook. I am most thankful for her invaluable assistance with this one.

MAIN DISHES

Lasagna

Have on hand 24 ounces mozzarella cheese, either fresh or in packaged slices. Using fresh mozzarella adds a more delicious flavor, especially for the topping.

Cook 8 lasagna noodles al dente in salted water (1 teaspoon salt). Drain and rinse in cool water and set aside. (A recent alternative is to simply use lasagna noodles that do not require cooking. Your choice!)

Cheese Mixture:

1 pound Ricotta cream-style cheese

3 lightly beaten eggs

2 teaspoons salt

½ teaspoon pepper

2 tablespoons chopped fresh parsley

½ cup grated Parmesan cheese

½ cup grated Romano cheese

Mix together and set aside.

Sauce:

1 pound ground beef

1 pound Italian sausage

2 cloves garlic, minced

1 heaping tablespoon each of chopped fresh parsley flakes, basil, and oregano

1 teaspoon salt

1 tablespoon chili powder

1 (20 ounce) can diced tomatoes

1 cup pesto

In a large skillet, brown the meat slowly. Drain and dispose of any liquid. Add the remaining ingredients and simmer uncovered until thick – 45 minutes to 1 hour.

In 1975 Judy Jackson, Charlie's sister-in-law, served this lasagna when Betty, Charlie, Fred, and I stopped by on our way home from Williamsburg.

Judy's college roommate, who was Italian, had shared her family recipe for lasagna. It quickly became a favorite in our family. Over the years, however, we have learned that substituting Connie's Savory Bolognese for the sauce makes the dish even more delicious.

Two years ago my granddaughters, Leslie and Kelli, experienced a fun evening at the Bay with Connie making her Savory Bolognese.

Leslie took very detailed notes and made the recipe on her return to Birmingham. She now loves to make lasagna using Connie's savory meat sauce and has become very proficient, enough so that before her wedding, she impressed her fiancé Harrigan and his parents with a lasagna dinner. It was a huge success!

MAIN DISHES

Assemble in a lasagna pan in layers as follows:

⅓ of meat sauce, layer of noodles, ½ of cheese mixture, 10 ounces mozzarella cheese,

⅓ of meat sauce, layer of noodles, remaining cheese mixture, 10 ounces mozzarella cheese,

remaining ⅓ of meat sauce

top with remaining mozzarella cheese

The lasagna may be assembled and refrigerated overnight. Before cooking, let the lasagna come to room temperature. This recipe also freezes well.

Bake at 350° for 45 minutes. Let stand 15 minutes before serving.

Yields 8 to 10 servings

Pesto

3 ounces vegetable oil

¼ cup pine nuts

3 garlic cloves

3 cups fresh basil leaves

½ stick unsalted butter

½ cup olive oil

½ cup grated Parmesan cheese

salt & pepper to taste

In a non-stick skillet, slightly roast the pine nuts over low heat.

Combine the roasted pine nuts, garlic cloves, and basil leaves in a food processor. Use the pulse mode to coarsely chop before adding the butter and olive oil. Process until well mixed.

Pour the mixture into a mixing bowl. Stir in the Parmesan cheese. Add salt and pepper to taste.

MAIN DISHES

Herb Buttered Quail

8 quail, dressed

2 tablespoons butter, softened

2 tablespoons chopped fresh rosemary

½ medium onion, finely chopped

salt and pepper to taste

16 slices bacon

olive oil, for coating

Make herb butter by combining the butter, rosemary, and onion in a bowl; salt and pepper to taste. Divide the herb butter among the quail, placing equal amounts inside the bird cavities. Next wrap each bird with 2 slices of bacon and truss with kitchen string.

Brush each bird with olive oil and place on a rack inside a large pan lined with foil. The quail should not touch. Placing a large cube of French bread between quail will keep them upright and separated.

Cook at 350° for about 25 minutes until done. Remove from oven and brush again with olive oil.

In the 1960s and 1970s, our area was rich in coveys of quail.

Familiar was the sound of their echoing "bob-whites" around our rural acres. During quail hunting season, my sons would bring home their limits, clean them, and freeze the birds until the end of the season. At that time, we would have a huge quail dinner and invite friends and fellow hunters to join in our "Feast of the Coveys." Over dinner the hunters would contribute stories about their hunts, remarkably remembering in detail almost every covey they flushed!

For many years, quail have been scarce to non-existent in our area. Quail hunting now requires a trip to another area. My sons and grandson still bring their quail to me, and I love to use this recipe. It is an incredibly easy and tasty way to serve this delicacy.

Tangy Meat Loaf

2 pounds lean ground beef

3 tablespoons horseradish

1 teaspoon Tiger Sauce

½ cup ketchup

1 medium onion, finely chopped

¼ cup finely chopped celery

1 tablespoon chopped parsley

2 eggs, lightly beaten

¼ cup milk

1 teaspoon salt

½ teaspoon coarse ground pepper

¾ cup quick-cooking oatmeal

Topping:

⅓ cup ketchup

2 teaspoons mustard

1 tablespoon horseradish

3 tablespoons light brown sugar

In a large bowl combine all ingredients except the topping. Shape into 2 loaves; place into an oblong baking dish and cook at 350° for 40 minutes.

Meanwhile combine the remaining ketchup, mustard, horseradish, and brown sugar. Pour this mixture over the loaves and continue to cook for 15 minutes. Place the meat loaves on a serving dish.

Yields 8 servings

Everyone has various meat loaf recipes, and I am no exception.

I like the tangy taste the horseradish gives to this one.

Bacon Quiche

My granddaughter Ashley married Justin in May of 2012.

That year they began a tradition of hosting a family Christmas breakfast at their home. She had mastered my cinnamon roll recipe in an earlier one-on-one lesson. Among other delicious dishes, she served this bacon quiche and shared her fabulous recipe with me!

1 pound bacon

1 refrigerated pie pastry

1 tablespoon butter

¼ cup sliced green onions

6 eggs

1½ cup heavy whipping cream

¼ cup unsweetened apple juice

⅛ teaspoon salt

⅛ teaspoon black pepper

2 cups shredded Swiss cheese

Cut the bacon into ½-inch pieces and fry until crisp. Drain on paper towels and set aside.

Sauté the green onions in the butter until tender. Set aside.

Line a 9-inch pie plate with the refrigerated pie crust, flute the edges, and set aside.

In a large bowl, whisk the eggs. Slowly add the cream and juice and blend well. Stir in the crisp bacon, sautéed green onions, salt and pepper. Pour the mixture into the pie shell and sprinkle the cheese on top.

Bake at 350° for 40-45 minutes or until a knife inserted in the center comes out clean. Let rest 10 minutes before cutting.

Baked Ham

6 to 8 pound cured ham, butt portion

1 tablespoon whole cloves

1 (8 ounce) can crushed pineapple, drained

¾ cup brown sugar

2 tablespoons Worcestershire sauce

Prepare the ham by scoring the visible fat which lines the top of the ham. Punch a clove into each diamond shaped scoring. Place the ham on a rack in a roasting pan that has been lined with heavy foil.

In a small bowl combine the drained crushed pineapple, brown sugar, and Worcestershire sauce. Spoon the mixture generously over the ham, reserving any left for basting during cooking.

Bake in a 325° oven, allowing 15 minutes per pound of ham. If the ham begins to brown too much, it can be covered with a tent of foil.

Yields 12 to 15 servings

With the advent of the spiral-cut ham, it became both easy and convenient to serve ham.

There is still, however, no equal to the aromas and the succulent taste of a home-cooked ham. Choose your favorite brand and rediscover baked ham.

MAIN DISHES

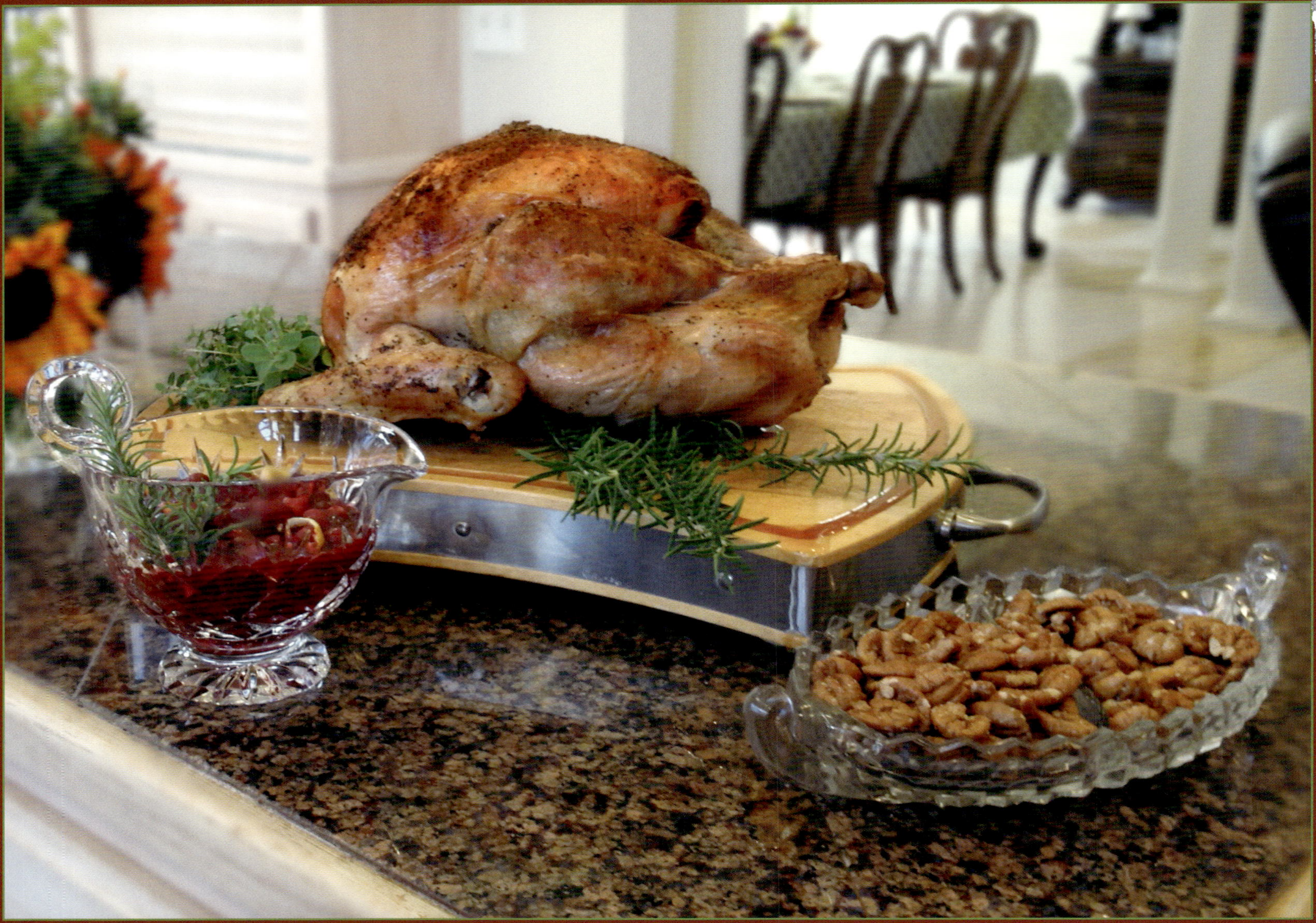

HOLIDAY DINNER

As Americans, we are so blessed with plenteous food. No longer do we have to wait for special occasions to enjoy certain foods. Due to freezers, refrigeration, and other food preservation processes, we have access to foods both in and out of season.

Some foods are identified with particular holidays. New Year's Day traditionally includes black-eyed peas and greens to ensure good luck for the coming year. For Easter, we dye boiled eggs and bake hams. Americans must have hot dogs at Fourth of July celebrations. At Christmastime, we make our family favorites of special desserts.

Accordingly, no other food can take the place of turkey at Thanksgiving. How interesting that the turkey almost became our national symbol, losing out to the American eagle. The turkey, however, does reign supreme as the national bird of choice during the holiday season of Thanksgiving through Christmas.

The traditional holiday dinner for my family always includes roasted turkey, cornbread dressing, giblet gravy, and cranberry sauce. Other sides may come and go, the desserts may vary, but tradition dictates the turkey dinner is constant.

As we gather around the table for Thanksgiving dinner, let us give thanks for the food before us, for the family and friends beside us, and for the love we share among us.

Roasted Turkey

Cranberry Sauce

Giblet Gravy

Classic Cornbread Dressing

Roasted Turkey

Holidays call for special foods that vary by family traditions.

In my family both Thanksgiving and Christmas dinners traditionally included roasted turkey with all the trimmings: dressing, giblet gravy, and cranberry sauce. Typically there were also dishes of ham, candied sweet potatoes, macaroni and cheese, Charleston Delight salad, green beans or butter peas, and a few dessert choices for later in the day. But always, always we had the turkey and "fixings".

Cooking the giblets and turkey or chicken parts for broth:

Wash the giblets and neck from the turkey. Extra turkey legs or chicken parts may also be purchased to make additional broth for the dressing and giblet gravy. Place all the giblets and parts in a large boiler with about 2 quarts of water. Add salt and pepper to taste. Cut an onion into 4 parts and cut 2 ribs of celery into 3-inch sections; add these to the boiler. Bring to a boil over medium heat; cover and simmer until all parts are done.

Remove the giblets and parts and set aside until needed. Remove the onion and celery and dispose of them. To the remaining liquid add the pan drippings from the roasted turkey. This becomes the broth to be used in the Classic Cornbread Dressing and the Giblet Gravy recipes.

12 to 15 pound fresh or frozen Butterball turkey

1 stick butter, melted

2 medium onions

3 ribs of celery

salt

coarsely ground pepper

Thaw the turkey carefully according to directions from Butterball. Note that it takes about 4 days in the refrigerator to thaw the turkey safely. Remove all giblets and turkey parts from the cavity; wash and set in refrigerator to be cooked later for additional broth and giblets for gravy.

Wash the turkey completely. Blot dry with paper towels. Place the turkey, breast side up, on a rack in a roasting pan that has been lined with heavy foil. Cut the onions into halves and the celery into 2-inch sections and place them in both the cavity and under the skin of the neck area. Lift the wing tips up and over the back, tucking them under the turkey. Also tuck the legs under the flap of skin near the tail.

Slowly pour the melted butter over the turkey, completely covering its surface. Lightly salt and pepper.

Roast in oven at 325° until done. Cooking time will be between 3 to 3½ hours, depending on the size of the turkey. A meat thermometer inserted into the thigh will read 185° when done. You may also test for doneness in old-fashion ways: 1) When pressed, the meat on the leg will be soft and 2) When moving the drum leg up and down, the joint will easily give. If the turkey begins to brown too much, place a tent loosely over the bird.

Remove the turkey from the oven. Cover with a layer of foil, and place several dishtowels over the foil. Let rest at least 45 minutes before slicing. Choose a 'designated slicer' before time, so that person can have the knife sharp and a two-tined fork ready!

Yields about 20 servings

MAIN DISHES

Cranberry Sauce

3 cups fresh cranberries

2 tablespoons water

½ cup sugar

juice of ½ orange

3 tablespoons fresh orange zest

½ teaspoon cinnamon

¼ teaspoon ginger

⅛ teaspoon ground cloves

Reserve 1 cup of the fresh cranberries.

In a small saucepan, combine 2 cups of the cranberries with the remaining ingredients. Stirring occasionally, cook over medium heat until the mixture begins to thicken and the cranberries pop open.

Add the reserved cup of cranberries, and continue to cook 4 minutes. Serve warm or cold.

Want a tart cranberry sauce for the traditional holiday turkey or ham?

This recipe is both sweet and tangy, with a freshness that cannot be emulated in the canned versions. Connie and Kelli collaborated in presenting this modification of a family favorite.

Sue Cannon

Holiday Menu
Roasted Turkey 350° 4 hrs.
Classic Cornbread Dressing 375° 45 min.
Giblet Gravy
Cranberry Sauce
Sweet Potato Casserole with Pecan Topping 350° 35 min.
Fresh Green Beans
Charleston Delight Salad
Nan's Famous Yeast Rolls 350° 20-25 min.
Desserts
Lovie's Pecan Pie
Cheesecake Supreme
  - Blueberry Topping

Dinner for 12
7:00 PM

MAIN DISHES

Giblet Gravy

3 cups broth and giblets from Roasted Turkey recipe (page 134)

¼ cup uncooked cornbread dressing

3 tablespoons cornstarch

⅓ cup milk

3 hard-boiled eggs, chopped into small pieces

salt and pepper to taste

Measure 3 cups of broth and heat in a medium boiler. Trim the gizzard; then dice all the giblets and some of the meat from the neck. Add these to the broth, along with the dressing mixture, and simmer over low heat for about 10 minutes.

Mix the cornstarch and milk together; then, stir into the heated broth until thickened and smooth. Remove from heat and add the chopped eggs. Lastly, add salt and pepper to taste.

Serve warm in a gravy boat along with the Classic Cornbread Dressing.

This is how my mother made giblet gravy, and it still works for me!

A few years ago, however, Steve Valerius introduced me to Minor's products. I discovered Minor's turkey gravy base, and now sometimes use it as a shortcut base to which I add my own giblets and chopped eggs. So easy... and yet so tasty!

Classic Cornbread Dressing

1 (8-inch) pan cornbread, broken into large pieces

1 (14 ounce) package Pepperidge Farm cornbread stuffing

6 slices white bread, pulled into large pieces

1 stick butter, melted

1 cup chopped onion

1 cup chopped celery

¼ cup chopped bell pepper

3 eggs, lightly beaten

turkey broth and drippings

chicken broth, if needed

¾ cup milk

4 green onions with tops, chopped

salt and coarse ground pepper to taste

meat from the cooked turkey or chicken parts, chopped

In a very large mixing bowl, combine the cornbread, stuffing mix, and white bread. Set aside. (One box of Jiffy cornbread mix will make this amount of cornbread.)

Instructions for making the turkey broth accompany the Roasted Turkey recipe (page 134). Reserve 3 cups of the broth for the Giblet Gravy.

In a large skillet over medium heat, sauté the onion, celery, and bell pepper in the butter until crisp tender. Add 4 cups of broth to the skillet and heat. Pour this mixture over the bread mixture and stir together.

Stir in the lightly beaten eggs; add the milk and green onions. At this point add extra broth, either turkey broth or chicken broth, to achieve a richly moist mixture.

Any extra turkey or chicken parts left from making the broth can be chopped and added to enhance the flavor of the dressing. Add salt to taste and coarse ground pepper generously.

Pour into 1 large or 2 smaller casserole dishes that have been sprayed with Pam. Bake at 375° for about 45 minutes until lightly browned, yet still moist.

This rich, flavorful dressing is the perfect pairing with the Roasted Turkey.

It is completely Southern when covered with Giblet Gravy and a bit of the orange-flavored cranberry sauce on the side. My husband, who did not especially care for turkey, loved this dressing. He would have been content with just a plate of dressing and giblet gravy for his holiday dinner!

Pizza, Anyone?

Anyone in America over two years old knows at least one Italian word – pizza! Just saying or hearing it immediately lights up eyes and brings smiles to both young and old faces. The mere mention of the word brings warm, fuzzy thoughts of a happy meal, pizza party, and comraderie! Since six billion pizzas are consumed by Americans each year, the facts speak blatantly for popularity of the Italian pies.

Pizza is a universal favorite food that dates as far back as ancient times. Research reveals its prominence in history, dating from a precursor flatbread from the ruins of Pompeii 79 A. D. and on through ancient civilizations to modern times. Naples lays claim to creating flatbread topped with herbs and oils, then later adding the myriad of toppings available in our present world. The addition of tomato sauce was not possible until explorers in the 16th century brought the first tomatoes to Italy from South America. Fortunately, the Italians overcame their initial resistance to the perceived poisonous tomato – a fruit when eaten raw, a vegetable when cooked.

The design for modern pizza originated in 1889. As the story goes, the working class in the poor districts of Naples required food that could be easily prepared and eaten quickly, frequently as they walked on the street. It seems that the royalty became tired of their diet of rich French cuisine. Chef Raffaele Espisito prepared three pizzas with different toppings for King Umberto and Queen Margherita. Their favorite was called pizza mozzarella at that time and featured the colors of the Italian flag – white cheese, red tomatoes, and green basil. Pizza Margherita became the new name and is still a popular choice on pizza menus.

Italian immigrants brought their cultural cuisine to America. The first retail pizza place was opened in New York City in 1905. The burst of popularity of pizza, however, exploded post World War II. American soldiers who spent time in Italy returned home with a great fondness for the Italian pie. Pizza, thereafter, became a national meal.

The most pizza fun, for me, includes those great times getting together with family and friends to make our own pizzas. Cooking in our Big Green Eggs locally or using the authentic fornos at the villas of our vacations in Tuscany, both venues provide excellent opportunities for great fun and entertainment.

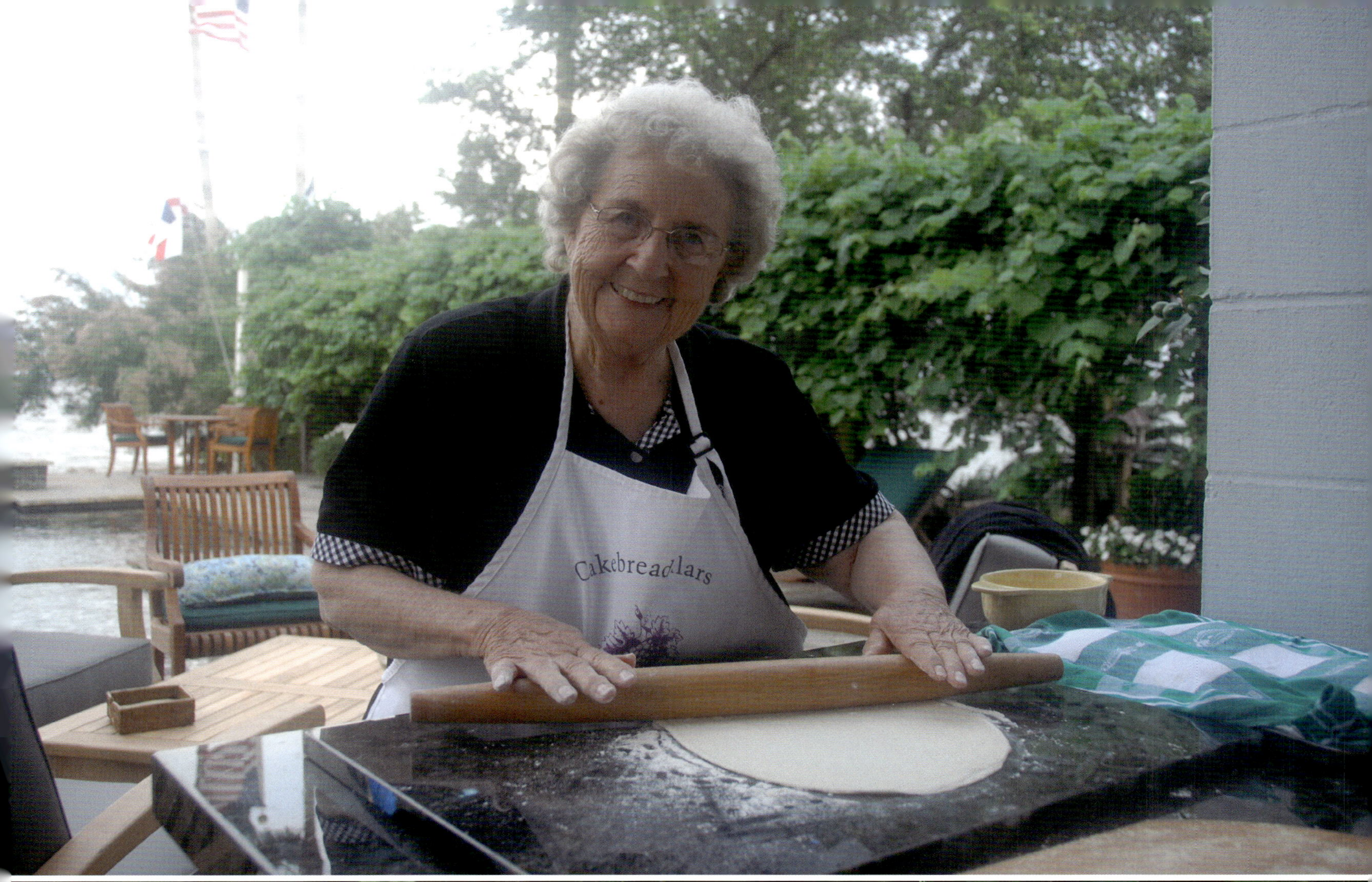
Cakebread

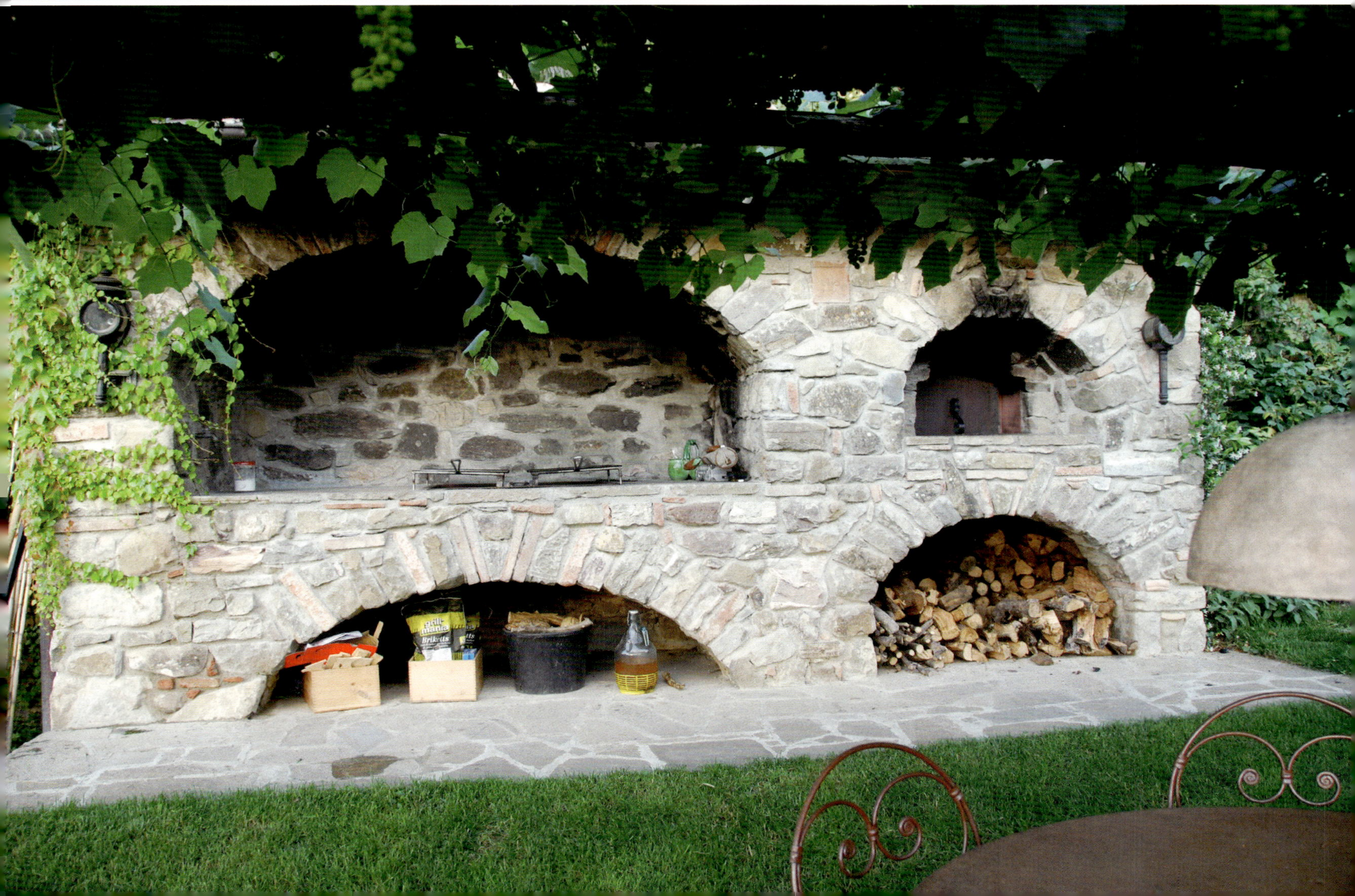

Pizza Dough

1 (¾ ounce) package active dry yeast

1¼ cups lukewarm water

4 cups unbleached "00" flour

2 teaspoons fine sea salt

2 tablespoons extra-virgin olive oil, plus extra

Sprinkle the yeast over the warm water; let stand until creamy, 5 to 10 minutes.

If the yeast does not appear creamy, start over.

In a large bowl, whisk together the flour and salt; form a well in the center. Add the yeast mixture and 2 tablespoons olive oil. Stir just until the dough comes together. Place the dough onto a lightly floured surface and knead vigorously for 10 minutes.

Cover with a damp dishtowel and let rest for 10 minutes. Knead vigorously again for 10 minutes more, forming the dough into a ball.

Lightly oil a large bowl; place the ball of dough in the bowl and turn to lightly coat with oil. Cover the bowl tightly with plastic wrap and refrigerate overnight.

Punch the dough down, fold the sides in, and turn the dough. Cover the bowl tightly again; refrigerate at least 4 hours or up to 24 hours.

Divide the dough into 4 pieces and shape them into balls. Place the balls on a lightly floured surface, leaving a few inches between them. Loosely cover with a damp dishtowel (not terry cloth). Let rise at room temperature until doubled, about 2 hours.

Special Equipment:

    a pizza stone and peel

    Big Green Egg, kitchen oven, or a forno

Yields 4 crusts

The special "00" flour is available at specialty stores.

It produces a pliable dough that is easy to work with. The result is a tender, yet sturdy, crust that is crisp. Bread flour can be substituted, if necessary.

MAIN DISHES

Assembling Pizza

Pizza toppings are many and varied. Choose your favorites and prepare them while the dough is rising. It is important that all topping ingredients are ready to be added when the dough is rolled into a crust. Also, plan the timing for the pizza stone to be very hot before the first pizza is ready for the oven – 1 hour at 500°. These pizzas are thin-crusted. The recipe makes 4 crusts, thereby providing several possible toppings!

Step 1:

On a lightly floured work surface, place one of the balls of pizza dough and begin to shape the crust. Using a floured rolling pin, roll the dough into the desired shape. You may choose a 10-inch round, an oblong, or even an interesting amorphous shape. Transfer the rolled crust to a peel, which has been sprinkled with cornmeal. Gently shake the peel to insure that the crust does not stick.

Step 2:

Working fairly quickly, brush the crust with olive oil; then, sprinkle lightly with kosher salt. Brush on a layer of marinara sauce.

Step 3:

Immediately add the toppings of choice.

For a sausage-pepper pizza, add red, green, and yellow peppers that have been sautéed. Combine with cooked crumbled Italian sausage. Top with fresh mozzarella slices or shredded mozzarella.

For a margherita pizza, place fresh tomato slices, fresh mozzarella slices, and basil leaves over the top.

Or create a topping with your own favorites: shrimp and artichoke, or pepperoni with bell pepper, or just vegetables, etc.

Step 4:

Slide the pizza carefully from the peel onto a very hot pizza stone, which has been placed in the lower third of the oven and heated at 500° for 1 hour. Cook until done, checking at 3 minutes. When done, slide the pizza onto a clean peel to remove it from the oven. Slide onto a cutting board. Drizzle the pizza with olive oil; sprinkle with grated Parmesan cheese and add crushed red pepper flakes to taste.

When it comes to grilling and smoking, the Cannon family men are masters. Beginning with Fred, then his sons, and then his grandson, the "Cannon Connection" seems to have that inherent gene which connects them to long-handled tongs and spatulas. They believe that every home should have a Weber gas grill and a Big Green Egg!

In order to share their expertise in outdoor cooking, I have used observation and interrogation to borrow from the knowledge and techniques they use. They have some basic rules: 1) Use the appropriate cooker. 2) Select good cuts of meat. 3) Treat the meat to its best advantage. 4) Match temperature to desired result.

1) There are two kinds of outdoor cookers: grills and smokers. Gas grills, whether propane or natural gas are best for hamburgers, steaks – thinner cuts of meat that require higher temperatures for shorter periods of time. A smoker, which uses charcoal, is appropriate for larger cuts of meat that require controlled temperatures for longer periods of time – such as turkeys, fresh pork hams or Boston butts.

2) Invest in good cuts of meat. For beef, choose either prime or choice. Avoid the select grade. Look for marbling in steaks; buy lean ground beef. Buy good quality pork with a healthy color and that is well within the expiration date.

3) Use individual recipes to determine the preparation of the meat. Some cuts require rubs, and some require marinades. Also, a good rule of thumb is to set the prepared meat out of the refrigerator 1 hour before cooking. This allows for more even cooking due to its room temperature throughout.

4) The recipe will indicate the proper cooking temperature to achieve the desired doneness. While most cookers have built-in gauges, a thermometer probe will ensure the perfectly cooked meat. Remote thermometers are especially efficient, allowing you to monitor from a distance.

In 1972, we were introduced to the Kamado ceramic grill – forerunner to the now popular Big Green Egg. To the delight of family and friends, Fred regularly smoked turkeys, fresh pork hams, ribs, and Boston butts. He literally used the Kamado until it fell into pieces 12 years later. At this point we began buying Big Green Eggs.

Twenty years later we are still believers in the Big Green Egg motto: The Ultimate Cooking Experience. Each of us has owned small and/or large Big Green Eggs. When grandson Steve bought his first house, we thought he needed his own. He has become proficient in its use, especially for wild game from his hunting. Nephew Mike, who attends the annual EGGtoberfest in Atlanta, is our expert on the wide array of foods he cooks on his Big Green Egg.

The popularity of outdoor kitchens attests to a universal love of outdoor grilling and smoking. You are invited to share these family recipes and tips for good food, fun, and fellowship on the patio.

GRILLING & SMOKING

Grilled Steaks

Baby Back Ribs

Famous Fajitas

Pork Tenderloin with Fresh Herbs

Smoked Boston Butt

Beef Tenderloin
Champagne Horseradish Sauce
Port Wine Reduction Sauce

> When Cannons want to celebrate, grilled steaks are always a favorite!
>
> John is our steak chef-of-choice. His slightly charred medium-rare steaks are, beyond all doubt, the very best. He chooses prime or choice cuts of beef to have that perfect rib eye or filet, and he credits the drizzling of honey for the flame nicely charring the steaks to grilled perfection.

Grilled Steaks

1¼-inch cuts of rib eye steaks or 1½-inch cuts of filet mignon steaks

soy sauce

Worcestershire sauce

Tex Joy steak seasoning

honey

minced garlic, optional

coarse ground black pepper

For optimum success in grilling, place the steaks in an uncovered dish in the refrigerator for several hours. At 2 to 4 hours before grilling, marinate them. On one side sprinkle generously with soy sauce and Worcestershire. Next, shake on a moderate amount of Tex Joy and drizzle with honey. Turn the steaks over and repeat the marinade procedure. If you choose to add garlic, spread a little on and around the steaks.

Return the steaks to the refrigerator and allow them to marinate uncovered from 2 to 4 hours. Remove the steaks from the refrigerator an hour before grilling. Having the meat at room temperature is important for controlling even doneness.

Heat the grill to 500° so that the steaks will sizzle when placed over the flame.

Sprinkle generously with coarsely ground black pepper as you place the steaks on the grill. When you turn the steaks over, dribble a little of the reserved marinade over them.

For a medium rare steak, grill about 7 minutes on each side, turning the steak only once. Adjust the time for the doneness you prefer. For ultimate enjoyment, place steaks directly from the grill onto warmed plates.

The Italian Stripe

A trip to Italy leaves an indelible mark on the soul.

As a part of a Grand Tour of Europe in 1992, we visited the four major cities: Rome, Milan, Florence, and Venice. I was completely overwhelmed with the reality of just being there. The ancient history of Rome, the romantic atmosphere of Venice, and the enduring artistry of Florence provoked feelings of wondrous awe that I was actually walking through the pages of history I had studied from childhood.

A few years later, I realized my dream of returning to Italy. Instead of the tour mentality, my later trips allowed more involvement in the Italian culture and more personal interaction with its people. On several "Girls' Trips" we have leased villas in different regions of Tuscany. Our favorite day might include lunch in a Chianti setting, shopping in a hilltop medieval village, and relaxation at the villa. On market days in the Tuscan villages, we would follow the example of the native people in buying whatever was fresh for our dinner. Those evenings of cooking with friends at the villa created cherished memories.

We learned how truly delicious fresh Asiago tastes when bought from our favorite cheese vendor. Many vineyards also made delicious cheeses, which they paired with their wines. We discovered that Chianti wines are truly fabulous as we visited famous wineries and vineyards dating as far back as 400 years.

Our excursions left us with fond memories of a friendly people, who seemed very pleased when you would attempt to speak their language – no matter how rudimentary. (After our first trip, I had taken some college courses in the Italian language and culture.)

Cooking together – wherever we are – is always a fun time when we girls spend time in the kitchen. Our housekeeper at one of the villas taught us to make her Eggplant Parmesan. We did a cooking class with the chef at the Antinori Winery restaurant. Chef Fabrizio came to our villa to teach his fun class on making pasta. After enjoying the bistecca alla fiorentina at Buca dell'Orafo, a tiny trattoria near the Ponte Vecchio in Florence, we successfully created our own presentation.

Using the wonderful forno at the villas, we would spend a fun evening creating pizzas. Taking advantage of the delectable fresh mushrooms, we made some pretty amazing risotto dishes.

From its fascinating history to its incredible vistas, from its marvelous people to its awesome cuisine, our sojourns in Italy touched our souls and left us always planning our next visit.

Baby Back Ribs

3 slabs of baby back ribs

2 (5 oz.) bottles Tiger Sauce

honey

Tex Joy steak seasoning

coarse ground black pepper

Prepare the ribs by first cutting each slab into 2 or 3 sections. On the back side of the ribs, slit the membrane between the individual ribs.

Coat both sides of the ribs with Tiger Sauce. Sprinkle with Tex Joy seasoning and dribble with honey. Refrigerate for at least 2 hours. About an hour before cooking, set the ribs out to come to room temperature.

Meanwhile, build the charcoal fire in the Big Green Egg. When the temperature reaches 300°, sprinkle the ribs with the pepper and place them on the grill with the skin side down. Maintain the cooker at 300° and cook 45 minutes to an hour. Turn the slabs a few times to insure they are evenly charred and thoroughly cooked.

Wrap the cooked ribs in heavy foil and keep warm until ready to serve. If you have a warming drawer, put the cooked, foil-wrapped ribs on the low setting for about 30 minutes. Doing so not only further tenderizes them, but also heightens the mingling of pork and seasonings.

Cut into individual ribs. Serve with your favorite barbeque sauce, remembering Alabama's Dreamland!

For many years in our family, Fred – known as "Pop" to kids and friends alike – was an incomparable for Big Green Egg expertise.

Thankfully, his progeny aspires to match his excellence. Baby back ribs continue to be a huge family favorite and are requested frequently. Pop's ribs are always remembered, as well as Aunt Catherine's expected comment that each time his ribs were the best ones she had ever eaten.

GRILLING & SMOKING

Famous Fajitas

3 pounds skirt or flank steak, or chicken breasts

1 cup soy sauce

¼ cup Worcestershire sauce

4 garlic cloves, minced

4 tablespoons honey

1 cup coarsely chopped cilantro

1 large onion, sliced thin

1 large bell pepper, sliced thin

coarse ground black pepper

Make a marinade by combining the sauces, garlic, honey, and cilantro. If you are cooking a large quantity of meat, simply double the marinade recipe. Set aside while you prepare the meat.

Beef fajitas may be made of either skirt steak or flank steak. Lightly score the meat on front and back. Place in a large, shallow container and layer the onion and bell pepper slices over the meat.

Stir the marinade well and pour over the meat; refrigerate. Allow chicken breasts to marinate for 2 hours. Beef can be marinated additional time, even overnight. Remove the meat from the refrigerator 1 hour before grilling.

Sprinkle the meat generously with the black pepper before placing it on a gas grill, which has been heated to about 450°. Turn the meat only once at 5 to 7 minutes (depending on the thickness). Flip the meat over, dribble with marinade, and brown on the other side for about 5 minutes. Be careful to avoid overcooking. Wrap the meat in foil and let it rest a few minutes. Slice against the grain.

The sliced onions from the marinade are good sautéed with strips of bell pepper in a little olive oil. They are best when slightly undercooked and served crisp with the meat.

This recipe, given to Connie by friends after she moved to Houston in 1979, has been extremely popular and frequently used by our family for over three decades.

We love our Mexican food, and we use these meats in several favorite dishes – especially fajitas tacos and nachos.

GRILLING & SMOKING

Pork Tenderloin with Fresh Herbs

Tender, spicy, and succulent describe the smoked pork tenderloin.

Slices of the meat are great also for appetizers when paired with Nan's Famous Yeast Rolls or Rosemary Garlic Rolls.

Pork tenderloins without herbs can be cooked using the same recipe minus the rosemary and oregano.

They can be cooked 1 at a time, using either a Big Green Egg or a gas grill. On the grill, they need to be turned a couple of times so that all sides are exposed to the fire.

2 pork tenderloins

⅓ cup Tiger Sauce

soy sauce

1½ teaspoons dry mustard

Tex Joy steak seasoning

1 bunch fresh rosemary

1 bunch fresh oregano

coarsely ground black pepper

Coat the tenderloins generously with Tiger Sauce. Splash with soy sauce. Sprinkle with the dry mustard and Tex Joy. Place ½ of the rosemary and oregano sprigs between the tenderloins. Using kitchen twine, tie the meat together. Put the meat into a dish and place the remaining rosemary and oregano sprigs around the edges. Set into the refrigerator for at least 2 hours. Let the meat come to room temperature before cooking. Insert meat thermometer into thickest part of meat.

Build a fire in the Big Green Egg and regulate the temperature to 300° degrees. Sprinkle the tenderloin generously with the black pepper. Place the meat on a V-rack in the smoker. Cooking time will be approximately 45 minutes. The pork tenderloin is done when the meat reaches 160° degrees. Remove from heat and let rest for 15 minutes. Cut into ½-inch slices for serving.

GRILLING & SMOKING

Smoked Boston Butt

6 to 8 pounds Boston butt roast

1 (5 ounce) bottle Tiger Sauce

kosher salt

coarsely ground black pepper

Get out the Dreamland, or your favorite barbeque sauce, and enjoy the succulence of this pork as an entrée with sides – or as a great sandwich with chips.

Place the Boston butt in a large pan. Using the Tiger Sauce, completely coat the meat. Generously cover the entire surface with kosher salt; generously sprinkle with the pepper. Loosely cover the pan and place in the refrigerator to marinate for a couple of hours or overnight. Set out of refrigerator for an hour to allow the meat to come to room temperature.

Using a generous amount of charcoal, start the fire in the Big Green Egg. Adjust the draft door and daisy-wheel flue cover to maintain the cooking temperature to 300°.

Place a foil pan on the grill and add water about 1½ inches deep. Place a rack, preferably the V-Rack, in the pan. Lastly, place the meat, fat side up, on the rack. Insert the probe of a meat thermometer into the center of the roast.

Close the Big Green Egg and cook at the maintained temperature. Additional water should be added during cooking as it evaporates. Allow 3 to 4 hours cooking time. The meat thermometer will register 160° for well done pork. No thermometer? Use the "wiggle the bone" test. The meat begins to pull away from the bone when done. To rest the Boston butt for about 30 minutes, place the meat on a cutting board. Cover with a sheet of foil. Over this, spread a couple of dishtowels to hold in the heat. Remove the blade bone and slice, or use forks to pull the pork.

Beef Tenderloin

5 to 6 pound beef tenderloin

½ cup soy sauce

¼ cup Worcestershire sauce

2 ounces good bourbon

2 tablespoons honey

Tex Joy steak seasoning

1½ tablespoons minced garlic

¾ stick butter, softened

freshly ground black pepper

Prepare the beef tenderloin by turning the tapered end back onto the loin in order to make the entire length the same thickness. Tie with kitchen twine at 3-inch intervals. Place the tenderloin in a pan or dish large enough to accommodate its length.

Splash the meat with the sauces and bourbon. Spread the minced garlic over the meat and sprinkle with Tex Joy. Refrigerate for 3 to 4 hours, if possible. Remove from the refrigerator 1 hour before cooking. Coat the tenderloin completely with the softened butter. Sprinkle generously with the pepper. Drizzle with honey and insert a meat thermometer into the center of the tenderloin.

Meanwhile, build a charcoal fire in the Big Green Egg and adjust the heat to 300°. Place the meat on the grill and close the lid. Cook approximately 45 minutes, turning the meat several times to insure even browning. The meat thermometer will reach 145° for medium rare doneness. Allow the meat to rest on a cutting board for about 15 minutes. Slice and serve with Champagne Horseradish Sauce and Port Wine Reduction Sauce on the side.

The Big Green Egg deserves all accolades.

Turning the meat during cooking ensures charring on all sides and infuses the tenderloin with wonderful smoky flavor. The remote thermometer is a convenient and effective tool to make certain the meat is cooked to the desired doneness.

Champagne Horseradish Sauce

Great with beef!

2 cups sour cream

⅓ cup horseradish

1 tablespoon minced chives

1 teaspoon champagne or white wine vinegar

1 teaspoon salt

dash Tabasco sauce

Combine all ingredients in a bowl and whisk until well blended. Chill.

Port Wine Reduction Sauce

½ stick unsalted butter, divided

¼ cup finely chopped shallots

3 tablespoons Cognac or brandy

1 fresh rosemary sprig

1 cup ruby or tawny port

1½ cups beef stock

1 teaspoon coarsely cracked black pepper

salt to taste

This family favorite sauce accompanies the horseradish sauce for the succulent beef tenderloin.

Over medium-low heat, melt 2 tablespoons of the butter in a large saucepan. Sauté the shallots until soft, about 3 minutes. Add the Cognac and rosemary. Cook until the liquid evaporates. Add the port and bring to a simmer. Pour in the beef stock and boil until reduced to 1½ cups, about 20 minutes. Strain to extract all solids.

Bring the sauce to a boil and whisk in the remaining 2 tablespoons of butter. Add the pepper. Season with salt to taste.

The Chopping Block

In autumn of 1981, we built a house in the middle of our little pecan orchard. Great attention to detail went into planning the new house. This was to be my most perfect kitchen ever! It was the era of split-brick flooring, wallpaper, and cabinets galore. The kitchen was furnished with state of art appliances, including an ice machine and heat lamps shelved under a beautiful hood.

The most charming feature was a quaint little booth just right for two people to share a cup of coffee or a bowl of seafood gumbo for lunch. Situated under a window, the booth afforded nice views of the pecan trees and provided the first sightings of guests approaching our house. The Tiffany-style hanging lamp gave off a warm glow of coziness in the evenings. I loved my kitchen. It was exactly what I wanted. Perfect. Complete. Or so I thought.

One afternoon about two weeks after we moved in, some dear friends drove to our doorway. Before I could assimilate what was happening, a huge chopping block was delivered to the center of my kitchen. Oh. . . . I was overwhelmed by the generosity and specialness of their gift. The chopping block was made from a section of a cypress log from Louisiana. The top surface was inlaid with hardwood sections, and the whole was supported by three sturdy turned legs. The piece was especially made for us, and it did make a statement.

I must confess that on that particular day, I was secretly apprehensive as to how the piece would affect my carefully planned kitchen. Looking back, however, over the 20 years we lived in that house, the most important recollections of that kitchen are those concerning the little booth (whose cozy magnetism crowded in four persons at times) and the chopping block.

So many fond memories center around the chopping block. It became our island before they were standard fare in kitchens. It was a prep station, and it was a cooling station for pies fresh from the oven. The fudge cake brownies were assembled there. Mostly, though, the chopping block was where our smoked and roasted meats rested. At Christmas Freddy sliced the ham and John the turkey, side by side at the block. It was a little crowded at times. We all remember the time the Christmas Holiday china platter was accidentally tipped off the block. It was as if time stood still waiting for it to crash on the floor. Somehow, someway, Lisa caught the platter in midair!

How many pounds of meat passed across the butcher block, we can only wonder. We know, for sure, that our friends' gift was perfect in both reality and in our fondest memories. The butcher block now resides at our daughter's house on Galveston Bay. It is still in use for slicing smoked meats, and it still evokes those wonderful family memories.

When I began the organizational process in preparation for writing this cookbook, I was astonished that the desserts heavily outnumbered the content of any other section. My naturally curious mind was disturbed. Why and how did this imbalance occur? What does one do about the variation? My search for answers led me to my shelves of cookbooks and to my iPad.

Looking at comprehensive cookbooks, I found that desserts consistently comprised one-fourth of the total pages. As noted by one of the major cookbooks, a "look through the recipe files of any serious cook, and the desserts section will no doubt be bulging with entries."

The iPad, likewise, supports a history of desserts that received a major boost with the manufacture of sugar in the Middle Ages. Can you believe that the first apple pie recipe was printed in 1381? Desserts were cost-prohibitive for centuries, with only the very wealthy able to indulge. When the common ingredients for making desserts finally became available and affordable, they became staples in the modern household pantry.

The broad category of the dessert section covers all varieties of sweets, therefore necessitating a plethora of recipes. Even so, any one cookbook can only scratch the surface of cakes, pies, cookies, ice creams, candies, etc. Thereby, I rest my case: It is okay, even required, to have an extravagance of recipes for the sweet course, the finale to a great meal. (Not to mention those times that only a chocolate chip cookie can give you a warm, fuzzy feeling!)

DESSERTS

Cheesecakes

Cookies & Bars

Cakes & Frostings

Pies & Cobblers

Candy

Ice Cream

Cheesecake for dessert! Say no more, we are in store for the ultimate in dessert perfection!

Every creamy bite of rich cheesecake is a taste of delicious extravagance. No matter the flavor, no matter the topping, cheesecake is that special confection that every hostess aspires to serve to both family and guests.

After a few attempts with mediocre results, I found two recipes that were promising. No longer apprehensive, I began making really good cheesecakes. I began to use a little creativity and tweaked them into my own versions. One is the German Chocolate Cheesecake which is included in this section with my additions and changes. The second is the versatile Cheesecake Supreme. This recipe is excellent on its own, but goes into another dimension as you add your favorite toppings. Or choose the Chocolate Crumb Crust from the Pie Section for Turtle Cheesecake. Again, use this as a basic recipe and create your own perfect dessert!

For a time my granddaughter Lindsey would ask me to make cheesecakes for her special occasion entertaining. We did a one on one class during one of my trips to her home in Tampa. Since then, she goes to my dropbox for the recipes and wows her friends with her perfect cheesecakes! I am always delighted when she sends a text with photos of her creations.

Because they are aware of my passion for making cheesecakes, my family has showered my kitchen with springform pans in every shape and size. I love using every one – whether small, large, individual, round, or square. Although I use them all at different times, my favorite is the 9-inch one from Sur la Table. This springform pan is heavier and is also deeper than most. The extra depth is important to me, since I prefer taller cheesecakes.

Not all springform pans seal completely, thus allowing butter from the crust to leak out into the oven during the baking. To avoid having a messy oven and setting off the smoke detector, place the pan on a cookie sheet that has been lined with foil. Turn the foil up around the pan in a loose manner. As an additional benefit, the filled springform pan is much easier to handle while on the cookie sheet.

Happily, cheesecakes can be frozen for several weeks. Although they can be frozen in the springform pan wrapped tightly in heavy-duty foil, I prefer to transfer the cake from the pan to a round cardboard circle. First, quick-freeze the cooled cheesecake while still on the bottom part of the pan. Immediately, use a cake lifter, carefully inserted under the crust, to move the cake to the cardboard. Cover with plastic wrap. Lastly, wrap the cheesecake in heavy-duty foil and seal.

CHEESECAKES

Cheesecake Supreme
Fruit Toppings

Praline Cheesecake

Turtle Cheesecake

German Chocolate Cheesecake

Cheesecake Supreme

Crust:

    1¾ cups graham cracker crumbs

    ¼ cup sugar

    1 stick butter, melted and still warm

Filling:

    5 (8 ounce) packages cream cheese, softened

    1½ cups sugar

    3 eggs

    2½ teaspoons vanilla

Topping:

    2 cups confectioners' sugar

    3 ounces cream cheese, softened

    2 tablespoons butter, at room temperature

    1 tablespoon vanilla

To make the crust: Mix ingredients together and transfer into a deep 9-inch springform pan. Press the crumb mixture into the bottom and 1½ inches up the side of the pan. Use the bottom of a metal measuring cup to carefully press the crust into place. Place on a foil-lined cookie sheet, and fold the foil to make a bowl-like form around the springform pan. Bake at 350° for 5 minutes. Set aside.

To make the filling: Beat the cream cheese at a high speed of an electric mixer until smooth. Gradually add the sugar as you continue beating. Add the eggs 1 at a time. Stir in the vanilla and beat the mixture until fluffy – about 10 minutes. Pour the filling into the prepared crust.

Bake at 350° for 55 minutes. The center will not be completely set. Turn the oven off and leave the cake in the oven for 30 minutes with the door partially open.

Remove the cheesecake from the oven. Loosen from the side of the pan by running a knife around the edge; then loosen the spring. When the cheesecake is cool, remove the springform.

To make the topping: Beat the softened cream cheese and butter until smooth. Add vanilla and confectioners' sugar, beating until smooth and light. Spread over the top of cheesecake. Chill before serving.

Fruit: Before serving add fresh fruit or your favorite flavor of fruit pie filling. Blueberry and cherry are delicious options.

Optional Toppings: Flavors of cheesecake crusts and fillings are limited only by the imagination. This recipe is up to the challenge. Try the ones listed, or test your own creativity.

Praline: Make pralines as per the recipe listed under Candy. Stir only enough for icing consistency, rather than to candy dropping consistency. Pour over top of cooled cheesecake.

Turtle: Substitute a chocolate cookie crumb crust (page 200). Cover the cooled cheesecake with the praline topping. Cool to room temperature. Melt about 2 ounces of semisweet chocolate morsels or squares with 1 teaspoon of Crisco. Pour the chocolate into a quart Ziploc bag and seal. Cut a tiny hole in one corner of the bag and squeeze the melted chocolate to make crisscrossing lines over the praline topping.

For years, though I tried several recipes, I could not make a cheesecake that really pleased me.

One year my niece, Sheila Williams, brought one to our Christmas Eve party. Eureka! She had the perfect recipe all the time. I gave it the name "Supreme" because it is the best ever. I have taken the liberty to add some creative touches; nevertheless, her original recipe was my inspiration.

CHEESECAKES

German Chocolate Cheesecake

This treasured recipe is one that a gentleman from Jacksonville, Florida, submitted to Southern Living many years ago.

I had to put my touch on it, of course, but hats off to him for coming up with this original idea.

Crust:

    1 ¾ cups chocolate wafer crumbs

    ¼ cup sugar

    1 stick butter, melted and still warm

Filling:

    3 (8 ounce) packages cream cheese

    1 ¼ cups sugar

    3 tablespoons flour

    ¼ teaspoon salt

    4 eggs

    1 (4 ounce) package German's Sweet Chocolate, melted

    ¼ cup evaporated milk

    1 teaspoon vanilla

Topping:

    1 cup sugar

    ¼ cup plus 1 tablespoon milk

    2 egg yolks

    3 tablespoons butter

    1 teaspoon vanilla

    ½ cup flaked coconut

    1 cup chopped pecans

    extra pecan halves for decorating

To make the crust: Mix the ingredients and transfer into a 7-inch springform pan. Using the bottom of a metal measuring cup, push-press the crumb mixture into the bottom and 1½ inches up the side of the pan. Place on a foil-lined cookie sheet, and fold the foil to make a bowl-like form around the springform pan. Bake at 350° for 5 minutes. Set aside.

To make the filling: Beat the cream cheese at medium mixer speed until light and fluffy. Gradually add the sugar, flour, and salt. Add the eggs 1 at a time, beating for about 5 minutes. On a lower speed of the mixer, add the melted chocolate, milk, and vanilla; mix well. Pour the filling into the prepared crust.

Bake at 325° for 1 hour. Turn the oven off, but leave the oven door partially open. After 30 minutes, remove the cheesecake from the oven. Carefully run a table knife around the edges; then, loosen the springform sides of the pan and cool for 30 minutes. Lastly, remove the sides from the pan and let the cheesecake cool completely before adding the topping.

For the topping: In a heavy saucepan, combine the sugar and milk. Add the well-beaten egg yolks to the mixture and stir well. Cook over low heat, adding the butter as the mixture heats. Stir often until the mixture begins to thicken. Stir in the coconut and pecans until they are heated thoroughly. Remove from the heat and add the vanilla.

Cover the cooled cheesecake with the topping, perhaps allowing a little to drip down the sides. Decorate by placing pecan halves intermittently around the edge. Chill before serving.

In my cooking evolution, from the novice who knew almost less than nothing, to one who attained some level of success in pleasing family and friends, the key word has been "Passion"! I wanted very much to learn to prepare nice meals. I needed for my family and friends to enjoy the food and fellowship around the table, and I wished them to know that the time I spent in the kitchen was an expression of love.

Very early on I decided to try to make perfect cookies. As usual, I tried different recipes. Failing to find what constituted my perfect cookie, I began to experiment. My idea of a perfect cookie is a large one whose edges are a bit crisp and whose center is rather soft and chewy. Once I hit on a formula that was true to my expectation, then I could branch out into several kinds.

In my "practice makes perfect" research, I found that the variable was most often the flour, with humidity and altitude as significant factors. Also important is to use butter flavor Crisco. Be consistent with measurements. Be aware, as well, of the different egg sizes; the difference in medium, large, and extra-large eggs is enough to affect the consistency of cookie dough.

When my grandchildren were quite young, we began making cookies together. My kitchen had the neatest little booth that served as their prep area, and the mixer was nearby. After making our plan, they learned to measure dry ingredients and to take turns adding them to the mixer bowl. After the dough was mixed, they were so happy if I had to get something from the pantry. My momentary absence provided them a perfect opportunity to sneak chunks of the cookie dough. Even though their little cheeks were puffed out, they always believed that I never knew what they were doing!

One of our rituals of making cookies together is to bake three or four samples. This procedure allows you to check that the amount of flour is correct on any given day. It also is an opportunity for reward, as those first bites of warm cookies are truly the best! Simply set the sample cookies on a cutting board, cut each into six wedges, and start the tasting. My grandchildren loved this ritual when they were young; as adults, they still claim the samples.

Freezing Possibilities:

Since everyone loves a fresh-baked cookie, I came up with the idea of freezing the dough. In the early 1970s, I began the practice of freezing logs of cookie dough and sharing them with family and friends. As soon as the dough is made, divide it into equal parts and shape into logs. Wrap each log with foil, label with a magic marker, and place four logs in a gallon Ziploc. Freeze until needed. Set the logs out of the freezer for a few minutes; slice into desired sizes and bake as directed.

COOKIES & BARS

Oatmeal Cookies

Chocolate Chip Cookies

Chocolate Nut Cookies

Peanut Butter Cookies

Macadamia &
White Chocolate Cookies

Biscotti

Butter Cookies

Decorator Frosting

Noels

Lizzies

Praline Grahams

Caramel Squares

Fudge Cake Brownies with
Chocolate Frosting

Oatmeal Cookies

Oatmeal cookies were the first cookies that I learned to make.

This recipe is the result of many attempts to get them right. Flour is the critical ingredient; time of baking is also very important. Practice really does make perfect. I know, because for 60 years this recipe has ranked at the top of family favorites.

1½ cups butter flavor Crisco

1½ cups sugar

1½ cups light brown sugar

3 large eggs

2½ teaspoons vanilla

4 cups flour

1½ teaspoons salt

1½ teaspoons baking soda

1½ teaspoons cinnamon

3½ cups oatmeal, either quick or old fashioned

1½ to 2 cups chopped pecans

Using an electric mixer on medium speed, cream the Crisco and sugars until smooth. Beat in eggs and vanilla. Whisk the dry ingredients together in a separate bowl, and add to the dough 1 cup at a time. After each addition, mix until all the flour is incorporated.

Add the oatmeal, 1 cup at a time. Lastly, stir in the chopped pecans by hand.

Scoop about ¼ cup of dough for each cookie. Bake on a parchment lined cookie sheet at 350° for about 14 minutes, checking at 10 minutes. Do not overcook!

To freeze for baking later: Divide the cookie dough into 5 parts. Make a log of each part and wrap in foil. Use a black marker to identify, and place these logs in a gallon Ziploc bag. Freeze and bake later as needed.

Yields 24 large cookies

COOKIES & BARS

Chocolate Chip Cookies

1 cup butter flavor Crisco

1 cup light brown sugar

1 cup sugar

2 large eggs

2 teaspoons vanilla

3¼ cups flour

1 teaspoon salt

1 teaspoon baking soda

1 (11.5 ounce) package milk chocolate morsels

1½ cups chopped pecans

Cream the Crisco; gradually add the sugars, beating well at the medium speed of an electric mixer. Beat in the large eggs and vanilla until well mixed.

Add the baking soda and salt to 1 cup of the flour; stir into creamed mixture using a low speed on the mixer. Add the remaining flour, 1 cup and a time, stirring after each until all flour is incorporated.

Remove the bowl from the mixer and stir in the chocolate chips and pecans. (The newer Kitchen Aid mixer with the paddle beater can safely mix in the chips and pecans – a tremendous improvement that saves time and wrists!)

Line a large cookie sheet with parchment paper. Scoop the cookie dough with ¼-cup measuring cup (or equivalent ice cream scoop) and place 12 cookies to a large sheet. Do not mash down!

Bake in 350° oven for about 14 minutes, checking at 10 minutes. Cookies should be a bit crisp around the edge but still soft in the center. Do not over bake.

To freeze: Make logs of cookie dough and wrap in foil. Label with magic marker. Place the logs in a gallon Ziploc bag and freeze. When you are ready for fresh warm cookies, just slice and bake!

Yields 20 large cookies

My favorite chocolate chips are the Ghirardelli brand, all natural, smooth texture, and a bit larger.

Tip: Cookies are wonderful while still warm; for leftovers, try refrigerating and eating them cold!

COOKIES & BARS

Chocolate Nut Cookies

1 cup butter flavor Crisco

2 cups light brown sugar

2 eggs

2 teaspoons vanilla

4 squares semi-sweet chocolate, melted

3 cups flour

1 teaspoon salt

½ teaspoon baking soda

1½ cups chopped pecans

Using an electric mixer, thoroughly cream the Crisco and sugar; beat in the eggs and vanilla. Stir in the melted chocolate. Whisk the flour with salt and baking soda. Add in 1-cup increments until dry ingredients are completely mixed into the creamed mixture. Stir in the chopped pecans by hand.

Scoop about ¼ cup of dough for each cookie. Bake on parchment paper-lined cookie sheets in 350° oven. Start checking for doneness at 12 minutes, being careful to avoid over baking. This cookie is best when edges are a bit crisp and the center is soft. Practice will teach you to achieve this result.

To freeze for cooking later: Divide the dough into four parts. Make a log of each part and roll in foil, sealing at the ends. Mark foil with black marker to identify cookies. Place the 4 rolls in a gallon Ziploc bag and freeze. Since most cookies are best fresh and warm, bake only the amount you need each time.

Yields 18 large cookies

The original to this recipe used butter and was intended to be a thin, crisp cookie.

The taste was phenomenal, but the texture did not meet my criteria. Therefore, the changes resulted in a brownie-like cookie with crisp edges and soft center. This cookie ranks in the top 3 favorites with my family.

COOKIES & BARS

Peanut Butter Cookies

1½ cups extra chunky peanut butter

1½ cups butter-flavor Crisco

3 cups sugar

1 ½ teaspoons vanilla

2 large eggs

4½ cups flour

1½ teaspoons baking soda

1½ teaspoons salt

¼ cup boiling water

Using an electric mixer on medium speed, cream the peanut butter and Crisco; gradually add the sugar and beat until smooth. Stir in the eggs and vanilla.

In a separate bowl, whisk the baking soda and salt into the flour. Using the low speed on the mixer, add the dry ingredients to the creamed mixture in 1-cup increments. After the 2nd cup, add the boiling water and mix well. Continue adding the flour until all is incorporated.

Form the dough into 1½-inch balls and place on a cookie sheet that has been lined with parchment paper. Press each ball lightly with fork tines that have been dipped in sugar, making a crisscross design.

Bake at 350° for about 14 minutes. Begin checking at 10 minutes. Do not overcook!

Yields 36 large cookies

A friend from my high school days also became a teacher.

When a group of us got together a few decades later, she shared this recipe from her school cafeteria. Originally for 600 cookies, it has been adjusted to family size.

COOKIES & BARS

Macadamia & White Chocolate Cookies

Macadamia nuts became a key pantry item after I visited the Mauna Loa orchards in Hawaii with Lisa and 10-year-old Ashley in 1998.

Needless to say, my suitcase left the islands fully loaded with packaged nuts. On returning home, I added this cookie to my list of favorites.

1 cup butter-flavor Crisco

1 cup sugar

1 cup light brown sugar

2 eggs

1½ teaspoons vanilla

3 cups flour

1 teaspoon salt

1 teaspoon baking soda

1½ cups white chocolate chips

1½ cups chopped macadamia nuts

Using an electric mixer on medium speed, cream the Crisco and the sugars until smooth. Beat in the eggs and vanilla.

Whisk the flour, salt, and baking soda together in a separate bowl. Add in 1-cup increments to the creamed mixture until the dry ingredients are incorporated.

Stir in the chips and nuts by hand. Using a scoop, for each cookie place about ¼ cup of dough onto a parchment-lined cookie sheet.

Bake at 350° for about 14 minutes. Begin checking at 10 minutes. Do not over bake.

Yields 24 large cookies

COOKIES & BARS

Biscotti

1¼ cups flour

2 teaspoons baking powder

¾ cup sliced unbleached almonds

2 eggs

¾ cup sugar

⅓ cup melted butter

2 teaspoons vanilla

1½ teaspoons almond extract

1½ teaspoons grated orange rind

1 egg white, lightly beaten

In a large bowl combine the flour, baking powder, and almonds. Set aside. In a separate bowl, whisk together the eggs, sugar, butter, flavorings and orange rind. Stir this mixture into the dry ingredients until a soft, sticky dough forms.

Transfer the dough to a lightly floured work surface. With hands, form into a smooth ball. Divide the dough and roll each half into a 12-inch log.

Transfer the logs to a parchment paper-lined cookie sheet. Brush the tops with the lightly beaten egg white.

Bake at 350° until done, from 15 to 20 minutes. Remove from the oven and place the pan on a rack to cool for 5 minutes. Transfer each log to a cutting board. Cut diagonally into ¾-inch slices.

Place the cookies upright on the cookie sheet. Return to the oven and continue to bake for 10 to 15 minutes until golden brown. Cool on a cake rack.

During a trip to Tuscany in 2007 with Connie and friends, I became fascinated with the Italian language.

Already sure that I would return to Italy, I studied Italian language and culture at the University of South Alabama under Norma Regni Dixon – a delightful Italian lady who had married an American serviceman. Although she had come to America 40 years prior, she still enjoyed strong family ties to her native country. She shared this recipe with me after bringing delicious samples to class. The beautiful Italian biscotti jar in my kitchen is a treasured gift from a dear friend, Cindy Creech, on one of our trips to Tuscany.

COOKIES & BARS

Butter Cookies

2 sticks butter, softened to room temperature

2 cups sugar

2 eggs

2 teaspoons vanilla

6 cups flour

½ teaspoon baking soda

½ cup sour cream

Using an electric mixer on medium speed, cream the butter and sugar. Stir in the eggs and vanilla until well mixed. With the mixer on low speed, add the flour and baking soda 1 cup at a time. After the 3rd cup of flour, stir in the sour cream; then, continue adding the remaining cups of flour.

Divide the dough into 3 parts. Wrap each part in plastic wrap and place in the refrigerator for 1 to 2 hours. Remove 1 part at a time. Using only enough flour for ease of handling, gently roll the chilled dough onto a lightly floured surface until about ½ inch thick. Cut into shapes, frequently dipping the cookie cutter into flour. Carefully transfer the cut cookies to a cookie sheet lined with parchment paper.

Bake at 350° until done. The edges will just begin to brown slightly, but the centers will be soft. Begin checking at 10 minutes. Be careful to avoid overcooking.

This cookie recipe was our favorite for the traditional "Decorating Christmas Cookie Competition" observed on Christmas Eve.

Using holiday cookie cutters, I would bake five of each shape (with a few extras, of course) for my five grandchildren to decorate. Year after year they continued to come up with creative designs. One year, mistakenly thinking that they were grown and would no longer appreciate the activity, I did not plan to have the competition. Arriving at Nan's house with no cookies to decorate was not to be. They immediately made a quick trip to the grocery store for refrigerated cookie dough and decorator kits! Now I have great-grandchildren eager to carry on the tradition.

COOKIES & BARS

Decorator Frosting

½ cup white Crisco

1 pound confectioners' sugar

3 tablespoons milk

1 teaspoon vanilla

food coloring, as desired

Combine Crisco, sugar, milk, and vanilla in mixer bowl; beat at low speed until blended. Beat at high speed about 5 minutes or until the frosting is light and fluffy.

For decorating, food coloring may be added to the entire recipe or to any portion. Determine the colors needed; then, divide the frosting into the appropriate number of small bowls and add the colors accordingly.

Noels

2 sticks butter, softened

½ cup confectioners' sugar, plus additional

2 teaspoons vanilla

2 cups flour

1½ cups finely chopped nuts

Using an electric mixer on medium speed, cream the butter and sugar until well blended. Add vanilla. Lower the speed and gradually add the flour, beating until smooth. Stir in the nuts by hand.

Wrap the dough in plastic wrap and chill for at least 30 minutes. Form into 1-inch balls or crescent shapes. Place on a parchment-lined cookie sheet.

Bake at 350°. Begin checking at 8 minutes. The edges will just begin to brown a bit when done.

Have ready a cup of confectioners' sugar in a shallow dish. While the cookies are still warm from the oven, roll each through the sugar. Place on a rack to cool.

A great Christmas cookie! After trying various wedding-type cookie recipes, I declared this one to be my favorite.

My daughter-in-law, Faye, perfected the recipe for this delicious confection. It is an all-time family favorite.

Lizzies

½ stick butter

½ cup light brown sugar

2 eggs

1½ cups flour

1½ teaspoons baking soda

1 teaspoon cinnamon

¼ teaspoon ground cloves

¼ teaspoon nutmeg

1 tablespoon milk

⅓ cup sherry or bourbon

1 pound white raisins

1 pound pecan halves

½ pound candied pineapple

1 pound candied cherries (red and green mixed)

Chop the candied fruit and place in a large bowl. Add the pecan halves and raisins. Dredge the fruit and nuts with ¾ cup of the flour. Set aside.

Using an electric mixer on medium speed, cream the sugar and butter until smooth. Beat in the eggs until well mixed. Combine the remaining ¾ cup flour, baking soda, and spices; stir into the mixture. Add the milk and sherry. Blend well.

Pour the batter over the fruit and nuts and mix well. Drop by tablespoon on parchment-lined cookie sheet.

Bake at 325° for 20 to 23 minutes until lightly browned.

Delicious when served with sherry for dipping.

No one made fruitcake cookies better than my sister, Ruth.

Every Christmas for 45 years, she kept them in a plastic container with a small glass of sherry to preserve their moistness. She loved to serve them to her friends with a demitasse of coffee.

COOKIES & BARS

Praline Grahams

1 box graham crackers

1½ sticks butter

½ cup sugar

1 cup finely chopped pecans

Separate each graham cracker into 4 sections. Arrange with edges touching in a large jellyroll pan, using as many of the graham crackers as the pan holds. Set aside.

Melt the butter in a small saucepan. Stir in the sugar and pecans. Bring to a boil and cook 3 minutes, stirring frequently. Spoon the hot mixture over the graham crackers.

Bake at 300° for 12 minutes. Remove from oven.

Using a small metal spatula, lift the graham pralines from the pan. Place on wax paper to cool. Store in an airtight container.

Lisa, my daughter-in-law, introduced me to these delightfully quick cookies, which seem to just disappear from the cookie jar!

Caramel Squares

2 sticks butter

1 pound light brown sugar

2 eggs

2 cups flour

¼ teaspoon salt

2 teaspoons vanilla

1½ cup chopped pecans

In a heavy saucepan, melt the butter and sugar over low heat. Set aside to cool.

Using an electric mixer on the medium setting, beat the eggs. Add the cooled butter and sugar mixture; continue beating until smooth. With the mixer on low speed, gradually add the flour and salt. Stir in the pecans by hand.

Pour into a well-greased and floured 9 x 13 pan. Bake at 325° for 30 minutes. Cool in the pan before cutting into squares.

Home Ec was one of the classes for which I never had time – nor inclination – in high school.

I was privileged, however, later in life to have a former home economics teacher as a mentor and dear friend. When I met Floy Plonk in 1962, she was a couple of decades older than I was. During her last 25 years, she taught me as much about life as about cooking. This recipe is her version of blond brownies.

Fudge Cake Brownies with Chocolate Frosting

Thanks to Louise, my sister-in-law, I learned to make fudge cake in the 1950s.

Over the years, I tweaked the original recipe and added the decadent toppings. My grandchildren loved to cut the brownies in creative ways when they were young. They took pride in their presentations, as they loved serving the dessert at family dinners.

2 sticks butter

4 (1 ounce) squares semi-sweet chocolate

4 eggs

2 cups sugar

1 cup flour

⅛ teaspoon salt

2 tablespoons light corn syrup

1½ teaspoons vanilla

1½ cups coarsely chopped pecans

3 ounces marshmallow creme

Chocolate Frosting

In a small saucepan, melt the butter and chocolate squares. Set aside to cool.

Using an electric mixer on the medium speed, beat the eggs until frothy. Continue beating as you gradually add the sugar, corn syrup, and vanilla. Lower the speed of the mixer to stir in the flour and salt. Lastly, add the cooled chocolate mixture. When well blended, stir in the pecans by hand.

Pour the batter into a 9 x 13 pan that has been heavily coated with Crisco and sprinkled liberally with flour. Bake at 325° until done, about 45 minutes. Do not overcook.

Remove from the oven and run a knife around the edges to loosen the cake from the pan. Immediately turn the fudge cake out onto either foil or parchment paper that has been generously sprinkled with sugar.

Put dobs of marshmallow creme onto the hot slab of fudge cake and let set for a few minutes. Carefully spread the melting dobs to cover the cake, leaving about an inch around the edges.

Prepare the chocolate frosting. While still warm, pour in a back-and-forth motion over the cake. Leave a bit of the marshmallow creme peeping through the frosting. Use a knife to carefully spread icing to cover the edges and sides.

Chocolate Frosting:

¾ stick butter

1½ (1 ounce) squares semi-sweet chocolate

¼ cup milk

1 teaspoon vanilla

1 pound confectioners' sugar

Pour the sugar into the electric mixer bowl and make a well in the center.

In a small saucepan, heat the butter, chocolate, and milk. While still hot, pour the chocolate mixture over the sugar. Beat at medium speed until creamy; add the vanilla while still beating.

Immediately pour the frosting over the brownie slab as directed. Give the frosting a few minutes to set, then cut into squares.

These brownies are especially good served warm. For later servings, a few seconds in the microwave transforms this brownie into blissful comfort food.

COOKIES & BARS

Believe it or not, there was life before the plenitude of cake mixes found on the baking aisle of every grocery store. There was a time when all cakes, including birthday cakes, were baked in your own oven, rather than ordered from the bakery.

Many advantages surround these modern modes of serving delicious cakes. For example, the cake mixes provide not only time saving convenience, but also the consistency of pre-measured ingredients. Also, bakery cakes are readily available in today's world, even in grocery baking sections; and they are always perfect in appearance.

While acknowledging the expediency of these convenient cakes, I insist that "made from scratch" truly cannot be matched in taste. There is a gratification of the senses, a delightful pleasure, and a bit of nostalgia in a freshly baked cake. I would dearly love to once again experience the coconut cake at my mother's table. Another memorable dessert she made was a rectangular yellow layer cake with a cooked chocolate icing. Somehow, the top layer always seemed to split, which allowed the chocolate to pool. My brother Charlie and I always schemed to have our serving from that part of the cake.

The recipes in this section include cakes which are made completely from scratch as well as cakes which utilize cake mixes. I hope you will choose from each method.

Just saying . . . I have to confess that every year when March 22 rolls around, I really like a decorated birthday cake from Pollman's Bake Shop! The original bakery was already established when I moved to Mobile in 1947. For decades Mr. Pollman baked all the cakes himself, arriving at his shop at 4 o'clock every morning to make the "baked fresh daily" delicious cakes. On second thought, maybe I should also confess that the Mother's Day cakes are quite special, too. This year mine was decorated with beautiful pansies!

CAKES & FROSTINGS

Cream Cheese Pound Cake

Texas Cake

German Chocolate Cake with
Coconut Pecan Frosting

Carrot Cake Supreme

Banana Nut Cake

Cream Cheese Frosting

Deluxe Cream Cheese Frosting

Italian Cream Cake

Red Velvet Cake

Applesauce Cake with
Orange Coconut Icing

Sour Cream Coconut Cake

Bourbon Nut Loaves

Strawberry Cupcakes with
Strawberry Frosting

Cream Cheese Pound Cake

1 (8 ounce) package cream cheese, softened

3 sticks butter, softened

3 cups sugar

6 eggs

2 teaspoons vanilla

1 teaspoon lemon flavoring

3 cups all purpose flour

⅛ teaspoon salt

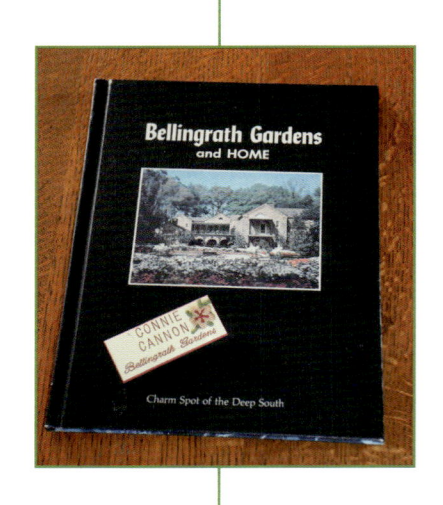

Beat the butter and cream cheese at medium speed with an electric mixer until light and fluffy. Gradually add the sugar, beating for 5 or 6 minutes until the mixture is smooth. Add the eggs, 1 at a time, beating after each until the yolks are blended into the batter. Stir in the flavorings.

Turn the mixer to a lower speed. Add the flour, along with the salt, in 3 increments. Mix until all the flour has been incorporated.

Choose either a tube pan or 2 loaf pans. Heavily coat each pan with Crisco and sprinkle generously with flour. Pour the batter into the pans. Bake at 325° until done, about 1 hour and 15 minutes.

Test doneness by checking the center top of the loaves. If not completely done, continue to cook 5 minutes at a time. For a tube pan, check by inserting a toothpick. If batter sticks to the toothpick, continue cooking 5 minutes at a time.

When the cake is done, place on a rack to cool for 20 minutes. Remove from the pan and finish cooling on the rack.

When my daughter was in college, she worked weekends as a tour guide at Bellingrath Gardens.

One of the older ladies who worked in the gift shop gave the basis of this recipe to her. With very few changes since 1978, this recipe has remained our favorite because of its rich flavor and tender texture.

CAKES & FROSTING

Texas Cake

1 stick butter

3 tablespoons cocoa

½ cup canola oil

1 cup water

2 cups flour

2 cups sugar

1 teaspoon baking soda

2 eggs, well-beaten

1 teaspoon vanilla

½ cup buttermilk

In a small saucepan, combine the first 4 ingredients. Bring the mixture to a boil; stir and set aside.

In the mixing bowl of an electric mixer, combine the flour, sugar, and baking soda. Add the eggs, vanilla, and buttermilk and beat at medium speed until well mixed. Stir in the chocolate mixture and beat until smooth.

Pour the combined mixture into an ungreased jelly roll pan. Bake at 400° for 15 minutes or until the center springs back when touched lightly. Remove from the oven and pour the hot frosting over the warm cake, which is still in the jelly roll pan.

Frosting:

1 stick butter

6 tablespoons buttermilk

2 tablespoons cocoa

1 teaspoon vanilla

1 pound confectioners' sugar

1½ cup chopped pecans

While the Texas cake is baking, prepare the frosting so that it is ready as the cake comes out of the oven.

Pour the confectioners' sugar into the mixer bowl and make a well in the center. Combine the butter, cocoa, and milk in a small saucepan. Place over medium heat and bring to a boil. Pour the hot mixture over the confectioners' sugar and beat at medium speed until smooth. Stir in the vanilla and pecans. Pour immediately over the hot cake.

My sister Ruth made this cake in the 1960s under the name Scotch Chocolate Cake.

In the 1990s, a friend reintroduced the cake to me under its new name. We love having the pecans in the frosting, rather than in the cake. An advantage for the cook is the quick and easy preparation and assembly.

CAKES & FROSTING

German Chocolate Cake with Coconut Pecan Frosting

German Chocolate Cake is one of those special recipes that cake mixes have been unable to duplicate.

The moist, flavorful finished cake from "scratch" is totally worth the extra time you invest in making this remarkably delicious dessert.

1 (4 ounce) package German's sweet chocolate

½ cup boiling water

2 sticks butter

2 cups sugar

4 eggs, separated

1½ teaspoons vanilla

2 cups flour

1 teaspoon baking soda

½ teaspoon salt

1 cup buttermilk

Melt the chocolate in the boiling water and set aside to cool.

In a medium bowl whisk the flour, baking soda, and salt together. Set aside.

In a clean mixer bowl, beat the egg whites until stiff peaks form. Set aside.

Using an electric mixer at medium speed, cream the butter and sugar until light and fluffy. Beat in the egg yolks; then, stir in the vanilla and chocolate mixture. Turn the mixer to a lower speed, and add the flour mixture to the creamed mixture alternately with the buttermilk. Lastly, fold the beaten egg whites into the cake mixture.

Pour the batter into three 9-inch cake pans, which have been greased with Crisco and sprinkled with flour. Bake at 350° for 30 minutes or until the cake layers spring back when lightly pressed.

Cool 10 minutes before removing the cake layers from the pans. Cool on cake racks before spreading the Coconut Pecan Frosting between layers and over the top of cake.

Coconut Pecan Frosting

3 cups sugar

¾ cup milk

5 egg yolks

1 stick butter

2 teaspoons vanilla

1½ cups flaked coconut

1¾ cups chopped pecans

Using a heavy saucepan, combine the sugar and ½ cup of the milk. Stir in the egg yolks until the mixture is smooth; then add the remaining milk. Place the butter in the mixture and turn heat to the medium-low setting.

Cook, stirring often, until the mixture begins to thicken. Add the pecans and coconut and continue cooking until the coconut is well heated. Remove from the heat and stir in the vanilla.

Spread generously between the layers of the German chocolate cake. Pour the remaining frosting slowly over the top and sides, using a spatula to cover the sides.

I was not pleased with the heavy consistency, nor the taste, of the original frosting recipe for German Chocolate Cake.

Using an idea from a wonderful neighbor in the 1950s, I began working on this recipe. I liked the more crisp consistency and taste, as well as the moistening effect on the layers. I have also paired this frosting with the Duncan Hines butter recipe golden cake mix, which I consider the very best cake mix ever!

Carrot Cake Supreme

A true confectionery delight! The glaze adds both moisture and flavor to this favorite cake.

3 large eggs

2 cups sugar

¾ cup canola oil

¾ cup buttermilk

2 teaspoons vanilla

2 cups flour

2 teaspoons baking soda

½ teaspoon salt

2 teaspoons cinnamon

2 cups grated carrots

1 (8 ounce) can crushed pineapple, drained

1 cup flaked coconut

1½ cups chopped pecans

Glaze

Deluxe Cream Cheese Frosting (page 187)

1 cup finely chopped pecans, optional for frosting

Whisk the flour, baking soda, salt, and cinnamon together and set aside.

Using an electric mixer on medium speed, beat the eggs, sugar, oil, buttermilk, and vanilla until smooth. Turn the mixer to a low speed. Add the flour mixture in 3 increments, beating until the dry ingredients are completely incorporated. Stir in the carrots, pineapple, and coconut; stir in pecans by hand.

Divide the batter into 3 cake pans that have been coated with Crisco and sprinkle generously with flour. Bake at 350° for 25 to 30 minutes until a wooden toothpick inserted in the center comes out dry. While the cake is baking, prepare the following glaze that is to be drizzled over the warm layers while still in their pans.

CAKES & FROSTING

Glaze:

¼ cup sugar

½ teaspoon baking soda

¼ cup buttermilk

½ stick butter

1 teaspoon white corn syrup

½ teaspoon vanilla

In a small heavy saucepan over medium heat, bring all the ingredients except vanilla to a boil. Stirring constantly, boil 4 minutes until the glaze is a golden color. Stir in the vanilla. Cool slightly before drizzling over the warm cake layers that are still in the pans.

Continue to cool the layers in the pans for 15 minutes. Remove from pans and place, glazed sides up, on cake racks. Cool completely before frosting.

Use the Deluxe Cream Cheese Frosting on page 187 to spread over the layers, top, and sides of cake. Garnish with pecans, if desired. Keep the cake refrigerated.

Banana Nut Cake

A friend from Arkansas shared her banana cake recipe with me in 1954.

With a few tweaks over the years, including the addition of pecans, this recipe has become a family favorite. My son Freddy always requested this cake for his birthday. His wife Lisa and daughter, Ashley, now make it for him.

¾ cup butter flavor Crisco

2¼ cups sugar

3 eggs

4 large bananas, mashed

3 cups flour

1½ teaspoons baking soda

1 teaspoon salt

1½ teaspoons cinnamon

2½ teaspoons vanilla

¾ cup buttermilk

1½ cup chopped pecans

Cream Cheese Frosting (page 187)

Whisk together the dry ingredients and set aside. Mash the bananas and set aside.

Using an electric mixer on medium speed, cream the Crisco and sugar until fluffy. Beat in the eggs, 1 at a time. Turn the mixer to a low speed. Add the dry ingredients, 1 cup at a time, alternately with the buttermilk. Stir in the vanilla and mashed bananas. Mix in the chopped pecans by hand.

Pour the batter into 3 layer cake pans that have been coated with Crisco and sprinkled with flour. Bake at 350° for 25 to 30 minutes, or until cake is firm when lightly pressed by fingers.

Cool in the pans for 10 minutes. Remove from pans and completely cool on racks. When stacking the cake, I like to put a dob of icing on the cake plate as an anchor. I place the first 2 layers with the tops down, then the 3rd layer with the top up.

Spread the layers and sides of the cake with Cream Cheese Frosting. Decorate with pecans, if desired.

CAKES & FROSTING

Cream Cheese Frosting

1 (8 ounce) package cream cheese, softened

1 stick butter, softened

1 pound confectioners' sugar

1 teaspoon vanilla

Beat the cream cheese and butter at medium speed of an electric mixer until creamy. Beating at low speed, gradually add the sugar. Add the vanilla and turn the mixer back to the medium speed. Continue beating until the frosting is light and fluffy.

Deluxe Cream Cheese Frosting

11 ounces cream cheese, softened

1½ sticks butter, softened

1 pound confectioners' sugar

1½ teaspoons vanilla

Using an electric mixer on medium speed, beat the cream cheese and butter until smooth and creamy. At a lower speed, gradually add the sugar. Stir in the vanilla and beat on medium speed until light and fluffy.

Variation: Pecan Cream Cheese Frosting

Stir 1½ cups chopped pecans into the finished Deluxe Cream Cheese Frosting.

The key word for this frosting is "deluxe"!

Italian Cream Cake

My sister Lucile was always the best cook in our family.

Like my mother, she could take the ordinary and turn that into something wonderful. This is her delicious recipe.

1 stick butter

½ cup Crisco

2 cups sugar

5 eggs, separated

2 cups flour

1 teaspoon baking soda

1 cup buttermilk

1 teaspoon vanilla

1 cup flaked coconut

1 cup chopped pecans

Cream Cheese Frosting (page 187)

1½ cups chopped pecans added to frosting recipe, optional

Whisk together the flour and baking soda. Set aside.

Separate the eggs, saving the yolks. Beat the egg whites until peaks form. Set aside.

Using an electric mixer at medium speed, cream the butter, Crisco, and sugar. Beat until the mixture is smooth. Add the egg yolks, 1 at a time, beating well after each. Turn the mixer to a lower speed. Add the flour and baking soda alternately with the buttermilk. Stir in the vanilla and coconut. Gently fold in the beaten egg whites. Carefully stir in the pecans until evenly distributed.

Divide the batter into 3 cake pans that have been coated with Crisco and sprinkled with flour. Bake at 350° for about 25 minutes or until done.

Cool in pans for 10 minutes before removing layers and placing them on cake racks to cool. Spread layers, top, and sides with Cream Cheese Frosting to which 1½ cups of chopped pecans have been added.

Red Velvet Cake

2½ cups flour

1 teaspoon baking soda

1 teaspoon salt

1 tablespoon cocoa

1½ cups canola oil

1½ sugar

2 large eggs

1 (1 ounce) bottle red food coloring

1 teaspoon vinegar

1 cup buttermilk

1½ teaspoons vanilla

Deluxe Cream Cheese Frosting (page 187)

1½ cups chopped pecans, small chop

Whisk together the flour, baking soda, salt, and cocoa. Set aside.

Combine the oil, sugar, and eggs; beat on medium speed of an electric mixer until smooth. Add the red food coloring and vinegar; beat well for 4 minutes. Turn the mixer to a lower speed and add the dry ingredients alternately with the buttermilk. Stir in the vanilla.

Divide the cake batter into 3 layer pans, which have been coated with Crisco and sprinkled with flour. Bake at 350° for 25 to 30 minutes. Test for doneness with a toothpick or by pressing a finger to test if the center of the cake will spring back. Cool in pans for 10 minutes. Remove from pans and cool completely on cake racks.

Stir 1½ cups of chopped pecans into the Deluxe Cream Cheese Frosting. Spread generously between layers and on top and sides of the cake.

This beautiful red cake with its creamy white frosting is spectacular for holidays, or for any special occasion.

Dorothy Rodgers brought this delicious version to one of our Standard Oil "Old Friends" reunions in the early 1990s. She liked to sprinkle pecans around on top of her frosting; I really like mixing the pecans into my frosting. Baking the cake in a 9 or 10-inch springform pan makes a lovely presentation, as well.

CAKES & FROSTING

Applesauce Cake with Orange Coconut Icing

1½ sticks butter

2 cups sugar

3 eggs

2 cups warm applesauce

3 cups flour

1½ teaspoons baking soda

1 teaspoon salt

1 teaspoon each of cinnamon, cloves, nutmeg, and allspice

1 tablespoon cocoa

1 cup buttermilk

1½ teaspoons vanilla

2 cups chopped pecans

2 cups chopped candied fruit, optional

If using the optional candied fruit, such as cherries and pineapple, place the fruit and pecans in a large bowl and dredge with ¾ cup of the flour. Set aside.

In a separate bowl, whisk together the remaining flour and all other dry ingredients. Set aside.

Using an electric mixer at medium speed, cream the butter and sugar until light and fluffy. Add the eggs and beat well. Turn the mixer to a lower speed and stir in the warm applesauce. Add the flour mixture alternately with buttermilk, beginning and ending with the dry ingredients. Stir in the vanilla. Lastly, stir in by hand the dredged pecans and the optional fruit.

Bake in pans that have been heavily greased with Crisco and sprinkled with flour. This cake is best in 3 layers, but may also be baked in 2 loaf pans or a tube pan.

Bake at 350° until done, about 25 minutes for layers and about 1 hour for tube or loaf pans. Cake will be firm to the touch when done. Cool in layer pans for 10 minutes, in tube or loaf pans for 20 minutes. Remove from the pans and cool on racks. Frost with Orange-Coconut Icing between the layers and on top of cake, letting it dribble down the sides.

When I was growing up, this cake was my family's special Christmas cake.

A few days ahead, my mother would bake two of these cakes — one in layers and one in a tube pan — and place them on the dining room buffet. To this day, the aroma of applesauce and orange zest takes me back to those happy holidays when we were all young. After my mother's death, I won a special place in my brothers' hearts when I began making her special applesauce cakes for them at Christmas.

Orange Coconut Icing

3 medium oranges

3 cups sugar

1½ cups flaked coconut

Prepare the oranges as follows: Zest the oranges and set the zest aside. Peel off the white layer of each orange. Grate the oranges, saving both the juice and bits of orange fruit. Remove any seeds. Add the zest to the mixture.

In a heavy medium saucepan, combine the orange mixture with the sugar. Bring to a boil over medium heat. Continue cooking, stirring frequently. When the mixture thickens to syrup consistency, add the coconut and cook 1 minute.

Remove from the heat and stir well. Spoon about ⅓ of the icing over each layer as you stack the cake. As the icing cools, it will harden somewhat and leave a piquant, zesty glaze crowning the cake.

Sour Cream Coconut Cake

1 box Duncan Hines butter recipe golden cake mix

3 large eggs

¾ cup water

7 tablespoons butter, softened

Mix the cake batter according to the directions on the box. Pour into two 9-inch cake pans that have been coated with Crisco and sprinkled with flour. Bake at 350° for 22 to 27 minutes. Cake is done when a toothpick inserted in the center comes out clean.

Cool in the pans for 10 minutes before turning layers out onto cake racks. When completely cool, split each layer in half horizontally.

The resulting 4 layers can be stacked, always placing the cut side down. Begin by using the bottom of each pan layer for the first 2 layers; then continue with the tops. Between each layer, spread the coconut icing. Follow directions for icing the top and sides.

Sour Cream Coconut Icing:

2 cups sugar

8 ounces sour cream

1 (12 ounce) package frozen coconut, thawed

½ teaspoon vanilla

¾ cup Cool Whip

In a medium bowl, whisk together the sugar, sour cream, vanilla, and coconut. Refrigerate until completely chilled. When the cake layers are completely cooled and split, remove the icing from the refrigerator.

Measure 1 cup of the icing into a smaller bowl; combine this cup of icing with the Cool Whip. Reserve this mixture for the top and sides of the cake. Divide the remaining icing, using ⅓ between each of the layers as you stack them. Use the reserved mixture to cover the top and sides of the cake. Refrigerate the finished cake 3 days for maximum taste.

I was first introduced to this recipe by my friend Floy Plonk in the 1960s.

My niece Sheila uses her mother's recipe with wonderful results. This version is a combination of the two. Coconut lovers will rejoice!

Bourbon Nut Loaves

1 pound candied red cherries, cut in half

1 pound golden raisins

4 cups coarsely chopped pecans

4 cups flour

2 teaspoons baking powder

4 sticks butter, softened

4 teaspoons fresh lemon juice

2¼ cups sugar

6 large eggs

1 cup bourbon

Combine the cherries, raisins, and pecans; dredge with 1 cup of the flour. Set aside. Blend the remaining flour and baking powder and set aside.

Using an electric mixer at medium speed, cream the butter with lemon juice. Add the sugar gradually, creaming until fluffy after each addition. Add eggs, 1 at a time, beating thoroughly after each. Turn the mixer to a lower speed. Add 1 cup of the dry ingredients at a time, alternately with the bourbon. Beat after each addition just until the batter is smooth.

Remove the bowl from the mixer. Stir in, by hand, the dredged fruit and nuts. Spoon the batter into 2 loaf pans that have been heavily coated with Crisco and generously sprinkled with flour.

Bake at 275° for approximately 2 hours. Test for doneness by inserting a toothpick; if it comes out dry, the cake is done.

Cool in the pans for 20 minutes, then remove from pans to a cake rack until completely cooled. Store in airtight containers or seal in foil wrap. These loaves freeze well.

These loaves are like pound cake with colorful fruit and nuts.

Sometimes instead of using raisins, I substitute ½ pound candied pineapple and ½ pound green cherries.

Although the alcohol content of bourbon cooks away, the flavor remains to lend special sapidity to the cake. The loaves make great gifts at Christmas. Use your creativity for special wrapping!

CAKES & FROSTING

Strawberry Cupcakes with Strawberry Frosting

1 quart fresh ripe strawberries

Pillsbury strawberry cake mix

½ cup water

½ cup strawberry puree

⅓ cup vegetable oil

3 eggs

Strawberry Frosting

Clean the fresh strawberries. Purée in a blender or food processor to make ½ cup and ¼ cup. Set aside.

Put the dry cake mix into an electric mixer bowl. Add the water, ½ cup of the strawberry purée, the oil, and eggs. Mix at low speed until all ingredients are incorporated. Turn the mixer to medium speed and beat 2 minutes.

Generously grease and lightly flour muffin tins with Crisco. Fill each cup ⅔ full. Bake at 350° until the centers spring back when pressed. The times will vary with the muffin size. Begin checking at 20 minutes for regular size.

Remove from the oven and let cool for 5 minutes. Use a table knife to run around each muffin tin, checking to see if muffins are loose from the pan. Using a table fork, lift each muffin onto a cake rack to cool. Cover the tops with Strawberry Frosting.

Strawberry Frosting

3 ounces cream cheese, softened

2 tablespoons butter, softened

¼ cup strawberry puree

3 cups confectioners' sugar, as needed

Using an electric mixer at medium speed, beat the cream cheese and butter until smooth and creamy. Stir in the strawberry puree. Beat in the confectioners' sugar, adding 1 cup at a time, until the desired consistency.

Generously frost the strawberry cupcakes. Set in a cool place to let the frosting set. Refrigerate any leftover muffins to keep the cream cheese frosting fresh.

For one of Connie's favorite desserts, I had to find a way to make these cupcakes special.

The addition of fresh strawberry purée in both the batter and the frosting enhance the plain muffin to a very-berry rendition!

During the Pie Era in my evolution of cooking, I dearly loved making pies, pies, and more pies! I wished for a small bakery in which I would just make pies: call in the morning and your pie of choice would be ready for pickup by mid-afternoon. (Too bad I did not have a cookie store idea during my Cookie Era!)

There are many synonyms for pies, all related to sweetness: sweet treat, confection, pastry, cobbler, and tart – to name a few. Pies are that special combination of tender, flaky crusts and delectable fillings. You can engage your imagination in choosing different combinations of crust, filling, and topping as noted in this section. If you feel a little adventuresome, have some fun creating your own versions.

These recipes have been my favorites over the past sixty-plus years. Using one of these, you can proudly serve, for example, your own homemade pecan pie. The Ultimate Chocolate Dream makes quite an impression on family and guests. Try the lemon pies with your seafood dinners. There is definitely a pie that pairs well with any chosen menu.

Don't forget to make the delicious fruit-in-season cobblers. Find fresh berries in the spring, peaches in the summer, and apples in the fall. Those deep-dish fruit pies will quickly become favorites, especially when topped with a scoop of Blue Bell homemade vanilla! I especially love putting together several cobblers, double wrapping them in heavy duty foil, and freezing them. I can personalize them with a signature heart when labeling with a magic marker. The best part, however, is sharing them with others who can bake and serve their cobblers warm.

PIES & COBBLERS

Pie Crusts

Flaky Pie Crust
Chocolate Cookie Crumb Crust
Graham Cracker Crumb Crust

Frozen Strawberry Pie with Coconut Crust

Cream Pies

Vanilla Cream Pie
Coconut Cream Pie
Banana Pudding
Meringue

Southern Chocolate Pie Filling

The Ultimate Chocolate Dream

Lovie's Pecan Pie

Autumn Apple Pie

Key Lime Pie

Clancy's Meyer Lemon Pie with Chantilly Cream

Lemon Blueberry Pie

Fruit Cobbler

Peach, Blueberry, Blackberry,
Very Berry, Dewberry

Pie Crusts

My favorite three pie crusts are:

1. a store-bought refrigerated crust
2. a homemade flaky crust
3. a cookie-crumb crust

Store-bought Refrigerated Pie Crust

The refrigerated section in the grocery store usually is well stocked with refrigerated pie crusts, each box containing 2 crusts. Follow directions for bringing to room temperature. I like to place 1 unrolled crust between 2 pieces of wax paper. Carefully use the rolling pin, beginning at the center, and roll in each direction to the desired shape and size.

Place the crust evenly in a pie plate and crimp the edges. If you are baking the pie crust before adding the filling, use a fork to prick the sides and bottom before cooking. Bake at 400° for 10 to 15 minutes.

If you are baking the filling in the pie crust, do not prick.

For double crust pies, do not crimp until the second layer of crust has been placed over the filling. Crimp at this time, and cut slits in the top crust to allow steam to exit.

For a special 2-crust pie, consider making a lattice top. Simply prepare the second crust using the wax paper method. Remove the top sheet of wax paper and cut the crust into strips ⅝-inch wide. Lay them over the filling to form a lattice.

If you need a crust for a larger pie dish, place 2 pie crusts together. Use the wax paper method and roll into the desired size and shape.

Flaky Pie Crust

2 cups flour

1 teaspoon salt

⅔ cup plus 2 tablespoons Crisco

4 to 5 tablespoons ice water

Combine the flour and salt. Cut in the Crisco with a pastry blender or 2 knives, until the mixture is crumbly. Using a fork stir in the ice water, 1 tablespoon at a time, until dry ingredients are moistened. Shape into 2 balls, wrap each in plastic wrap, and chill 30 minutes to 1 hour.

Remove the dough from the refrigerator and let stand briefly. Working with 1 ball of dough at a time, flatten and set the dough in the center of a work surface that has been sprinkled with flour. Sprinkle the top of the dough and a rolling pin with flour. Carefully roll from the center out, rolling equally in opposite directions until the dough forms a round shape about 2 inches larger than the pie plate. The resulting pie dough should be about ⅛-inch thick. The trick is to accomplish the finished pastry without using an excessive amount of flour in handling the dough.

To transfer the crust to the pie dish, carefully fold the dough in half and then fold in half again. Place the point in the center of the pie plate and unfold carefully, using your fingers to lightly mold to the pie plate shape. Take extreme care to avoid any break in the crust. If one should occur, wet your finger and carefully seal the break.

For a baked pastry shell, trim the excess dough from the edges, leaving enough to fold under and crimp. Prick the bottom and sides with a fork. Bake at 400° for 12 to 15 minutes until lightly golden.

For a pastry shell that is to be filled before baking, such as Pecan Pie, simply trim the edges and crimp. Make sure there are no breaks or holes in the dough. Do not prick the dough. Simply pour in the filling and bake according to pie directions.

Yields 2 pie crusts

The key to making good flaky pie crusts lies in the accurate measurement of all ingredients and in proper mixing.

Handling the dough takes a bit of practice. If you are short on time, or if you just don't really want to do that today, make a guilt-free purchase of refrigerated pie crust at your favorite grocery store. You may consider keeping an extra box in the freezer!

Chocolate Cookie Crumb Crust

Some recipes just seem more suited to a chocolate crust rather than the traditional graham cracker crust.

For example, a turtle cheesecake absolutely calls for a chocolate crust!

2 cups chocolate cookie crumbs, made from Oreo cookies

¼ cup sugar

¾ stick butter, melted

In a food processor, make 2 cups of cookie crumbs from Oreos. Combine the crumbs, sugar, and melted butter. Pour the mixture into either a pie dish or a springform pan. Use a metal measuring cup to firmly press the mixture onto the bottom and up the sides of the pan.

Bake at 325° for 10 minutes. Set aside to cool.

Graham Cracker Pie Crust

You can buy the graham cracker crumbs or you can make your own.

Simply break graham crackers into smaller pieces and feed them into the food processor in small amounts. Alternate from chopping to pulsing as needed to make perfect crumbs.

1¾ cups graham cracker crumbs

¼ cup sugar

1 stick butter, melted and still warm

Combine all ingredients and mix with a fork until all crumbs are moistened. Pour into either a pie plate or a springform pan. Spread the mixture and use a metal measuring cup to form the sides and to press the bottom into a firm layer.

Bake at 350° for 8 minutes. Set aside to cool. Use according to the selected recipe.

Frozen Strawberry Pie with Coconut Crust

2½ cups flaked coconut

1 stick butter, melted

1 (3 ounce) package cream cheese, softened

1 can Eagle Brand sweetened condensed milk

1½ cups purée made from 1 quart fresh ripe strawberries

3 tablespoons lemon juice

1 (8 ounce) carton Cool Whip

additional fresh strawberries for garnishing

A delightful frozen dessert for those hot summer months!

Spread the coconut evenly in a jelly roll pan and place in preheated oven at 350°. Toast 7 to 15 minutes until golden, stirring frequently. Place the toasted coconut in a bowl and combine with the melted butter. Next, press the coconut mixture firmly on the bottom and up the sides of a pie dish or springform pan. Set aside.

In a large mixer bowl, beat the cream cheese on medium speed until fluffy; gradually beat in Eagle Brand milk. Turn the mixer to a lower speed; stir in the puréed strawberries and lemon juice. Fold in the Cool Whip.

Pour the strawberry mixture into the coconut crust. Freeze 4 hours or until firm. Before serving, if desired, garnish with fresh strawberries and an extra dollop of Cool Whip. Keep any leftovers in the freezer.

Cream Pies

Cream pies are those satiny smooth fillings with both eye and taste appeal. They are easy to make and versatile to serve. Cream pies pair equally well with a baked crust or a graham cracker crumb crust. The toppings may vary from meringue to whipped cream. Their flexibility extends to individual servings in ramekins, pretty dessert bowls, etc. Use a little creativity and make a special dessert from these easy recipes.

Note several commonalities: using a heavy medium saucepan, making a paste first by whisking a small amount of milk with the dry ingredients, stirring constantly while the filling is cooking, etc. Also note that you are using only one pan for the entire recipe!

Remember your choices: choose the crust, choose the flavor, and choose the topping!

Vanilla Cream Pie

1½ cups sugar

½ cup flour

⅛ teaspoon salt

3 egg yolks

3 cups milk

½ stick butter

1 teaspoon vanilla

In a heavy saucepan, whisk the dry ingredients together. Stir in ½ cup of the milk to make a paste. Add the egg yolks and whisk briskly. Gradually stir in the remaining milk. Cook over medium heat, stirring constantly, until the mixture thickens and boils briefly.

Remove from the heat, and stir in butter and vanilla. Whisk until smooth. Pour the hot filling into a baked pie crust or graham cracker crumb crust. Choose a topping from these recipes: Meringue, Whipped Cream, or Chantilly Cream. Cool Whip is also an option.

Coconut Cream Pie

Use ingredients and directions for Vanilla Cream Pie. When you remove from heat, immediately stir in 1½ cups of flaked coconut with the butter and vanilla.

Banana Pudding

Make a recipe of the Vanilla Cream Pie and set aside.

In your preferred dish, make a layer of vanilla wafers. Slice 2 bananas over the vanilla wafers.

Pour the warm filling over the bananas and vanilla wafers. Spread the top with another layer of vanilla wafers.

Add meringue, if desired. The pudding may also be topped with a dollop of whipped cream, or simply served plain.

Banana pudding may also be assembled in small bowls for individual servings. Topped with a dollop of whipped cream, the servings have a bit more flair.

Meringue

4 egg whites

¼ teaspoon cream of tartar

⅓ cups sugar

½ teaspoon vanilla

Let the egg whites stand at room temperature for 30 minutes.

With an electric mixer at medium speed, beat the egg whites and cream of tartar in a grease-free bowl until soft peaks form. Turn the mixer to the high speed. Gradually add the sugar and beat 3 to 4 minutes until all is completely dissolved and until stiff peaks form. Stir in vanilla.

Quickly spread the meringue onto the hot filling, sealing it to the edges. Bake at 350° until the meringue is a golden brown. Cool at room temperature.

When using this meringue for coconut pie, sprinkle a little flaked coconut over the top before putting the pie in the oven to brown.

Southern Chocolate Pie Filling

1½ cups sugar

½ cup cocoa

½ cup flour

⅛ teaspoon salt

3 egg yolks

3 cups milk

¾ stick butter

1½ teaspoons vanilla

crust, as desired

topping, as desired

In a heavy saucepan, whisk the dry ingredients together. Stir in ½ cup of the milk to make a paste. Add the egg yolks and whisk briskly until well blended. Gradually stir in the remaining milk.

Cook over medium heat, stirring constantly, until mixture boils. Continue to stir and cook briefly, about half a minute.

Remove from the heat; stir in the butter and vanilla. Whisk until smooth.

Pour into your choice of crumb crust or baked pie crust. May be topped with meringue, whipped cream, or whipped topping. Chill before serving.

Chocolate cream pie filling can be used in many creative ways.

Individual servings are nice when topped with whipped cream and chopped roasted pecans. My favorite way is to use the filling in the Ultimate Chocolate Dream recipe.

The Ultimate Chocolate Dream

First Layer:

    1 cup flour

    1 stick butter

    ½ cup finely chopped pecans

Place the flour in a bowl; cut the butter into pats and add to the flour. Blend together, using either a pastry blender or 2 knives. Stir in the pecans. Press this mixture into the bottom of a 9 x 13 (or equivalent) ovenproof dish. Cook at 350° for about 15 to 20 minutes or until done. Edges will just begin to brown. Set aside to cool.

Second Layer:

    1 (8 ounce) package cream cheese, softened

    1 cup confectioners' sugar

    1 cup Cool Whip

Cream the cream cheese and sugar, beating until smooth. Stir in the Cool Whip. Spread evenly over the cooled first layer.

Third Layer:

    Southern Chocolate Pie Filling (page 204)

When the mixture has cooled, stir well and pour evenly over the second layer.

Topping:

1 (12 ounce) carton Cool Whip

½ cup finely chopped pecans

Cover the chocolate layer generously with Cool Whip (may not use all the 12 ounce carton). Sprinkle the top with chopped pecans. Refrigerate several hours.

This dessert lives up to the name! It is my favorite dessert – it has the crunch in the crust, the creamy layer, then chocolate at its best.

Add pecans in the crust and topping, and it becomes truly extraordinary. My first introduction to this "delight" was made with an instant chocolate pudding mix. My mind fairly screamed, "Why not use the scratch version of chocolate pie filling?" The difference is, in my opinion, well worth the effort.

PIES & COBBLERS

Lovie's Pecan Pie

For a really special treat, serve when the pie is still a bit warm.

A scoop of Blue Bell homemade vanilla ice cream may be added as a delicious topping for this luscious dessert! A dollop of homemade whipped cream is equally delightful.

For many years this pie was one of my signature desserts, delicious and yet so easy to make.

The recipe was given to me by Lovie, who worked for my sister Ruth in Jackson, Mississippi. Lovie's cooking was a legend. Her special direction, as she shared the key to her pecan pie, was to make sure to beat the butter into the mixture really well!

4 large eggs

1 cup sugar

1 cup white corn syrup

⅛ teaspoon salt

½ stick butter, melted

2 teaspoons vanilla

1½ cup chopped pecans

1 pie crust

Place a pie crust into a 9-inch pie plate and crimp the edges. Make sure that the crust is completely unbroken. Set aside. (Store-bought refrigerated crusts are great!)

Do not use the electric mixer! Whisk the eggs until well blended. Add the sugar and beat until thoroughly mixed. Stir in the corn syrup and salt. Whisk in the melted butter and vanilla, continuing to beat until all butter is completely incorporated. Stir in the pecans; pour the mixture into the crust.

Bake at 325° for 1 hour.

PIES & COBBLERS

Autumn Apple Pie

2 pie crusts

6 cups peeled Granny Smith apples, sliced

¾ cup sugar

½ cup light brown sugar

¼ cup flour

⅛ teaspoon salt

1 teaspoon cinnamon

¾ stick butter, melted

nutmeg and sugar for sprinkling over top

Line a pie plate with 1 of the pie pastries. If using the refrigerated kind, place the crust between 2 sheets of wax paper. Starting in the center, roll with a rolling pin in each direction. When the pie shell is the correct size and shape, place it evenly in the pie dish. Set aside.

Place sliced apples in a large mixing bowl. In a medium sized bowl, combine the dry ingredients. Whisk to mix together. Pour this dry mixture over the sliced apples and stir until the fruit is coated. Pour the melted butter in next and stir until combined. Spoon the mixture into the waiting pie shell.

Using the 2nd pie pastry, cut into strips about ⅝-inch wide. Lay the strips over the apple mixture in a lattice pattern. Crimp the edges. Sprinkle the top generously with sugar and sprinkle with nutmeg.

Bake at 350° for about 1 hour and 20 minutes or until bubbly and golden brown.

If pies were grouped by seasons, the apple pie would well represent Fall.

A visit to the apple orchards of North Carolina almost rivals the aroma that fills the house when this apple pie is baking.

PIES & COBBLERS

The Magic Ingredient

The ingredient called "magic" by dessert makers was developed in 1856 by Gail Borden. It is paradoxically both the oldest and the most contemporary product in the Borden line. The quality all-natural product was a sweetened condensed milk that required no refrigeration. Gail's first marketing venue was a pushcart in New York City. He named his new product Eagle Brand after the American eagle, the recognized symbol of pride and high quality.

Along the way to its pinnacle as a classic dessert ingredient, Eagle Brand made other footprints. It was praised by the military for saving many lives during the Civil War. Eagle Brand was also credited with significantly lowering the infant mortality rate. Before World War I, its principle use was as a sweetener-creamer for coffee. After that conflict, however, it became popular for use in ice cream – and remains so today.

So began the magic. In the mid-1920s, Borden was advertising Eagle Brand for making "glorious" pies. Borden Kitchens, in 1931, sought original recipes by offering $25 for those selected. They received 80,000 entries. By the 1940s homemakers were proudly serving Lemon Icebox Pie, which only required cooking to brown the meringue.

Elsie the Borden Cow came onto the scene in time for the 1938 World's Fair. She further promoted the popular Eagle Brand, eventually replacing the eagle as the logo on the label. Eagle Brand, however, remains the name – which still denotes pride, quality, and convenience. It is the basis for innumerable magic desserts on the contemporary scene.

Borden cookbooks date back to the early 1900s. The Borden kitchen selected some of the all-time favorites and developed new recipes for publication as Classic Desserts in 1984. The recipes from this little spiral hardback, along with the creamy richness of Eagle Brand, have worked their magic in the kitchens in which I have had the joy to fill so many empty pots.

My earliest memory of this magic ingredient dates back to the summer of 1943. My mother was delighted over the simple and easy way to make pies. One morning she made two lemon pies and sent me to deliver one to our new neighbor. That basic recipe remains the same: Mix together 3 egg yolks and a can of Eagle Brand sweetened condensed milk; stir in ½ cup of lemon juice; pour into a vanilla wafer crumb crust; top with meringue and brown in the oven.

My favorite Eagle Brand pies – Key Lime, Lemon-Blueberry, Clancy's Meyer Lemon, and Frozen Strawberry – take the initial recipe to a significantly higher level.

Key Lime Pie

1¾ cups graham cracker crumbs

¼ cup sugar

1 stick butter, melted and still warm

1 (6 ounce) can frozen limeade, partially thawed

1 can Eagle Brand sweetened condensed milk

1 (12 ounce) carton Cool Whip

green food coloring, optional

A refreshing summer pie using Borden's magic ingredient.

Combine the graham cracker crumbs, sugar, and melted butter; stir with a fork until well mixed. Pour into either a pie plate or springform pan. Spread the mixture, and use a metal measuring cup to form the sides and press the bottom into a firm layer. If using a springform pan, place it on a foil-lined cookie sheet.

Bake at 350° for 8 minutes. Set aside to cool.

In a large mixing bowl, whisk the limeade into the Eagle Brand milk. When well mixed, fold in the carton of Cool Whip. If desired, add green food coloring to tint the pie that delicate real lime color. Hint: add sparingly, 1 or 2 drops at a time of the green food coloring.

Pour into the graham cracker pie crust and refrigerate or freeze. Serve well chilled. Garnish as desired, with a dollop of whipped cream and/or a twist of lime.

PIES & COBBLERS

Clancy's Meyer Lemon Pie with Chantilly Cream

Located on Annunciation Street in New Orleans, Clancy's is an intimate neighborhood restaurant.

When Connie found their Meyer lemon pie recipe, we immediately began squeezing the lemons!

Crust:

    1¾ cups graham cracker crumbs

    ¼ cup sugar

    1 stick butter, melted and still warm

Filling:

    2 cans Eagle Brand sweetened condensed milk

    1¼ cups fresh Meyer lemon juice, strained

    zest of 2 lemons

    8 large egg yolks

Chantilly Cream:

    1 cup heavy whipping cream

    ½ teaspoon vanilla

    ¼ cup confectioners' sugar

To make the crust: Mix the graham cracker crumbs, sugar, and butter together. Transfer the crust mix to a 9-inch springform pan. Press the crumb mixture into the bottom and 1 inch up the sides of the pan. Use the bottom of a measuring cup to press the crust into place. Set aside.

To make the filling: In a large bowl, whisk the Eagle Brand milk with the lemon juice and set aside. Whisk the zest with the egg yolks in a medium bowl until pale, 30 to 60 seconds. Combine the 2 mixtures and whisk until well blended.

To assemble: Place the springform pan on a cookie sheet, which has been lined with foil. Slightly turn up the edges of the foil. Pour the filling mixture over the crumb crust. Carefully place in a 325° oven. Bake until the center jiggles slightly, about 25 minutes.

Remove from the oven and cool for 1 hour. Release the springform, after carefully running a knife around the edge. Do not remove the side of pan. Cool a few more minutes, then loosely cover the pan with plastic wrap. Be careful not to let the plastic wrap touch the top of the pie. Freeze at least 6 hours or overnight. To keep frozen for an extended time, wrap in heavy-duty foil.

To make Chantilly Cream: Pour the heavy whipping cream into a chilled bowl. Whip on low speed as you add vanilla and sugar. Increase to medium-high and continue to beat until soft stiff peaks form. Cover and refrigerate until needed.

To serve: Remove the side from the springform pan. Slice into desired sizes. Top each slice with a dollop of Chantilly Cream and serve immediately. Garnish with a sprig of mint leaves and a twist of lemon peel, if desired.

We only tweaked Clancy's recipe a wee bit. Although the filling requires only 3 ingredients, the lemons must be Meyer (a lemon variety that is a cross between a true lemon and an orange, resulting in a sweeter, less acidic flavor).

Lemon Blueberry Pie

Crust:

>1¾ cups graham cracker crumbs
>
>¼ cup sugar
>
>1 stick butter, melted

While the butter is still warm, stir in the graham cracker crumbs and sugar. Empty this mixture into a deep 9-inch springform pan. Using a metal measuring cup, press the mixture into the bottom and 1 inch up the sides of the pan. Place the springform pan on a foil-lined cookie sheet and bake the crust at 350° for 8 minutes. Set aside and cool completely.

Blueberry Filling:

>1½ pints fresh blueberries
>
>3 tablespoons blueberry preserves

Wash the berries and spread on paper towels to dry. Save a few berries for garnish. In a mixing bowl, stir the preserves into the remaining berries until well coated. Set aside.

Lemon Filling:

>2 (8 ounce) packages cream cheese, softened
>
>½ cup confectioners' sugar
>
>2 cans Eagle Brand sweetened condensed milk
>
>4 teaspoons grated lemon rind
>
>1 cup fresh lemon juice
>
>2 (3.4 ounce) packages Jell-O instant lemon pudding mix

Beat the cream cheese, powdered sugar, and Eagle Brand milk at medium speed until creamy. Add the grated lemon rind, lemon juice, and pudding mix; beat until well blended.

The idea for this excellent pie came from a Fourth of July pamphlet around 2002.

The hidden blueberry center is perfect with the tart-to-sweet citrus taste of lemons. Adapting the recipe to showcase its stellar qualities led me to choosing a springform for presentation.

Assemble as follows:

Pour ½ of the lemon filling into the cooled crust and spread carefully to the edge. Spoon the blueberry filling on next, leaving a 1-inch margin around the edge. Carefully spoon the remaining lemon filling over the top, beginning with the edge and working to the center.

Cover with plastic wrap or foil and chill at least 3 hours. To serve, carefully run a table knife around the edges and remove the springform. Cut into appropriate sized slices and add a dollop of whipped cream. Garnish with a blueberry and mint leaves.

The generous amount of the filling would allow, if you wish, for assembling 2 additional small individual desserts. Just spoon some of the filling into 2 pretty dessert dishes, topping them with blueberries and a dollop of whipped cream. Consider these a bonus!

Whipped Cream:

    1 pint heavy whipping cream

    4 tablespoons confectioners' sugar

    ½ teaspoon vanilla

Place the mixer bowl and beaters in the refrigerator to chill. Pour the heavy whipping cream into the chilled bowl; beat on medium speed of an electric mixer until soft peaks begin to form. Add the confectioners' sugar and vanilla. Continue beating until the desired consistency. Cover and keep chilled until needed.

The eye appeal of a bubbly, golden brown homemade fruit cobbler speaks straight to our sense of home and comfort. The aroma of a cobbler in the oven beckons everyone to the kitchen. Our taste buds ascend in culinary delight when we lift a spoon of warm cobbler, especially when topped with Blue Bell homemade vanilla ice cream.

When our family moved to Grand Bay in 1964, we built our house next to a large open field that was covered with wild dewberry vines. That first year we picked 30 gallons of the beautiful juicy berries. We shared them with friends, made jelly, and still had an abundance to freeze. I felt compelled to learn to make real cobblers. My search led me not only to developing a recipe for dewberry cobbler, but also to discovering a sort of formula that could be adapted for other fruits.

I no longer have access to wild dewberries. Instead, I now use either fresh or frozen fruits to make peach, blueberry, blackberry, and very-berry (combination blueberry-blackberry) cobblers. They all have flaky crusts with bubbly centers, and they have lattice tops sprinkled with sugar and nutmeg. Also, Blue Bell homemade vanilla ice cream should always be in the freezer!

After making a cobbler, you will understand its simplicity. Go for the refrigerated pie crust – in fact, it is good to keep a box or two in your refrigerator or freezer. For the bottom crust, place one refrigerated crust between two sheets of wax paper. Using a rolling pin, gently roll in opposite directions from the center out. Place the crust evenly in the cobbler dish. If you are using a rectangular or larger dish, use two pie crusts. Remove a bit from the side of each, and join them by overlapping. Roll between sheets of wax paper until you achieve the size and shape needed. For the lattice top, roll out the same way; then cut into even strips about ⅝-inch wide.

When fruits are in season, cobblers can be made ahead and frozen. After the lattice has been crimped and sprinkled with sugar and nutmeg, cover the cobbler with plastic wrap. Using heavy-duty foil, wrap and seal completely. Label with the contents and the date. I personalize mine by drawing a little heart! On the day you need this dessert, remove the cobbler from the freezer, unwrap, and thaw for 3 or 4 hours. Cook as directed. If you time the process correctly, you can have warm cobbler for dessert.

Cooking Tip:

Cobblers and fruit pies have a tendency to bubble over, causing messy spill-overs in the oven. A foil-lined cookie sheet placed under the cobbler or pie will avoid this problem.

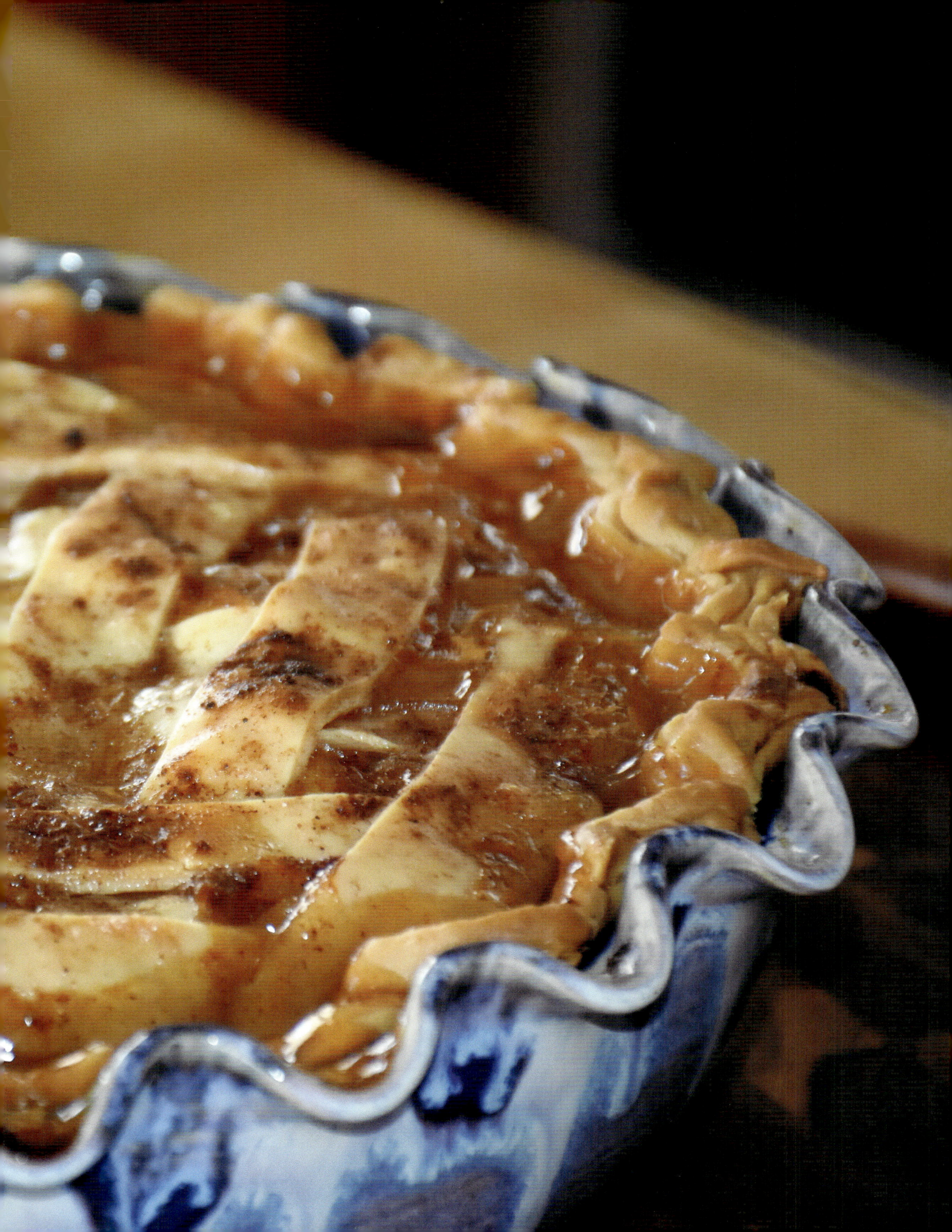

Fruit Cobblers

Fruit of choice, select one:

    7 cups sliced fresh peaches, not over-ripe

    6 cups blueberries

    6 cups blackberries

    4 cups blueberries plus 2 cups blackberries (very-berry)

    6 cups dewberries

⅓ cup flour (decrease to ¼ cup for blackberries)

¾ cup sugar

¾ cup light brown sugar

¼ teaspoon salt

1 teaspoon cinnamon

1 stick butter, melted

1 tablespoon fresh lemon juice

2 pie crusts, choose either homemade or refrigerated

nutmeg and sugar for sprinkling on lattice crust

Choose your crust. For speed and convenience, use the refrigerated pie crusts; they are excellent in both taste and texture. If you use my Flaky Pie Crust recipe, add 2 tablespoons light brown sugar with the flour and salt – my secret ingredient for cobbler crust! Line your cobbler dish with 1 of the pie pastries.

In a large bowl, place the fruit of choice. In a medium bowl, combine the dry ingredients and whisk together. Pour this dry mixture over the fruit and stir until all fruit is coated. Pour the melted butter and lemon juice over the fruit mixture; stir until combined. Pour the entire mixture into the cobbler dish that has been lined with the 1st pie crust.

Using the 2nd pie crust, cut into strips about ⅝-inch wide. Lay the strips over the fruit in a lattice pattern. Crimp the edges. Sprinkle generously with sugar, then sprinkle with nutmeg. Place the cobbler on a foil-lined pan and bake at 350° until bubbling and golden brown. Depending on the depth of the cobbler dish, the cooking time usually is from 1 hour 15 minutes to 1 hour 45 minutes.

Delicious served warm. Blue Bell homemade vanilla ice cream takes it over the top!

PIES & COBBLERS

Just the idea of homemade candy invokes happy memories of a long-ago time when my sisters filled the kitchen with the joy of making Christmas candies. Having brought in all the special ingredients, they began the prep work that is so important. According to their expertise, you cannot stop once the candy making process begins.

Every flat surface in the 1940s kitchen was covered with selected ingredients and the necessary paraphernalia for making the designated recipes. It was a major production, and they had wisely chosen a sunny Saturday for the project.

Working together in sync, they began the mixing, stirring, and testing. Soon the house was filled with wonderful aromas, made even more special by the chatter and laughter flowing from the kitchen. My brothers came home from work just in time to wheedle sample tastings. It was a memorable time.

When I grew up, married, and started my own family, I wanted to make those Christmas memories for my children and their friends. Later on, I wanted to build a bank of memories from which my grandchildren could draw. At the present time, my great-granddaughters are just reaching the "cooking with Nan" age.

The tips for optimizing success in candy making used by my sisters are much the same today: have all ingredients ready before beginning, use heavy cookware and wooden spoons for stirring and pick a sunny day.

Most of the best candy recipes are those that have been passed down and around: down from mothers, aunts, and grandmothers; around from friends to friends. Sometimes the ingredients are just written on a paper napkin or the back of a bank deposit slip, but you will know how to put them together.

At Christmas you can select a few of your favorite recipes. Make the candies and put together a cake plate or tier of assorted tasty treats. Don't forget to make enough to share a few with neighbors and friends. I am always delighted when my neighbor Teresa and her daughter, Dannielle, share their wonderful treats with me at Christmas.

CANDY

Creamy Pralines

Peanut Butter Balls

Chocolate Fudge

Candied Pecan Halves

Homemade Turtles

Haystacks

Martha Washington Candy

Peanut Brittle

Creamy Pralines

1 cup sugar

1 cup light brown sugar

¼ teaspoon salt

½ cup evaporated milk

2 tablespoons light corn syrup

½ stick butter

1½ teaspoons vanilla

2 cups pecans, either whole or chopped

Measure the first 5 ingredients, combining them in a heavy skillet. Place over low heat and stir with a wooden spoon until the sugars dissolve. Turn up the heat slightly and let the mixture come to a boil, stirring frequently. The mixture needs to cook only for a very short time. With a cup of cool water handy, begin to test for the soft ball stage after 2 minutes. A couple of drops will stick together to form a soft ball when dropped into the cool water. Change the water between testings.

When the candy mixture reaches the soft ball stage, immediately remove from heat. Stir in the butter until melted, then add vanilla and pecans. Begin to stir with a wide wooden paddle, scraping the bottom of pan often and stirring in wide circles. When the mixture begins to thicken, make periodic tests for readiness.

On a flat surface, place a long piece of wax paper that has been smeared with butter. Coat 2 soup spoons with softened butter – use 1 for spooning and 1 for guiding the candy onto the wax paper. When the praline mixture tests for readiness, the candy will hold its shape as it is spooned onto the wax paper.

You will need to work fast to ladle all the candies. If the mixture begins to set too quickly, give it a good stir with the wooden paddle, then continue dropping. You can make the large pralines, or you may want to do small ones to include on a tray of treats.

This candy treat always reminds me of my first trip to New Orleans!

Watching the ladies as they stirred those huge pots at the French Quarter Market was fascinating. I have to admit that I am more fond of the creamy pralines rather than the sugary ones they were making. I was beyond delighted when I learned to make my own. Remember, some recipes take practice – so persevere. You can make perfect ones!

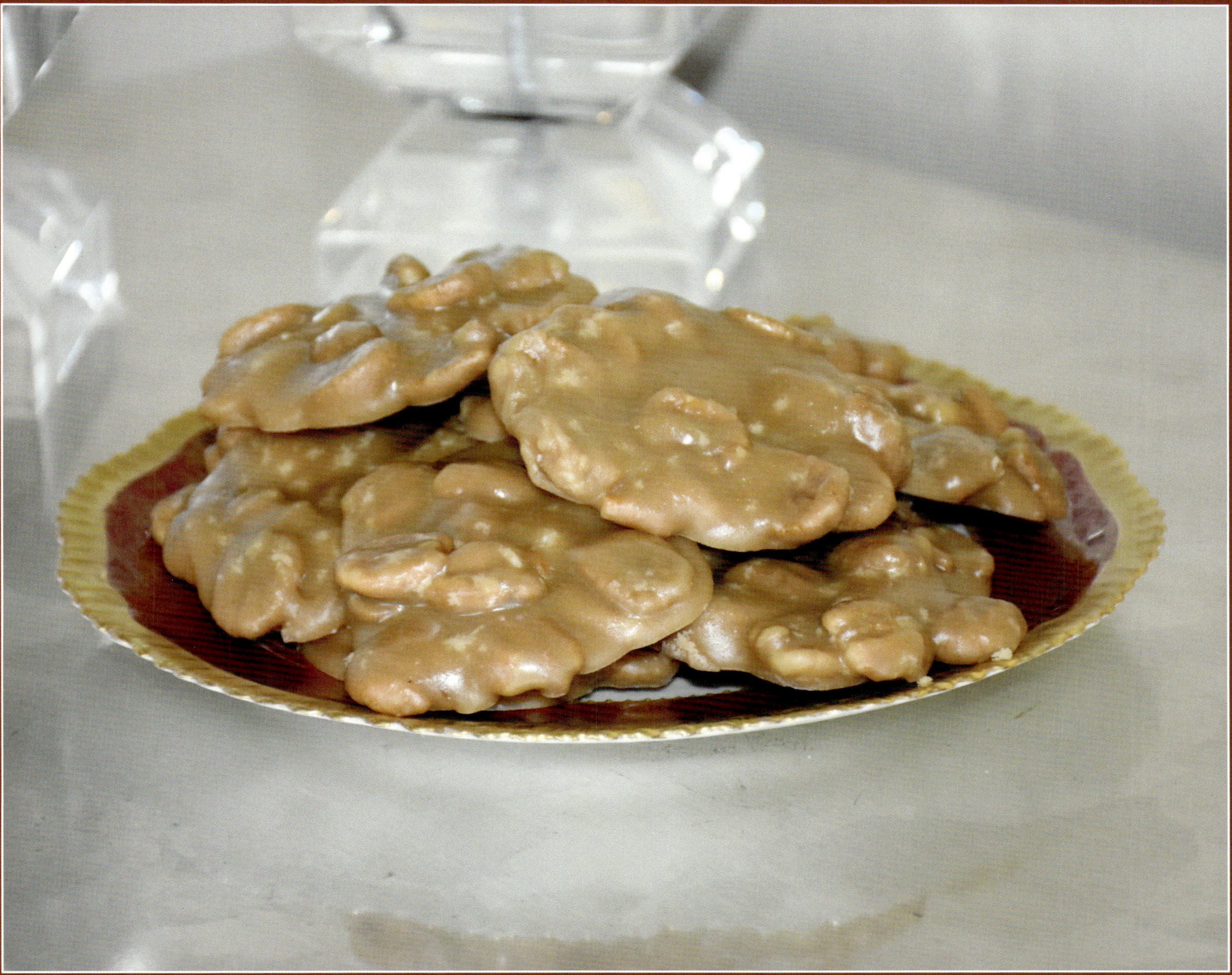

Peanut Butter Balls

1½ cups peanut butter, creamy or crunchy (Jif extra crunchy for me!)

2 sticks butter, softened

1 pound box confectioners' sugar

1 (11.5 ounce) package chocolate morsels, milk chocolate or semi-sweet

¼ block of paraffin, cut into small pieces

Using an electric mixer, cream the butter and peanut butter. Add the confectioners' sugar 1 cup at a time, beating at medium speed until well blended. Shape the mixture into small balls and place them on a cookie sheets lined with wax paper. Chill for 2 hours.

In the top of a small double boiler, place the paraffin. Bring the water to a boil in the lower pan. Place the top pan over the boiling water and turn the flame to low. Heat until the paraffin melts, stirring occasionally. Gradually add the chocolate morsels, stirring until all are melted and smooth. Remove the entire pan from the heat, leaving the chocolate mixture over the hot water.

Working quickly, drop 1 or 2 of the chilled balls into the chocolate mixture. Use a fork to lift each chocolate covered ball and place it on a cookie sheet lined with wax paper. When all are coated, place the cookie sheet in the refrigerator until the chocolate is set.

These tasty little treats have been a holiday favorite since the 1970s, and remain my daughter's favorite candy.

Since the recipe makes so many, some may be stored in the refrigerator until needed. Recycled jelly jars with colorful tops are just the right size containers to fill for sharing with friends.

Chocolate Fudge

2 cups sugar

½ cup evaporated milk

1 stick butter

1 (11.5 ounce) package chocolate morsels, semi-sweet or milk chocolate

1 cup marshmallow creme

1 teaspoon vanilla

1½ cups chopped pecans

Combine the sugar, evaporated milk, and butter in a heavy saucepan or skillet. Bring to a boil, stirring frequently. Cook, stirring constantly, until a few drops in cool water become a soft ball.

Remove from the heat and immediately stir in the chocolate morsels until smooth. Next, stir in the marshmallow creme and vanilla; lastly, add the chopped pecans. Pour the candy mixture into a buttered dish. After the candy has set, cut into pieces.

Using marshmallow creme and chocolate morsels has made fudge a never-fail recipe.

The old-fashioned method was a bit intimidating. In high school days, my girl friends and I often had to eat our cooked fudge with spoons. Just imagine the excitement when this foolproof, never-fail recipe became available!

Candied Pecan Halves

½ cup sugar

1 cup light brown sugar

⅛ teaspoon salt

½ cup sour cream

2½ to 3 cups pecan halves (may be lightly toasted, if desired)

In a heavy skillet combine the sugars, salt, and sour cream. Cook over medium heat, stirring frequently, until the mixture boils. Continue stirring until a few drops form a soft ball when dropped in cool water.

Remove from heat. Stir in the pecan halves until all are well coated. Pour the candy onto parchment paper and spread into a single layer. When cooled, break the pecans apart.

In 1969, my friend Marilyn Hatchett taught me to make this special recipe.

Her father was the founder of Dees Pecan Company of Grand Bay, and she is the ultimate expert on all things pecan. She graciously shared many recipes with me. When friends dropped in, I could quickly make these treats while Fred made the coffee.

Homemade Turtles

1 (14 ounce) package caramels

2 tablespoons plus 1 teaspoon evaporated milk

2½ cups pecan halves

1 (11.5 ounce) package chocolate morsels, semi-sweet or milk chocolate

¼ bar paraffin, cut in small pieces

Unwrap the caramels and place them in a small heavy saucepan. Add the evaporated milk and set over low heat. Stir with a wooden spoon until the caramels melt and the mixture is smooth. Remove from heat and stir in the pecan halves. Using buttered spoons, drop by small amounts onto wax paper that has been coated with butter. Allow the candies to set for at least 15 minutes before coating with chocolate.

Put the paraffin in the top of a small double boiler. Bring water to a boil in the lower part of the double boiler. Place the top pan over the boiling water and turn the heat to low. Heat until the paraffin melts, stirring occasionally. Gradually add the chocolate morsels, stirring until melted and the mixture is smooth. Remove the entire pan from the heat, leaving the chocolate mixture over the hot water. Keep the mixture smooth by frequent stirring.

Working quickly with 1 or 2 at a time, drop the candies into the chocolate coating mixture. Use a fork to lift each candy and place it on a cookie sheet lined with wax paper. When all are coated, leave them until the chocolate is firm. If needed, they can be placed in the refrigerator for a few minutes.

As far as candies go, this recipe always gets an outstanding rating.

These homemade turtles have been one of our special Christmas candies for many years. They remain John's favorite, even above marshmallow fudge!

CANDY

Haystacks

2 (11.5 ounce) packages butterscotch morsels

½ cup peanut butter

1 large can chow mein noodles

1 cup salted peanuts

Pour morsels into a large mixing bowl. Microwave 1 to 1½ minutes and stir. Continue microwaving 15 seconds at a time and stirring until the morsels are completely melted and mixture is smooth.

Stir in the peanut butter until blended. Add the chow mein noodles and peanuts and stir until well coated.

Drop by large spoonfuls onto a wax paper-lined cookie sheet. Place in the refrigerator a few minutes until set.

This salty, crunchy treat really appeals to kids who want to cook.

My grandchildren always chose one recipe for us to make when they came to visit. The haystacks were often chosen. We fondly remember those times when we made them together.

CANDY

Martha Washington Candy

2 pounds confectioners' sugar

1 stick butter, room temperature

1 can Eagle Brand sweetened condensed milk

4 cups finely chopped pecans

1 tablespoon vanilla

3 cups chocolate morsels, milk or semi-sweet chocolate morsels

¾ bar paraffin, cut into small pieces

In a large bowl, whisk the Eagle Brand, vanilla, and butter together until smooth. Add the confectioners' sugar 1 cup at a time, stirring after each addition until well mixed. Lastly, stir in the pecans.

Make small balls of the mixture and place them on a cookie sheet lined with wax paper. Place in the refrigerator for about 20 minutes.

Place the paraffin in the top of a small double boiler. Bring water to a boil in the lower pan. Place the top pan over the boiling water and turn the heat to low. Heat until the paraffin melts, stirring occasionally. Gradually add the chocolate morsels, stirring until all are melted and smooth. Remove the entire pan from the heat, leaving the chocolate mixture over the hot water.

Working quickly, drop 1 or 2 balls at a time into the chocolate. Use a fork to lift each chocolate covered ball and place it on a cookie sheet lined with parchment paper. Keep the chocolate smooth by stirring from time to time. Also, place the double boiler back on the heat if the chocolate gets too thick. When all the candies are coated, place the cookie sheet in the refrigerator a few minutes until chocolate coating is set.

Nostalgia demands that I include this candy.

The recipe, from the 1930s, is so old that the directions do not mention using an electric mixer. My older sisters, Lucile and Ruth, made this candy every Christmas when I was a child. Sometimes they would add chopped cherries or peppermint flavoring. They were in the kitchen having fun, while I probably had to polish the dining room furniture.

Peanut Brittle

1 cup sugar

1 ½ cups raw peanuts

½ cup light corn syrup

1 square inch paraffin, cut in small pieces

pinch of salt

1 teaspoon baking soda

Butter a large cookie sheet and set aside.

In a cast iron skillet, combine all the ingredients except the baking soda. Cook over medium heat, stirring occasionally, until the syrup begins turning a light amber color.

Remove from the heat and quickly stir in the baking soda. Immediately pour the mixture onto the buttered cookie sheet and spread as thin as possible. Set aside to cool.

When cool, lift the sheet of brittle using a metal spatula. Turn the brittle over and break into pieces with the back of a metal spoon. Store in an airtight container.

Pick a bright sunny day and have fun making this candy; my sister Lucile finally taught me to make her recipe when I was about 50 years old!

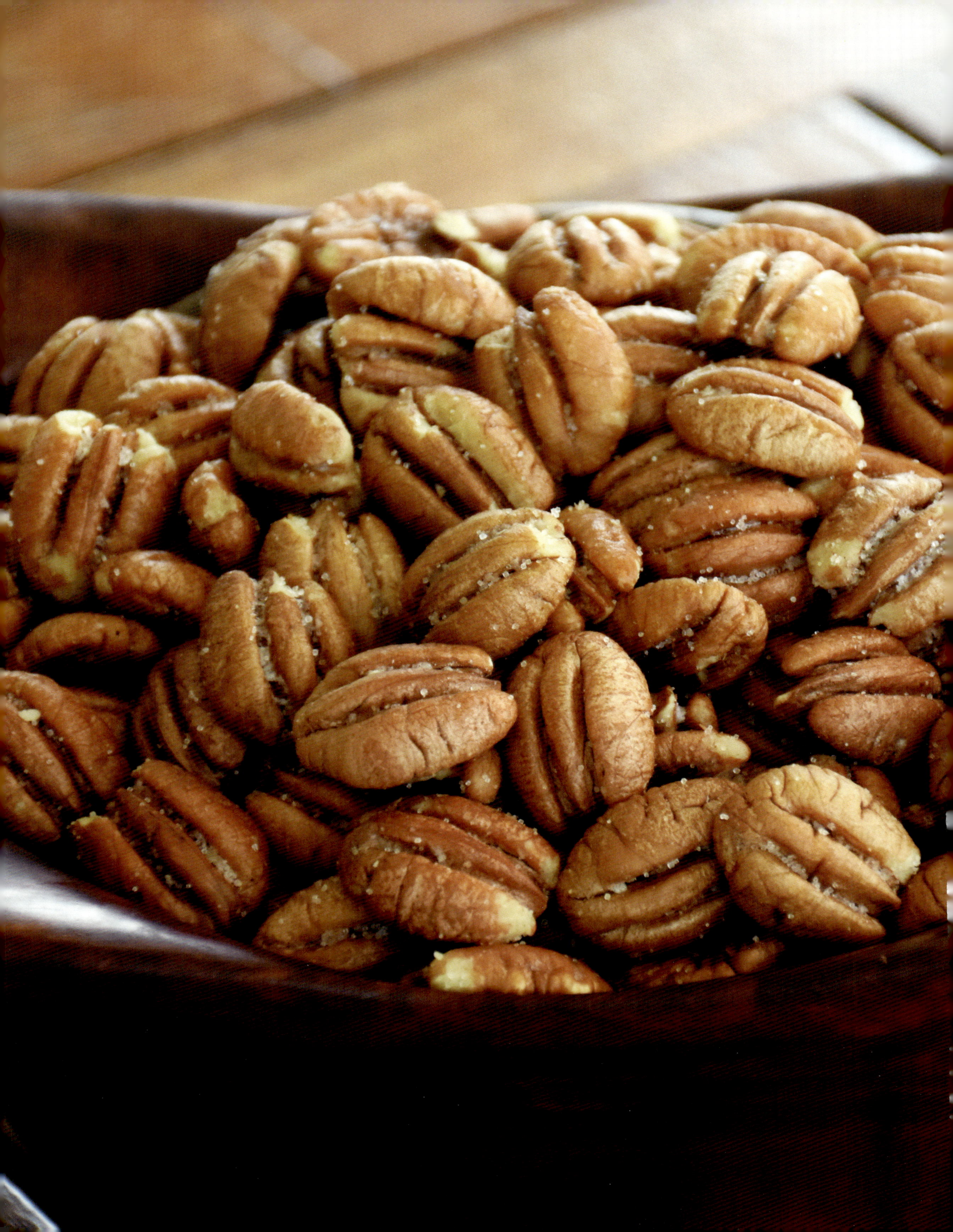

Favorite Ingredient

I love cooking with pecans! While I am aware of the good taste and nutritional value of walnuts and almonds, I must confess that both these nuts pale in appeal when compared to the oval, smooth-shelled pecans.

Pecans and I have a history. In my adolescent years in the Mississippi Delta, pecans were not that plentiful. Since harvest season for pecans precedes the Thanksgiving and Christmas holidays, my family would get a bag of the nuts to use in baking the holiday goodies. With a hammer, we would carefully crack and shell the pecans; then we would wait for my mother and sister Lucile to make candies, applesauce cake, and pecan pies.

After I married, I continued the holiday tradition and used pecans as I learned to cook. In 1964 we moved to Grand Bay in South Mobile County. Pecan orchards were everywhere! That is when I really fell in love with pecans. Fred would go to the orchards and buy 100 pound sacks of pecans for me. My sons would crack them on the new Rocket pecan cracker. By then I had learned to cook pretty well, and I just went crazy using all those delicious nuts.

Not many years passed by before I really wanted my own orchard. In 1975 we bought 11 acres of land in Irvington, just a few miles closer to Mobile. There were 52 huge pecan trees on the property. Although Hurricane Frederick did significant damage to the orchard, the remaining trees produced more pecans than even I could use.

After I retired from teaching, we bought a commercial pecan cracker and sold our cracked pecans. We delivered hundreds of pounds to Texas every year. For a month during the holiday season, we had a weekend booth at the Mobile Flea Market where we sold cracked and shelled pecans, pralines, and pecan pies. I loved interacting with customers and sharing recipes.

This phase lasted about five years before we sold our orchard. We bought an adjoining two and a half acres, built a new house, and went out of the pecan business. Pecans are still my favorite ingredient for cooking. However, these days the harvest is much less. We still have the commercial cracker, but I now shell the pecans and share them with family and friends.

Although there are many varieties of pecans, I have never eaten one that I did not like. My very favorite ones are Elliotts, a dome-shaped small pecan. This variety has more oil content than the popular Stuart. They also have a great shell-out rate of 50% or better.

I just love pecans! They are my favorite ingredient for cooking! The proof lies in the many recipes which appear in my cookbook. If a normal recipe calls for one cup of pecans, you can be sure that I use at least one and a half cups – or maybe two.

Homemade ice cream is not only a welcome treat any day of the week, it is a well-known culinary instrument of social bonding. We first learned this fact when the young married couples class in our church loved to gather for ice cream socials during the summer months. Whether a party of 30 on a set night, or an impromptu get-together of a handful of couples on Sunday afternoon, our group did some great bonding over the old-fashioned crank machines. As the years went by, our group scattered to other areas; however, we never outdistanced the friendships that were nourished during those times.

Since those early years, we have replaced the hand-crank with electric ice cream freezers. We have worn out a few of those using the traditional old-fashioned recipes. A few years ago on a stroll around Williams-Sonoma, I discovered the modern ice cream makers. That very day I took one home with me and tried it out. I love the modern way: no ice, no salt – just plug in, pour in your flavor of the day, and wait 30 minutes. The result – you have 1½ to 2 quarts of wonderful frozen delight. You just have to remember to keep the special canister in the freezer!

I did my part in making sure all my family members have this modern machine in their pantries. To accommodate recipes for the smaller machine, I have included my two quart ice cream recipes in this section. These are easily doubled when you wish to use a gallon freezer.

And don't forget – you still can have that special bonding. Invite some people over!

ICE CREAM

Old-Fashioned Vanilla
Ice Cream

Fruit Options

Tumbleweeds

Orange Sherbet

Strawberry Gelato

Chocolate Ice Cream

Modern Two Quart Ice Creams

Vanilla

Fruit Options: Peach,
Strawberry, and Blueberry

Old-Fashioned Vanilla Ice Cream

4 large eggs

1 cup sugar

¼ teaspoon salt

2 tablespoons vanilla

½ pint heavy whipping cream

2 cans Eagle Brand sweetened condensed milk

1 to 1½ quarts whole milk

Using an electric mixer at medium speed, beat the eggs until blended. Add the sugar gradually and beat 4 minutes. Stir in salt, vanilla, and whipping cream and beat 2 more minutes.

Turn the speed to low and add the Eagle Brand milk. Gradually add 3 cups of the whole milk, beating on low speed until well mixed. Pour the mixture into the gallon freezer container. Add additional whole milk to fill the container to no more than ⅔ full.

Follow directions on your ice cream maker. Alternately layer 4 thick layers of ice with 4 thin layers of ice cream salt. Continue this layering as the ice melts during freezing.

Ice cream is best when allowed to ripen for about an hour. Simply remove the dasher, place a layer of foil over top, and replace the lid. Pack with more ice and salt, cover with a thick towel and then wait. (If you can!)

Yields 1 gallon

Fruit-Flavored Ice Creams:

This Vanilla Ice Cream is quite versatile for adding fruits to make different flavors:

1. Use 2 cups less milk.

2. Select a fruit and purée to make 3 cups; sweeten to taste. Chill.

Fruits may be either stirred in during mixing or added after the mixture has begun freezing.

Tumbleweeds

vanilla ice cream

3 ounces Kahlua

1½ ounces Crème de Cacao

nutmeg for sprinkling

Fill the blender with ice cream, but do not pack down. Add the liqueurs and blend until smooth.

Pour into champagne glasses, sprinkle with nutmeg, and serve.

A favorite at Christmas Eve parties during the 1970s.

We were living in our renovated 1913 Dutch Colonial house in Grand Bay during those happy times. The Christmas crystal was, of course, a ruby-red Fostoria – perfect for the Tumbleweeds and the season!

Orange Sherbet

6 (12 ounce) cans of orange soda, chilled

1 can Eagle Brand sweetened condensed milk

1 large can crushed pineapple, undrained

small bottle maraschino cherries, cut in half – optional

Reserve 2 cans of orange soda. Combine the remaining ingredients in a gallon freezer container. Add only enough of the reserved orange soda to fill the container ⅔ full.

Freeze according to the manufacturer's directions on your ice cream freezer, alternating 4 thick layers of ice with 4 thin layers of ice cream salt.

Yields 1 gallon

Beginning in the 1950s, this was a popular recipe for a tasty alternative to ice cream.

The citrusy, tart-to-sweet taste is summer-perfect!

Strawberry Gelato

1 quart fresh ripe strawberries

2 eggs

1 cup sugar

1¼ cups heavy whipping cream

1 cup whole milk

1 vanilla bean

juice of 1 lemon

Wash the strawberries. Remove the stems and any white or green places, leaving only the very ripe parts. Use a blender or food processor and purée to obtain 1½ cups. Set aside.

Beat the eggs until fluffy; gradually add the sugar and beat 4 minutes. Stir in the heavy cream and whole milk and beat for 2 minutes.

When well mixed, pour the mixture into a heavy saucepan and place over medium low heat. Whisk constantly until the mixture is ready to boil, but do not boil. Remove from heat.

Make a slit in the vanilla bean. Scrape the bean from the hull; whisk the scrapings into the warm mixture. Set aside, whisking occasionally until the mixture cools down. Add the juice of 1 lemon, whisking throughout.

Chill the mixture in the refrigerator.

Pour the chilled gelato mixture into the freezer canister, filling only ⅔ full. Freeze in the modern ice cream machine for about 35 minutes.

Yields 2 quarts

For a larger quantity, you can double the recipe and freeze the gelato in an old-fashioned gallon freezer.

On a Girls' Trip to Italy in 2011, Chef Fabrizio did a hands-on cooking class at our villa one evening.

We requested that he teach us to make gelato. This is his recipe for the fantastic dessert we made for our dinner. Italians are pretty adamant that Americans cannot duplicate their gelato. The reason they espouse is the difference in their ingredients, mainly that their cows produce a superior cream. We can only try our best!

Chocolate Ice Cream

2 quarts chocolate milk

1 can Eagle Brand sweetened condensed milk

1 (12 ounce) carton Cool Whip

Combine all ingredients and stir until well mixed. Pour the mixture into the 1-gallon freezer canister, making sure the container is no more than ⅔ full.

Follow the manufacturer's instructions for freezing. For an electric ice cream freezer, alternate 4 thick layers of ice with 4 thin layers of ice cream salt. Add more layers as the ice melts. Most machines cut off when the mixture is frozen.

If you want to wait a bit before serving, remove the dasher. Cover the top with foil and replace the lid. Repack ice and salt around the container. Cover all with newspaper or a heavy towel. Will ripen in about an hour.

Yields 1 gallon

My niece Betty Murray, visiting from Jackson, MS, introduced us to this refreshing ice cream treat that tastes very much like a frostie.

Her preview of the recipe sounded good enough for the guys to run to the nearest store for ingredients. An hour or so later, we were looking out over Mobile Bay enjoying our own frostie treat!

Modern Two Quart Ice Cream

Vanilla Base:

2 large eggs

½ cup sugar

⅛ teaspoon salt

½ can Eagle Brand sweetened condensed milk

1 cup heavy whipping cream

2 cups whole milk

1 tablespoon vanilla

Using an electric mixer at medium speed, beat the eggs until light and fluffy. Gradually add the sugar and salt, beating 4 minutes until well mixed. Stir in the Eagle Brand milk. Add the heavy whipping cream and beat until blended. Turn the mixer to a lower speed; add the vanilla and milk.

Assemble the frozen canister in the modern ice cream machine. Turn on the machine. Pour the ice cream mixture through the top opening, filling the canister only ⅔ full.

The mixture will take about 35 minutes to freeze. Turn the machine off and remove the dasher. The ice cream is ready to serve, but will continue to harden in the canister for a short time if left covered.

The Vanilla Base becomes the base for making many delicious flavors using chilled fresh fruit:

1. Decrease the whole milk to 1 cup.
2. Add the specified sweetened fruit.

Peach: Peel 2 ripe peaches and remove the seed. Purée the peach, adding ½ cup sugar. Chill.

Strawberry: Clean 1 pint of berries. Mash or purée, adding ½ cup sugar. Chill.

Blueberry: Boil 1½ cups of blueberries, ¼ cup water, and ½ cup sugar for 5 minutes. Cool. Purée and add 1 tablespoon fresh lemon juice. Chill.

Pour into the frozen canister as directed and freeze.

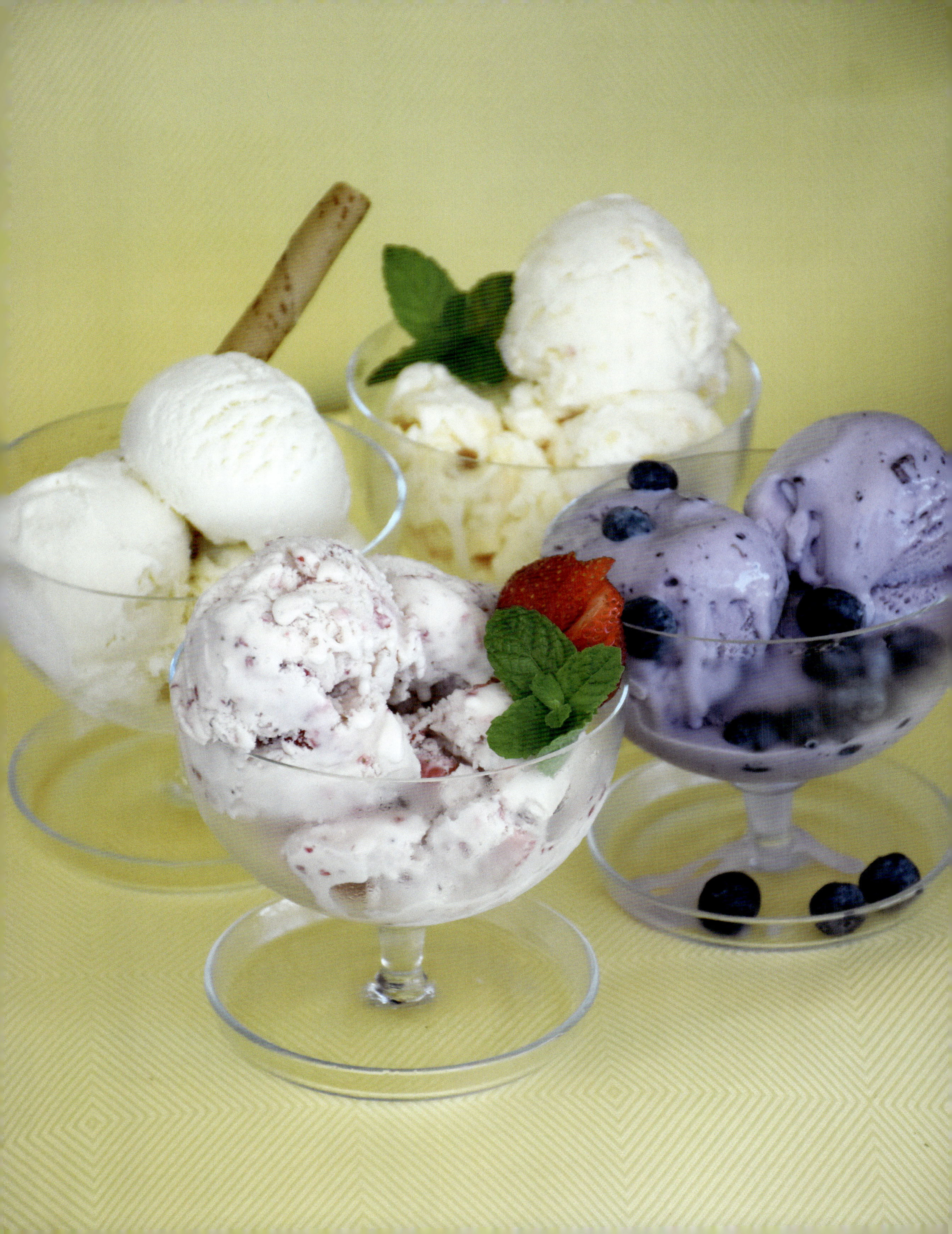

RECIPE INDEX

Appetizers
Crab, Shrimp & Avocado Cocktail 31
Crabmeat Gruyere Tarts 30
Fajitas Nachos 32
Firecrackers 25
Grilled Shrimp with Bacon 27
Holiday Cheese Wafers 21
Hot Crab & Shrimp Dip 20
Hot Pepper Jelly 35
Parmesan & Rosemary Crackers 22
Roasted Pecans 28
Roquefort Logs 33
Sausage & Cheese Balls 34
Shrimp Dip 26
Smoked Cheddar Cheese Spread 29
Swedish Meatballs 23
Three Cheese Pimento 24

Breads
Banana Nut Bread or Muffins 47
Blueberry Surprise with Lemon
    Blueberry Sauce 50
Cinnamon Rolls 41
Focaccia Bread 40
Hush Puppies with Crabmeat 44
Nan's Famous Yeast Rolls 38
Old-Fashioned Jalapeño Cornbread 43
Orange Carrot Muffins 48
Peach or Pear Preserves 49
Pumpkin Bread 46
Rosemary Garlic Rolls 39
Speedy Jalapeño Cheese Cornbread 42
Uncle Charlie's Hush Puppies 45

Soups & Salads
Absolutely Delicious Salad Dressing 64
Ambrosia 78
Bleu Cheese & Spicy Pecan Salad 66
Blueberry Salad 77
Charleston Delight 79
Chicken & Andouille Gumbo 60
Chicken Salad 68
Chicken Tortilla Soup 62
Clam Chowder with Dill 59
Coca Cola Party Salad 75
Cole Slaw 73
Comeback Salad Dressing 65
Crab Tower Salad 70
Crispy Pickle Slices 72
Frozen Pink Salad 79
Pineapple Salad 76
Poblano Crab Soup 58
Roux 61
Shrimp Salad 69
Southern Broccoli Salad 74
Spicy Pecans 67
Uncle Charlie's Chili 57
Vegetable Beef Soup 56
West Indies Salad 63

Veggies & Sides
Baked Beans 92
Candied Sweet Potato Rounds 90
Fried Apples 95
Fried Okra 84
New Potatoes in Cream Sauce 89
Potatoes au Gratin with Fresh Herbs 88
Risotto with Wild Mushrooms 93
Sautéed Squash with Onions 87
Southern Creamed Corn 82
Southern Peas or Butter Beans 85
Spiced Peaches 94
Sweet Potato Casserole
    with Pecan Topping 91
Turnip or Collard Greens 86

Seafood
Baked Stuffed Shrimp 112
Barbequed Shrimp 111
Crab Royale 108
Crab Stuffing 109
Crawfish Etouffée 114
Favorite Seafood Cocktail Sauce 100
Fried Fish or Oysters 100
Fried Shrimp or Crab Claws 101
Jumbo Lump Crab Cakes
    with Lemon Remoulade 106
Oysters Rockefeller 115
Shrimp Fettucine 113
Stuffed Flounder 110
Sue's Seafood Gumbo 104

Main Dishes
Bacon Quiche 130
Baked Ham 131
Boston Butt, Oven Roasted 119
Classic Chicken Pot Pie 121
Classic Cornbread Dressing 137
Country Fried Steak 124
Cranberry Sauce 135
Giblet Gravy 136
Herb Buttered Quail 128
Lasagna 126
Osso Bucco 122
Party Chicken 120
Pizza 140
Roasted Turkey 134
Savory Bolognese 125
Standing Rib Roast 118
Tangy Meat Loaf 129

Grilling & Smoking
Baby Back Ribs 146
Beef Tenderloin 150
Champagne Horseradish Sauce 151
Famous Fajitas 147
Grilled Steaks 144
Pork Tenderloin with Fresh Herbs 148
Port Wine Reduction Sauce 151
Smoked Boston Butt 149

Desserts
Cakes & Frostings
    Applesauce Cake with
        Orange Coconut Icing 190
    Banana Nut Cake 186
    Bourbon Nut Loaves 193
    Carrot Cake Supreme 184
    Cream Cheese Frosting 187
    Cream Cheese Pound Cake 180
    Deluxe Cream Cheese Frosting 187
    German Chocolate Cake with Coconut
        Pecan Frosting 182
    Italian Cream Cake 188
    Red Velvet Cake 189
    Sour Cream Coconut Cake 192
    Strawberry Cupcakes with
        Strawberry Frosting 194
    Texas Cake 181

Candy
    Candied Pecan Halves 223
    Creamy Pralines 220
    Chocolate Fudge 223
    Haystacks 225
    Homemade Turtles 224
    Martha Washington Candy 226
    Peanut Brittle 227
    Peanut Butter Balls 222
Cheesecakes
    Cheesecake Supreme 158
        Fruit Toppings 159
    German Chocolalte Cheesecake 160
    Praline Cheesecake 158
    Turtle Cheesecake 158
Cookies & Bars
    Biscotti 169
    Butter Cookies 170
    Caramel Squares 175
    Chocolate Chip Cookies 165
    Chocolate Nut Cookies 166
    Decorator Frosting 171
    Fudge Cake Brownies 176
    Lizzies 173
    Macadamia & White
        Chocolate Cookies 168
    Noels 172
    Oatmeal Cookies 164
    Peanut Butter Cookies 167
    Praline Grahams 174
Ice Cream
    Chocolate Ice Cream 235
    Modern Two Quart Ice Cream
        Blueberry Ice Cream 236
        Peach Ice Cream 236
        Strawberry Ice Cream 236
        Vanilla Ice Cream 236
    Old-Fashioned Vanilla Ice Cream 232
        Fruit Options 232
    Orange Sherbet 233
    Strawberry Gelato 234
    Tumbleweeds 233
Pies & Cobblers
    Autumn Apple Pie 207
    Clancy's Meyer Lemon Pie
        with Chantilly Cream 210
    Cobblers
        Blackberry Cobbler 216
        Blueberry Cobbler 216
        Dewberry Cobbler 216
        Peach Cobbler 216
        Very Berry Cobbler 216
    Cream Pies
        Banana Pudding 203
        Coconut Cream Pie 203
        Southern Chocolate Pie Filling 204
        Vanilla Cream Pie 202
    Frozen Strawberry Pie
        with Coconut Crust 201
    Key Lime Pie 209
    Lemon Blueberry Pie 212
    Lovie's Pecan Pie 206
    Meringue 203
    Pie Crusts
        Chocolate Cookie Crumb Crust 200
        Flaky Pie Crust 199
        Graham Cracker Crumb Crust 200
    The Ultimate Chocolate Dream 205

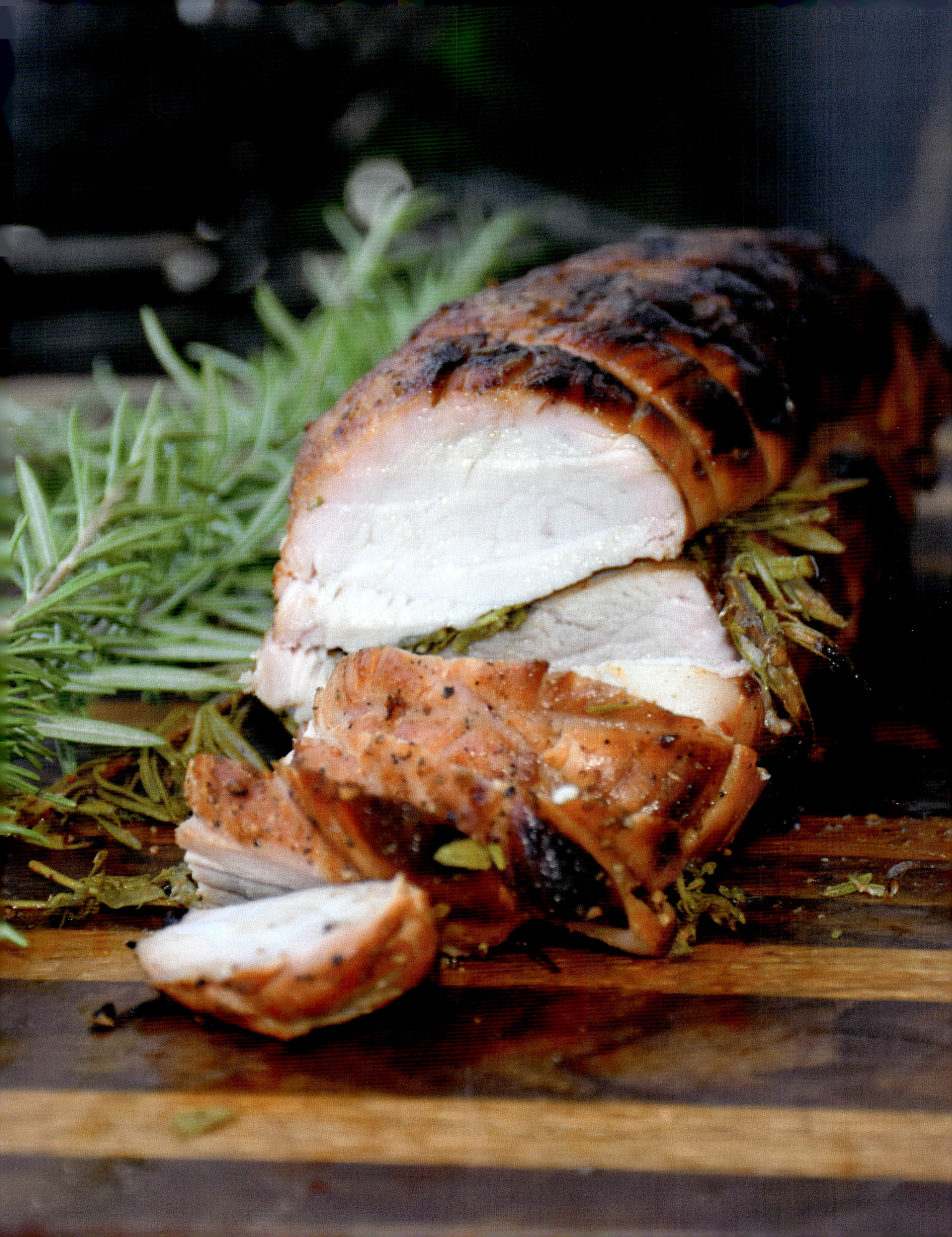

INDEX

A

Ambrosia 78
Appetizers
  Cheese Spread, Smoked Cheddar 29
  Cheese Wafers, Holiday 21
  Crab & Shrimp Dip, Hot 20
  Crab, Shrimp & Avocado Cocktail 31
  Crabmeat Gruyere Tarts 30
  Fajitas Nachos 32
  Firecrackers 25
  Hot Pepper Jelly 35
  Meatballs, Swedish 23
  Parmesan & Rosemary Crackers 22
  Pecans, Roasted 28
  Roquefort Logs 33
  Sausage & Cheese Balls 34
  Shrimp, Grilled with Bacon 27
  Shrimp Dip 26
  Three Cheese Pimento 24
Apples
  Applesauce Cake 190
  Autumn Apple Pie 207
  Fried Apples 95

B

Beef
  Beef Tenderloin 150
  Fajitas, Famous 147
  Roast, Standing Rib 118
  Steak, Country Fried 124
  Steaks, Grilled 144
  Vegetable Beef Soup 56
Beef, Ground
  Bolognese, Savory 125
  Chili, Uncle Charlie's 57
  Lasagna 126 – 127
  Meatballs, Swedish 23
  Meat Loaf, Tangy 129

Bread
  Banana Nut Bread or Muffins 47
  Blueberry Surprise with Lemon
    Blueberry Sauce 50
  Cinnamon Rolls 41
  Cornbread, Old Fashioned Jalapeno 43
  Cornbread, Speedy Jalapeno Cheese 42
  Focaccia Bread 40
  Hush Puppies, Uncle Charlie's 45
  Hush Puppies with Crabmeat 44
  Orange Carrot Muffins 48
  Pumpkin Bread 46
  Rosemary Garlic Rolls 39
  Yeast Rolls, Nan's Famous 38

C

Cakes
  Applesauce Cake 190
  Banana Nut Cake 186
  Bourbon Nut Loaves 193
  Carrot Cake Supreme 184 – 185
  Cream Cheese Pound Cake 180
  German Chocolate Cake 182
  Italian Cream Cake 188
  Red Velvet Cake 189
  Sour Cream Coconut Cake 192
  Strawberry Cupcakes 194
  Texas Cake 181
Candy
  Candied Pecan Halves 223
  Creamy Pralines 220
  Chocolate Fudge 223
  Haystacks 225
  Homemade Turtles 224
  Martha Washington Candy 226
  Peanut Brittle 227
  Peanut Butter Balls 222
Cheesecakes
  Cheesecake Supreme 158 – 159
    Fruit Toppings 159
    Praline Cheesecake 158 – 159
    Turtle Cheesecake 158 – 159
  German Chocolate Cheesecake 160 – 161
Chicken
  Chicken & Andouille Gumbo 60
  Chicken Pot Pie 121
  Chicken Salad 68
  Chicken Tortilla Soup 62
  Party Chicken 120
Chowder
  Clam Chowder 59
Cobblers
  Blackberry Cobbler 216 – 217
  Blueberry Cobbler 216 – 217
  Dewberry Cobbler 216 – 217
  Peach Cobbler 216 – 217
  Very Berry Cobbler 216 – 217
Cookies & Bars
  Biscotti 169
  Butter Cookies 170
  Caramel Squares 175
  Chocolate Chip Cookies 165
  Chocolate Nut Cookies 166
  Fudge Cake Brownies 176
  Lizzies 173
  Macadamia & White Chocolate Cookies 168
  Noels 172
  Oatmeal Cookies 164
  Peanut Butter Cookies 167
  Praline Grahams 174
Crab
  Crab Cakes, Jumbo Lump 106 – 107
  Crab Claws, Fried 101
  Crab Royale 108
  Crab, Shrimp & Avocado Cocktail 31
  Crab Stuffing 109
  Crab Tower Salad 70
  Crabmeat Gruyere Tarts 30
  Hot Crab & Shrimp Dip 20
  Hush Puppies with Crabmeat 44
  Poblano Crab Soup 58
  Seafood Gumbo, Sue's 104 – 105
  Stuffed Flounder 110
  West Indies Salad 63
Crawfish
  Crawfish Etoufée 114

D

Dressing
  Classic Cornbread Dressing 137

F

Fish
  Fried Fish Fillets 100
  Flounder, Stuffed 110
Frostings
  Chocolate Frosting 177
  Coconut & Pecan Frosting 183
  Cream Cheese Frosting 187
  Decorator Frosting 171
  Deluxe Cream Cheese Frosting 187
  Orange Coconut Icing 191
  Sour Cream Coconut Icing 192
  Strawberry Frosting 195
  Texas Cake Frosting 181

G

Gumbos
  Chicken Andouille Gumbo 60
  Roux 60, 105
  Sue's Seafood Gumbo 104 – 105

INDEX

I

Ice Cream
  Chocolate Ice Cream 235
  Modern Two Quart Ice Cream 236
    Blueberry Ice Cream 236
    Peach Ice Cream 236
    Strawberry Ice Cream 236
    Vanilla 236
  Old Fashioned Vanilla Ice Cream 232
    Fruit Options 232
  Orange Sherbet 233
  Strawberry Gelato 234
  Tumbleweeds 233

J

Jellies & Preserves
  Hot Pepper Jelly 35
  Peach or Pear Preserves 49

M

Muffins
  Banana Nut Muffins 47
  Orange Carrot Muffins 48
  Pumpkin Muffins 46

O

Oysters
  Fried Oysters 100
  Oysters Rockefeller 115

P

Peaches
  Peach Cobbler 216 – 217
  Peach Ice Cream 236
  Spiced Peaches 94
Pecans
  Candied Pecan Halves 223
  Creamy Pralines 220
  Lovie's Pecan Pie 206
  Roasted Pecans 28
  Spicy Pecans 67
Pesto 127
Pickle Slices, Crispy 72
Pies (see also Cobblers)
  Autumn Apple Pie 207
  Cream Pies 202
    Banana Pudding 203
    Coconut Cream Pie 203
    Southern Chocolate Pie Filling 204
    Vanilla Cream Pie 202
  Key Lime Pie 209
  Lemon Blueberry Pie 212 – 213
  Meyer Lemon Pie, Clancy's 210 – 211
  Pecan Pie, Lovie's 206
  Strawberry Pie, Frozen 201
  The Ultimate Chocolate Dream 205
Pie Crusts
  Chocolate Cookie Crumb Crust 200
  Coconut Crust 201
  Flaky Pie Crust 199
  Graham Cracker Crumb Crust 200
Pie Toppings
  Chantilly Cream 211
  Meringue 203
  Whipped Cream 213
Pizza
  Pizza Dough 140
  Pizza, Assembling 141
Pork
  Bacon Quiche 130
  Boston Butt, Oven Roasted 119
  Boston Butt, Smoked 149
  Ham, Baked 131
  Pork Tenderloin with Fresh Herbs 148
  Ribs, Baby Back Smoked 146
  Sausage
    Blueberry Surprise 50
    Chicken & Andouille Gumbo 60
    Sausage & Cheese Balls 34
Potatoes
  Candied Sweet Potatoes Rounds 90
  New Potatoes in Cream Sauce 89
  Potatoes au Gratin with Fresh Herbs 88
  Sweet Potato Casserole
    with Pecan Topping 91

Q

Quail
  Herb Buttered Quail 128

R

Risotto
  Risotto with Wild Rice 93
Roux
  Roux for gumbo 61, 105

S

Salads
  Ambrosia 78
  Blue Cheese & Spicy Pecans 66
  Broccoli Salad, Southern 74
  Charleston Delight 79
  Chicken Salad 68
  Cole Slaw 73
  Congealed
    Blueberry Salad 77
    Coca Cola Party Salad 75
    Pineapple Salad 76
  Crab Tower Salad 70 – 71
  Frozen Pink Salad 79
  Shrimp Salad 69
  West Indies Salad 63
Salad Dressings
  Absolutely Delicious Salad Dressing 64
  Comeback Salad Dressing 65
  Vinaigrette, White Wine 31
Sauces
  Champagne Horseradish Sauce 151
  Cranberry Sauce 135
  Giblet Gravy 136
  Lemon Blueberry Sauce 51
  Lemon Remoulade 107
  Pesto 127
  Port Wine Reduction Sauce 151
  Seafood Cocktail Sauce, Favorite 100

Shrimp
  Barbequed Shrimp 111
  Crab, Shrimp, & Avocado Cocktail 31
  Fried Shrimp 101
  Grilled Shrimp with Bacon 27
  Hot Crab & Shrimp Dip 20
  Seafood Gumbo, Sue's 104 – 105
  Shrimp Dip 26
  Shrimp Fettucine 113
  Shrimp Salad 69
  Stuffed Shrimp, Baked 112
Soups (see also Gumbos)
  Chicken Tortilla Soup 62
  Chili, Uncle Charlie's 57
  Clam Chowder with Dill 59
  Poblano Crab Soup 58
  Vegetable Beef Soup 56

T

Turkey
  Dressing, Classic Cornbread 137
  Giblet Gravy 136
Roasted Turkey 134

V

Veal
  Osso Bucco 122 – 123
Vegetables
  Baked Beans 92
  Butter Beans, Southern 85
  Collard Greens 86
  Creamed Corn, Southern 82
  Crispy Pickle Slices 72
  Fried Okra 84
  Peas, Southern 85
  Risotto with Wild Mushrooms 93
  Squash with Onions, Sautéed 87
  Turnip Greens 86

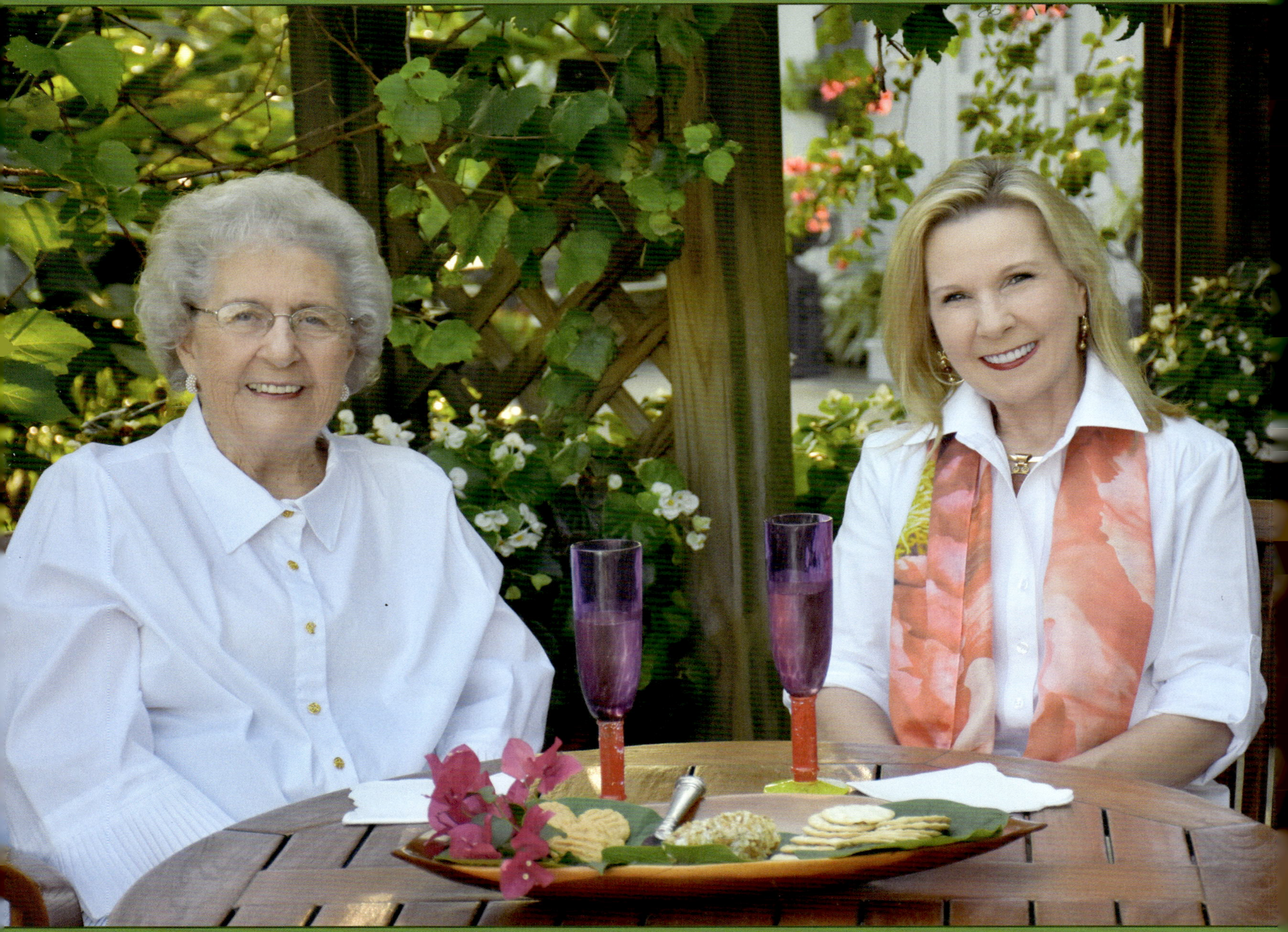

Copyright © 2015 by Sue Collins Cannon and
Connie Cannon Valerius.

All rights reserved. No part of this publication may be reproduced or transmitted in any form or by any means, electronic or mechanical, including photocopying, recording, or by any information store and retrieval system, without the expressed written permission of
Sue Collins Cannon or Connie Cannon Valerius.

Inquiries or requests to the printer should be addressed to:

Bayside Printing Company, Inc.
160 Lockhaven Drive
Houston, TX 77073
(281) 209-9500
www.BaysidePrinting.com

Produced by Bayside Printing Company, Inc.
Photographs © 2015 by Connie Cannon Valerius
Recipes © 2015 by Sue Collins Cannon
(except for those credited within this book)

Printed in the United States
ISBN 978-0-692-57074-6

First Printing in November 2015

Reflections & Recipes

Looking back over the many years of cooking for family and friends, I can truly say that the reflections are equally as important as the recipes. How apt is the phrase that food is memories. With both my mind and my heart engaged, I have strolled down memory lane while writing the recipes, sharing the stories, and cooking the foods for the photographs. I have also remembered the wonderful people who were my mentors and supporters. I am deeply appreciative of the most valuable lesson I learned, that the passion for cooking is about more than just the food. Always, the people sitting in the chairs at the table are vastly more important than the meal on the table. I believe that food served with laughter also feeds the soul. The food that I prepare and the recipes that I share, therefore, are gifts from my heart. May your life be enriched, as mine has been, by love, laughter, and a passion for cooking.